Bicycle Touring Holland

Bicycle Touring Holland

With Excursions into Belgium and Germany

Katherine Widing

Van der Plas Publications / Cycle Publishing, San Francisco

Printed in Hong Kong

Publisher's information:
Van der Plas Publications / Cycle Publishing
1282 7th Avenue
San Francisco, CA 94122
USA
http://www.cyclepublishing.com
E-mail: con.tact@cyclepublishing.com

Distributed or represented to the book trade by:
USA: Midpoint Trade Books, Kansas City, KS
UK: Chris Lloyd Sales and Marketing Services/Orca Book
          Services, Poole, Dorset
Australia: Tower Books, Frenchs Forest, NSW

Cover design:
Yvo Design, San Francisco

Photographs by the author
Maps by Yuki Kawaguchi, San Francisco

Publisher's Cataloging in Publication Data
Widing, Katherine. Bicycle Touring Holland: with excursions into Belgium and Germany.
1. Bicycles and bicycling — handbooks and manuals.
21.6 cm. 296 p: Bibliographic information. Includes index.
I. Title
II. Authorship
Library of Congress Control Number: 2005920664
ISBN 1-892495-46-5

To Joan Marsden,
for getting me started in the travel book biz, and
Clay Hubbs
for encouraging me to write, publishing my first magazine article, and for having
the foresight to create *Transitions Abroad* magazine years ahead of its time.

Acknowledgments

There have been a great many people who have helped, encouraged, and offered advice throughout the course of this book. Firstly, to my adopted Dutch family, André Vagevuur, Greetje Dekker, and their daughters Dewi and Nora: *dank u wel* for your hospitality, translation help, and for my *gezellig slaapkamertje*. Big thanks to Jason and the great group of cycle touring enthusiasts at The Bike Peddler in Santa Rosa, California, and to Mark Bakker and his partner Natascha at Bakker Fiets in Hilversum. And thanks to Ortlieb for making the best waterproof panniers and handlebar bags on the planet.

And *een grote dank u wel* to all the wonderful *Vrienden op de Fiets* who open their homes and their hearts to cyclists. They are truly friends. I thank every one that I stayed with. A special *bedankt voor alles* to Henny Boers in Harlingen; Jan Willem and Marijke Ruegebrink in Zutphen; Betty Bakker in Enkhuizen; Berend and Greetje Dijkstra in Borger; Gijsbert and Deet Kraay on Texel; Reiner van der Wal, Ditteke and Carel Slooten, and Jannette Oussoren in Gouda; and Peter Guertens and Anke Verhees in Maastricht. And to Henk Kroes and his wife Swaentsje, friends to both cyclists and skaters: there is something magical about being in the right place at the right time. Thanks for a splendid afternoon.

I would also like to give particular mention to the people in the VVV and ANWB offices for their invaluable information, and special thanks to Bianca Helderman of the Netherlands Tourist Board in New York, Janine Winkens-Arets at VVV Zuid Limburg, and Anya Speerstra at VVV Workum.

And to my husband Jerry, thanks yet again for supporting this *fietser* in her quest to cycle every corner of the Netherlands.

Table of Contents

Introduction: How to Use This Book

This book is designed for all touring cyclists—novices, experts, and anyone in between. It is intended for the person who wants to cycle in the Netherlands for a single day or for several weeks or even months.

The first five chapters of the book introduce the cyclist to the Netherlands, explain the practicalities of cycling there, and give information on preparation and planning, where to eat and sleep, and more.

The second part of the book contains route information. The routes are broken up into days of varying length. Several "days" within a route can be done as day trips by starting at a railway station and then returning to the start town by train. Each day begins and ends at a location with a variety of accommodations and eating establishments and sightseeing opportunities. The majority of these overnight stops are accessible by train. For those wishing to rent bikes, bicycle shops with rentals are listed. Riding levels differ, weather conditions vary, some days have many points of interest, and some days are longer, but towns with amenities en route are noted so that days can be broken up. As well as the longer routes, several day trips are described, either as a stand-alone ride or as an optional day trip on a longer route.

Each route description gives detailed directions to follow and highlights interesting sights, lodging, eating options, and points of interest along the way. At the end of each day, information about the stopover place is listed: tourist information, bicycle shops (with rentals, if applicable), and accommodations and places to eat.

The route directions are provided in the form of a cue sheet for each section, to be read in conjunction with the text and a route map. The route maps in the book are for general orientation only. In addition, the reader should obtain a detailed map of the area, such as those recommended at the start of each route. If you're ever in doubt or feel you are lost, ask someone. People are friendly and willing to help. At the beginning of each day, decide how far you intend to go, being careful not to overestimate. You are here to experience the Netherlands, so allow yourself time to stop and smell the tulips, so to speak. It is also important to arrive at your destination early enough in the day to allow yourself time to settle in, relax, visit the tourist information office, and enjoy the sights.

Goede Reis!

Symbols Used in the Cue Sheets

N/S/E/W North/South/East/West

L	Left
R	Right
VL	Veer Left
VR	Veer Right
CS	Continue Straight
RA	Roundabout
U	U-turn or U-turn maneuver (often when coming off a bridge or freeway overpass)
T	City, town or village
SS	Sightseeing/Point of interest
SS L or SS R	Sightseeing/Point of interest is on the left or right
#	Refers to number on ANWB *paddestoel* (mushroom) or signpost (see below)
ST	Side trip (not included in day's total distance)
RT	Round trip (round trip distance of side trip)
A4	Freeway number
N123	National (major) road number
E7	International road number (always in addition to the A or N number for the same road)
K43 / sign "K43"	*Knooppunt* 43 / to *Knooppunt* 43 (*Knooppunt* means node—an element of the bicycle route network)
!	Attention required (easily missed, tricky turn, or difficult navigation); explained in text
/	Street continues straight, but name changes, e.g. Kerkstraat/Emmalaan/N123 (Kerkstraat becomes Emmalaan, becomes N123)
sign "Alkmaar"	Bicycle-specific directional sign on post or *paddestoel* indicates to (town of) Alkmaar (*paddestoel* means mushroom—a low mushroom-shaped direction sign specifically for cyclists and walkers)
dir. "Edam"	General directional sign indicates to (town of) Edam

Using the Cue Sheets

Each day always begins and ends at either a VVV Tourist information office or a railway station.

The routes used in the book are not always the shortest way from point A to point B, but they are the most scenic. The routes use the quieter roads and bicycle paths whenever possible, and often detour for a worthwhile sight.

Distances are given in tenths of kilometers (100 m), but if there is a short distance within that 100 m, it is indicated in meters. For example:

21.3   L   Kerkstraat (30 m), R Dorpsstraat

means:

"Turn left at 21.3 km into Kerkstraat; then, after 30 m, turn right onto Dorpsstraat."

Always assume you will continue straight unless a turn is indicated. Continue Straight (CS) is used as a point of reference or as a marker if there is ambiguity at an intersection.

Bicycle-specific ANWB signpost. Here, all signs are in red, meaning they are all bicycle-specific, whereas other signposts also include general traffic signs, in black.

Knee-high ANWB *paddestoel* (mushroom) signs are used in scenic areas because they are less obtrusive then regular signposts and quite convenient for cyclists and walkers.

The # symbol followed by a four- or five-digit numbers refer to the number on the ANWB signpost (see Chapter 3, page 31). If there are four digits, it usually refers to a general signpost for motor vehicles; when there are five digits, it usually refers to a bicycle-specific signpost. When there are two sets of numbers, the second set refers to a new, updated number in the same location.

Sightseeing en route is indicated by SS L or SS R, with the point of interest to the left or the right of the route respectively. Once you have done your sightseeing, continue (straight) on the route.

Street names are often installed on buildings. In rural areas, roads are often unmarked. A bike path will sometimes have a name ending in -pad (path), but it will usually be unnamed.

You will find yourself on many streets and roads with ANWB or LF recreational cycle route signs (see page 44). Often, these signs are used in the cue sheets as a reference. Sometimes you will follow just one, and sometimes you will follow the signs for several turns. In the case of the LF1, you will follow a section of the route. On the Hanzeroute, you will follow the LF3 for the entire trip. ANWB bike routes sometimes overlap. Follow the signs only as directed. If you were to continue following the route signs when they are not listed in the cue sheet, you may not find your way back to the route described in the book.

The cue sheets are set up for use with a bicycle computer to record your progress, to be reset to 0.0 at the beginning of each day's ride. But beware: individual

Side-by-side comparison of maps. Below: Sample section of a typical route map from this book. Right: the same area as shown in a detailed map at scale 1:100,000 (i.e., 1 cm on the map represents 1 km in the terrain, or 1 in. on the map represents about 1.6 miles).

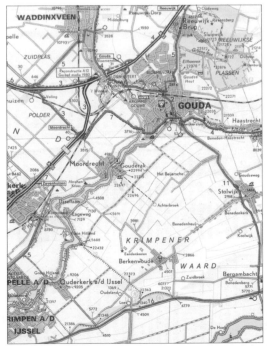

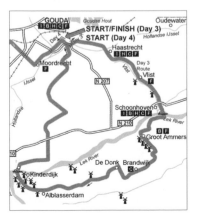

computers vary in their accuracy. A turn may be indicated as 7.9 km, but your computer may have turned over that extra few meters to show 8.0 km.

Don't forget that crossing the street to go to a bakery or to check out a beautiful building façade without removing your computer can add 30 m, 40 m, or more to your computer. Looking around a town for a café or going to a museum without removing your computer will also add distance to your tripmeter.

Maps

The route maps in this book are for general orientation only, and intended to be used in conjunction with a more detailed map, such as the *ANWB/VVV Toeristenkaart* (see pages 47–48). The route is indicated by a heavy amber line (or, in the case of an alternate route or side trip, a dashed amber line), while all the general information is in black, or in the case of water bodies, grey. The list below shows the symbols used on the maps.

Symbols

Services:

I   Tourist information (VVV)

B   Bike shop

H   Lodging (hotels, hostels, pensions, B&Bs)

C   Camping

F   Food (restaurants, cafés, take-outs, bakeries, food stores)

Other symbols:

 Boat/ferry

 Hunebed

 Tulip field

 Windmill

1.

The Netherlands and Bike Touring

THERE IS an old Dutch saying "The Good Lord made the earth, and the Dutch made Holland." This of course refers to the elaborate land reclamation projects where the Dutch have added land to enlarge and protect their country. If a cyclist were to coin this phrase, it would have to be re-written as "The Lord made the earth, and the Dutch made Holland heaven for cyclists." One can appreciate this after riding for as little as a few hours in this country where the cyclist has top priority in the hierarchy of vehicles on the road.

Cycle touring is an exciting and rewarding way to travel. Your bicycle gives you independence, and traveling by bicycle lends a totally different perspective to towns, country roads, sights, and life in general. While on two wheels, you have time to inhale and experience. Plus, you are physically active and traveling as the locals do.

The Netherlands is one of Europe's, if not the world's, premier cycling destinations. Over the years, I have made numerous trips to the Netherlands. Each time, no matter what the season, the bicycle has been my transport choice. Being on a bicycle affords opportunities to see this country as the Dutch do. And on a daily basis, over 4 million Dutch get on their bikes to ride to work, shop, or enjoy

Serene cycling on a coastal bike path en route to the island of Marken (Waterland Day Trip, page 65).

their scenic country. They can't all be wrong! The land is mostly level, making it easy to cycle, and the superb network of car-free bicycle paths ("*fietspad*," or in the plural, "*fietspaden*") crisscross the country.

From over the handlebars, all those stereotypical images of cows, canals, windmills and tulips take on a different perspective as you glide through miles and miles of brightly colored tulips, or are intoxicated by the overpowering scent of a field of hyacinths. Imagine cycling alongside a canal surrounded by lush green pastures of placid cows grazing, against a backdrop of stately windmills, or watching a farmer tilling muddy soil wearing, what else but those most practical of Dutch footwear, clogs. The countryside and the storybook villages lend themselves to cycling. In this country, where the bicycle reigns supreme, even cycling in larger cities is a breeze.

Cycling the Netherlands is possible for cyclists at any level. Distances between villages are small, making distances manageable for the novice, and most of the country is essentially level. Experienced cyclists will relish the extensive network of bicycle paths and the marked long-distance routes. Anyone and everyone will enjoy the scenery and feel part of the bicycle-friendly culture, apparent wherever you go.

In the Netherlands you get the feeling that cycling is "the thing to do." In most countries, as a cyclist you stand out, but in the Netherlands, you blend in: cycling is the norm! Everyone, it seems, rides a bike, from 2-year-olds to grandmothers. It's a way of life. People use their bikes to commute, shop, carry a load of vegetables or tools to a neighboring farm, or even to pull a windsurfer to a nearby lake. Most of the population owns a bicycle, and up to 40% of the population get into the saddle on a daily basis. The Dutch are friendly, and you quickly feel accepted as you pedal throughout the country. The people are welcoming and language shouldn't be a problem, as English is widely understood in the Netherlands.

Not an uncommon sight in the Netherlands: Mother takes the kids along on the bike when running errands in Den Bosch. And no, in Holland, not many cyclists wear helmets.

Practically Speaking

Bicycle shops everywhere offer repairs and rentals, as do many railway stations, most of which also offer secure bicycle parking facilities. There are plenty of bicycle paths to get you off the beaten track. Where there are no bicycle paths, there are numerous quiet rural backroads.

Touring by bike allows a choice of budget. On your bike, you have virtually no transportation costs. The rest is up to you. For the lower budget traveler, the bike offers an easy means to transport camping equipment and personal gear. If you choose to stay in hotels, bed and breakfasts, or with Dutch cyclists (*Vrienden op de Fiets*, see page 36), all you need to carry is your clothing and daily essentials.

In the Netherlands, cyclists have privileges often not afforded to the motorist. One-way street signs, for example, often have a sign underneath with a picture of a bike and the word *uitgezonderd* (translation: bicycles excepted). Bicycle paths in rural areas are sometimes better paved than the dirt road for vehicles that runs alongside it. In most cities and towns, bicycle-parking facilities can be found in the center where it can be impossible to park a car. Where traffic construction diverts cars many kilometers out of their way, the cyclist is hardly disrupted, as special bike detour routes are often set up through the construction site.

As a cyclist, you will feel like royalty with the incredible network of bicycle paths, special amenities for cyclists, compared to other countries where cyclists are often viewed as second-class citizens and a hindrance to cars. And, while on the subject of royalty and bicycles, Queen Beatrix is known to be at her happiest when she is cycling in the Dutch countryside. As a cyclist in the Netherlands, you will feel safer and more comfortable than you could ever imagine, whether in rural areas, or even in a big city like Amsterdam.

The Netherlands is culturally diverse, has a rich history, interesting architecture, a variety of cuisine, has some of the world's finest museums, and the Dutch have one of the most progressive lifestyles in Europe. All things considered, tour-

No bridge, no problem! Crossing a canal near Delft by means of a *voetveer* (literally pedestrian ferry), which takes pedestrians and cyclists only.

ing the Netherlands by bicycle will provide you with an unforgettable experience. Pack your panniers and find out!

And Belgium

Some of the routes in this book dip into Belgium. The Belgians are also very fond of cycling, but more for short local trips, rather than for long-distance bicycle touring. Belgians love bicycle racing, and Belgium has produced several international cycling champions, including Eddie Merckx, who is considered a national hero in Belgium.

Flanders, the Northwestern part of Belgium, borders on the Netherlands and has a lot in common with its bicycle-conscious neighbor. Although road surfaces are usually good, many roads in Flanders maintain one tie with the past: cobblestones.

Here too, you are never far from a town or a village, and the extensive canal system offers idyllic cycling under a canopy of shady trees. Rolling hills define cycling in Belgian Limburg in the Northeast, while in the West. you can ride along the beach and visit to the jewel of Flanders, the medieval town of Bruges.

Germany Too

Germany borders the Netherlands to the east, and also has a lively bicycle culture. Except for the language change and the different road signs, it may be hard to tell that you've crossed into another country on the South Limburg route, which slips over the border for a visit to the historic city of Aachen.

Cycling along a quiet tree-lined country lane on the way to Bruges, Belgium.

2.

Pre-Departure Planning

A certain amount of planning and organization is important for bicycle touring. Many matters apply to any type of trip, such as deciding when to go, purchasing tickets, official documents, budget, etc. For a bicycle tour, there are additional considerations, such as weather, terrain, equipment, and physical ability.

Everyone has different needs and expectations. It isn't necessary to plan your trip down to the tiniest detail. In fact, you don't want to be too rigid, as part of the fun of bicycle touring is flexibility. This chapter covers some of the essentials, and extras, to help you plan and ensure smooth cycling.

Be prepared to share the bike paths with more than just cyclists. En route to Heusden, sheep relax along the bike path.

Climate

The Netherlands' proximity to the sea and the warm North Atlantic Gulf Stream ensure a temperate maritime climate; moderate temperatures, with mild winters and cool summers. Summer temperatures never rise much above 25°C (80°F). Normally, winter temperatures don't fall below the freezing point, but It is not unusual to see snow in winter, but it usually melts fairly quickly. Rainfall is evenly distributed throughout the year, averaging 762 mm (30 in.) annually. April and May receive the least precipitation.

Wind is commonplace, especially along the coast, particularly Zeeland, North Holland and Friesland. The prevailing winds are from the west or southwest, and coastal gales are most frequent in autumn and winter. As well as giving temperature and precipitation, daily weather reports indicate the wind direction and the wind force.

When to Go

Although cycle touring in the Netherlands is possible year-round, the weather conditions are most favorable between mid-April and early October. If you want to see the tulip fields in bloom, mid-April or early May would be the time to go.

The summer months, June, July and August are optimal: the weather is mild and the days are long. Attractions and lodgings are busiest in summer while everybody is on vacation. The peripheral months of May and September are excellent choices. Temperatures are pleasant, accommodations and sights are less crowded, and often price breaks on lodgings and airline travel are available.

Late-September and October see a drop in temperatures. However, this time can also have its charm. Although the mornings can be crisp, it usually warms up during the day. The crowds are gone, so it's easier to find accommodations. It is more difficult to camp at this time, as many campgrounds close for the season.

Rain and wind are your biggest adversaries, but neither should be a deterrent. Flexibility and patience are the keys. If it is windy, take it slowly or, if possible, alter the direction of your route. If you encounter a sudden cloudburst, then find shelter in a café, or linger in a museum. If several days of rain are on the horizon, try to reach an interesting town where you can spend a day or two.

Resources

Knowing about your destination will enhance your travel experience. Books and maps are invaluable. This book offers detailed cycling and route information, plus sightseeing highlights for locales en route. There are abundant supplemental publications available such as the *Michelin Green Guide: Netherlands* (general tourist information), the *Insight Guide: Holland* (background information), and the *Norton Blue Guide: Holland* (rich in cultural and historic detail). Two good all-round general guidebooks are *Lonely Planet: Netherlands* and the *Rough*

Guide: Netherlands. For a complete listing, see Further Reading in the Appendix, page 289).

Maps are even more important than guidebooks, both for planning and while on the road. Specific map-related information is provided in Chapter 5.

The Netherlands has National Tourist Offices in many countries. The official website of the Netherlands Board of Tourism is www.holland.com, and the official site for Amsterdam Tourism is www.visitamsterdam.nl, and then click on the tab for English. Both sites are packed with useful information.

Throughout the book, websites for individual tourist offices for towns, lodgings, restaurants, museums, bike shops, and other organizations and facilities are listed. Some websites are in Dutch only, but with the help of a dictionary, even those are usually easy to navigate. Some useful websites:

www.ns.nl	Dutch railway; schedules, prices, station facilities
www.detelefoongids.nl	The Dutch telephone book
www.freedict.com/onldict/dut.html	Online Dutch-English dictionary
www.thehollandring.com	Interesting expat website and all things Dutch
www.learndutch.org	Learn Dutch online
www.ntfu.nl	Dutch Bicycle Touring Union. Events & general information
www.vriendenopdefiets.nl	Cycle-friendly lodging in people's homes (see page 36)
www.fietsvakantiewinkel.nl	Shop with maps, books, planning information for cycling trips, tours, and more (see page 184)

Documents

Your most important and essential document is your passport. Check to make sure it is valid for the duration of your trip. If you do not have a passport yet, apply

Be Prepared

Some of the most important items you are carrying are your documents. It's a good idea to photocopy the passport pages that have your photo, passport number, the date and place of issue. Make two copies, one to leave with someone you can contact from on the road, and carry the other one with you, separate from your passport. This will be helpful for more efficient replacement should your passport be lost or stolen. Also do this for other important documents, such as airline tickets, hostel card, etc. Do the same with the list of the numbers of traveler's checks, credit cards, and ATM cards.

for one well in advance, as the process can be time-consuming.The Netherlands does not require a visa for most nationalities, but check with your travel agent, airline, or consulate as to whether one is required.

Other documents you may wish to consider are the Hostelling International card, available from Hostelling International Offices, online at www.hihostels.com, official hostels in your country, or most official hostels in Europe. If you are a student, an International Student Card can be useful for discounts. For campers, an optional document is a Camping Card International, CCI (previouly Camping Carnet). It can be used in place of a passport if the campground requires you to leave one, and some campgrounds offer discounts for holders of this card. Information on purchasing a card is available at www.campingcardinternational.org. In the Netherlands, you can buy a CCI card from ANWB offices (see pages30–31).

Protect your valuables (passport, airline ticket, credit cards, cash) by wearing a money belt or pouch concealed under your clothes. While cycling, you may wish to take it off and keep it in your handlebar bag, but as soon as you stop or leave your bike, put it back on! Be aware of pickpockets, especially in crowded tourist areas.

Another consideration in personal safety is health. Medical facilities in Europe are excellent. Check your health insurance policy prior to departure for international benefits and coverage. If you are not adequately covered, you may wish to consider additional travel insurance.

Money Matters

Traditionally, one of the safest ways to take money is the traveler's check. Converted into Euros at banks, exchange bureaux or post offices, you will typically be charged a small commission or fee for the transaction. Cross traveler's check numbers off after cashing them, and keep numbers separate from your traveler's checks.

Nowadays, credit cards and ATM (debit) cards are another option. They are not accepted as widely in the Netherlands for payment as in many other countries. Instead, the Dutch use a so-called PIN card, similar to a debit card. Don't count on paying with a credit card in small family-run establishments, and the Dutch railways only accepts credit cards for international journeys, while cash or PIN card payment is required for domestic journeys.

Plan ahead so that you are not short of cash for weekends and public holidays when banks are closed.

Planning Your Budget

The amount of money you spend is an individual decision. Major variations in cost depend on where you sleep and eat.

Accommodation and food costs are a daily occurrence, but extra costs to consider are sightseeing entrance fees (museums, castles etc.), unexpected bicycle repairs, books or maps, laundry charges, souvenirs, and so on.

In addition to your airline ticket, there are some other transport charges to consider. Allow for trains and ferries, as well as public transport within a large city. There will be an additional charge for your bicycle on trains and some ferries.

Transporting Your Bicycle

If you are taking your own bike, the first decision will be how to prepare it for travel. Although some airlines will accept your bike for shipment as is, most require a bike box. Some airlines charge substantial fees, and airline regulations change often, so check this when purchasing your ticket. You can purchase bike boxes from most airlines (fees vary) at the airport. If you return from Amsterdam's Schiphol Airport, the bike boxes (for all airlines) are available from the KLM oversize luggage counter for €20. Some airlines sell their own bike boxes.

The standard airline bike box is a simple, large cardboard box. You will only have to remove the pedals, turn the handlebars sideways, deflate the tires, put your bike in the box, and tape it up. However, these boxes are not very sturdy, and do little to protect your bike. A shipping carton obtained from a bike shop is sturdier, but requires more disassembly of the bike to fit. Hard cases built specifically for bikes provide the best protection, but they are expensive and bulky—and they must be stored somewhere at your destination until you return.

Fitting the bike into the airline box is not a complicated process, but don't leave it to the last minute, as it can take much longer than you might anticipate the first time you do it. You should pad the bike as well as you can, and the dead space in the box can be used for packing panniers, sleeping bags, etc. Do not leave any parts (pedals, for example) loose in the box as it is not uncommon for it to arrive at the destination with holes in the cardboard. Clean your bike before packing.

Folding bikes can make the shipping process simple. Several companies now produce good-quality bikes that fold and fit into hard cases that are within the airlines' allowance for regular baggage. You can simply check these as you would a normal suitcase. No one can tell there's a bike inside, and it is in a protective hard case. Bike Friday (www.bikefriday.com) is a good example. These bikes are somewhat expensive, but worth considering if you do a lot of traveling.

Itinerary and Route Planning

The routes in this book guide you through the Netherlands. Time may allow you to choose them all, sections of some, or combine them with a larger European tour. Whatever the case, you will need to do some research (see Resources, page 18). Basic reading and referring to maps will help you decide what suits you best.

Maps are invaluable in planning, and you should try to obtain as many maps as possible prior to departure. The maps in this book are guides, and should be used with the maps suggested at the beginning of each route. Details on these maps can be found in the map sections specific to each ride.

Consider your own time restrictions, and if part of some routes or regions interest you, cycle that portion then take a train and pick up a route in another area. The Dutch rail system is extensive and bicycle-friendly. (see Transporting your Bike by Train, Chapter 5)

It is also important to plan rest days into your itinerary. You will enjoy the trip more if you don't feel the pressure of being behind schedule. Allow yourself the flexibility to stay longer than planned in a place that turns out to be more interesting than you anticipated, stay an extra day when you discover a festival or special event, or make a detour or side trip that you hear about while underway. Also allow for less desirable delays such as bad weather, mechanical problems or illness.

Bicycle touring gives you the independence to go where you like, when you like—but only if you give yourself that flexibility by allowing enough time.

How Far Should You Go Each Day?

Everyone is different! Ability, endurance and interests are an individual question. Some cyclists will ride greater distances and treat it as a challenge, some people will meander through the countryside at a much slower pace, and cover less distance. Some days have so many sights that your day's overall mileage will decrease; some areas with less to see allow you to speed up. Don't be discouraged if you don't go far in a day, as long as you've enjoyed what you've done. Pace yourself to your own satisfaction, but plan for an end of day arrival in time to set up your tent, find lodging, buy supplies for the evening, or get to the tourist office before it closes.

Physical Conditioning

In order to complete the tours in this book, you don't have to be a Tour de France contender. All you need is to be prepared both physically and mentally. It won't

In the provinces of North and South Holland, tulip fields make for a colorful visual treat in early spring.

take you long to determine your comfort level, and beginning with reasonable fitness will allow you to enjoy your trip all the more.

Some training is necessary before departure. If time doesn't allow extended rides, then do what you can, even an hour every couple of days will suffice. Begin with short rides and build up. Then, as departure approaches, add the panniers with weight, so that you get a feel for the difference in handling the loaded bike.

If this is your first tour, take it step by step as suggested above. If you are camping, and have never cycle-camped before, try a short practice weekend trip.

Once you arrive, don't push yourself too hard in the initial days. It can take a few days to get over jet lag, and get used to full cycling days. If you have not had a chance to do a lot of preparation, consider starting with day trips from a base city or shorter days.

Touring Equipment

For touring in the Netherlands, a good quality bike of any type will work, as long as it fits and is comfortable. Some things you should look for in any bike you choose include a sturdy frame, wide range of gears, good brakes, a comfortable saddle, the right tires for touring, fenders and, again, the proper fit for you.

Preparing Your Bike

Any bike, new or old, can be customized or personalized. A comfortable saddle is paramount. Handlebars can also be switched on virtually any bicycle. If you find the right bike, but want different handlebars, talk to your dealer.

For touring in the Netherlands, it is an absolute necessity to have fenders, or mudguards. They reduce the amount of water and road dirt that sprays you when the roads are wet. Full (attached) fenders are the most effective; clip-on versions are inadequate.

Although a kickstand may not hold up a fully loaded bike, it's handy to store your bike in a place with nowhere to lean your bike, which is the case in most hotels and hostels.

Racks, Panniers, and Bags

A rear rack is essential. Whether you need a front rack depends on what type of touring you will be doing. If you are camping, there is no question: you will need both front and rear racks. If you travel light, you can probably manage with just rear panniers and a handlebar bag.

Any good rear rack will work. There are two types of front racks. One style is similar to a rear rack but shorter; the other is the so-called low-rider rack, which places the weight of the panniers close to the center of the wheel. The latter type does not affect the steering as much.

23

There are many panniers (bike bags) to choose from. Look for a larger pair for the rear and a smaller pair for the front. They need not be the same brand or style. It is worth paying more for high-quality panniers. Most will be weather resistant but not rainproof. Ortlieb (www. ortlieb.de) offer the only truly waterproof panniers and other bags. They are available worldwide, although it may take some searching.

Handlebar bags provide quick access to your camera and other necessities. When selecting your handlebar bag, there are three things to keep in mind:

❑ It should have a of a waterproof map-holder on top.
❑ It should be easy to take off the bike and put back on.
❑ Bigger is not necessarily better, because too much weight makes the bike hard to maneuver.

Other Items

You will also need the following items: a helmet, water bottles, a bell, lights, a pump, a lock, a tool kit, and a bicycle computer.

Most Europeans do not wear helmets. Regardless of what the locals are doing, play it safe and wear a helmet.

A bell is required by law in the Netherlands. The same applies to front and rear lights, even if you are not planning on riding at night.

Most bikes have two bottle cage mounts. Drink frequently, even if you don't feel thirsty, to avoid dehydration.

A bike lock is an unfortunate necessity. Make sure the pump fits the type of valve used on your tires. It is also essential that you have the tools to do the most basic repairs, such as fix a flat tire.

A bike computer is essential for following the directions in this book. It lets you know how far you've ridden, which is essential for navigation, and how fast, which can help with planning. Set it to read in km rather than miles, because that's the reference used in the cue sheets in this book and all signs along the road.

The number of optional accessories is endless. Some you might want to consider are described below.

Compasses help with navigation. There are bike bells available which incorporate a compass.

A small handle-mounted rear view mirror allows you to monitor traffic (or your cycling partner) behind you without constantly turning your head.

Bungee cords allow you to strap almost anything onto your racks.

A waterproof saddle cover will keep the saddle dry when you leave the bike outside (plastic bags also work).

Something else to consider is a rack trunk—a bag or case that fits on top of the rear luggage rack. They are great for holding lunch, rain-gear and other items you may need during the day.

Tools & Repairs

One advantage to cycling in the Netherlands is that you are never far from a bike shop. The popularity of bicycles, both for sport and transportation, ensures that even most small towns have a bike shop. Therefore, an elaborate array of tools is not necessary. You should carry the following:

❏ spare tube
❏ tube repair kit
❏ tire levers
❏ spare spokes (tape to frame)
❏ spoke wrench
❏ phillips and regular screwdrivers
❏ adjustable wrench
❏ allen wrenches
❏ lubricant
❏ pliers
❏ duct tape
❏ plastic ties of various lengths and sizes

Many companies make combination tools, which include most of the basic tools in extremely compact packages.

In addition, you may want to carry extra brake pads and cables, a chain link removal tool, a crank bolt tool, and freewheel tools.

Packing

Packing what you need, or anticipate needing, is an important part of planning. For the most practical use of your garments, dress in layers. This is particularly ef-

Fully loaded touring bikes in front of the Bicyclists statue in Bruges, Belgium.

fective when you start out on a cool morning, and can peel off clothing as the day warms up.

Mostly you will be dressed for cycling, but you will need casual clothes while off the bike, and you may wish to take an outfit for the evening in fabrics that don't wrinkle.

The most important thing to keep in mind is that everything you pack, you will have to carry, so pack lightly and evaluate each item by asking, "Do I really need this?"

❑ Padded cycling shorts are available both in lycra with padded chamois or, if you prefer the look of ordinary shorts, with a sewn-in padded lining.

❑ For cooler weather, take long lycra cycling pants.

❑ For wet weather, take a waterproof (or at least water-resistant) jacket, and rain pants.

❑ Consider a pair of waterproof booties that fit over your shoes.

❑ If your ears get cold, take a headband.

❑ Instead of jeans or casual pants, think about convertible pants with zip-off legs; a two-for-one deal, long pants and shorts.

❑ For cooler weather, take a warm hat and regular gloves, or full-finger cycling gloves. Padded cycling gloves reduce jarring, protect your hands if you fall and prevent sunburn.

❑ Hard-soled cycling shoes help you pedal more efficiently and ultimately avoid knee problems. Soft-soled shoes or sandals should be taken for while off the bike.

❑ Camera film is expensive in Europe, so stock up before you leave.

❑ Also take spare batteries for items such as digital camera, bike headlamp or flashlight.

❑ Ziploc bags are great for organizing and keeping things dry, and garbage bags can be used for picnicking on damp grass, extra ground cover when camping, or lining panniers.

❑ A flashlight is handy, or substitute with your detachable bike headlight.

❑ If you take a Swiss Army knife or scissors, remember to put them in your checked luggage, because they'll be confiscated if you try to carry them on board.

Washing Your Clothes

Be prepared to wash your small items by hand and (hopefully) dry them overnight. Two useful items are concentrated tube soap and an expandable clothesline. From time to time you will need to stop at a self-service laundry. Many campgrounds have washing facilities, as do some hostels. If you need to find a self-service laundry, the word in Dutch is *wassalon*. Washing powder is usually available at the laundry in small packets, or purchase the smallest amount possible at a supermarket prior to visiting the laundry.

Drying Tip: If you have a wet or damp item, it is possible to dry it as you ride, by tucking it under a bungee cord, or by using the mesh outer pocket found on some panniers.

❑ Take extra passport photos for hostel cards, and certain discounted cards and passes.

Once you have compiled your personal list, practice packing everything into your panniers. This is important for two reasons. First, you need to know that it all actually fits. Remember to leave some room for food and additional items you'll collect en route. Second, there is an art to packing panniers. Weight distribution is very important on a bike, and the time to figure what goes where, is before you leave. Try to keep roughly equal weight in the left and right panniers. Cyclists disagree on the front and back weight ratio. Many feel that all your heavy items should be in the rear, while others feel it should be an almost equal distribution. Try both and see which feels better to you. Unless you have waterproof panniers, line your panniers with large plastic bags for extra protection. The lists below are suggested packing lists; these will vary with individual needs.

Clothing
❑ 1 rain jacket
❑ 1 pair rain pants
❑ 3 T-shirts or cycling jerseys
❑ 2 pairs padded cycling shorts
❑ 1 pair long cycling pants
❑ 1 fleece jacket or 1 sweatshirt
❑ 1 long sleeve (capilene-type fabric) top
❑ 1 pair regular shorts and/or 1 skirt
❑ 1 pair jeans or long pants
❑ 1 bathing suit
❑ underwear (for women include 2 sports bras)
❑ 3 pairs socks
❑ 1 pair cycling shoes
❑ 1 pair walking shoes or sandals and/or thongs
❑ 1 pair cycling gloves
❑ 1 sunhat
❑ 1 bandanna or scarf

Personal
❑ toiletries kit
❑ first aid kit
❑ dental floss (also handy for tying or repairing things, or as a clothes line)
❑ towel and soap
❑ toilet paper
❑ towelettes/waterless hand sanitizer
❑ expandable clothesline
❑ tube detergent
❑ sunglasses
❑ sunscreen

❑ insect repellent

Miscellaneous
❑ camera and film
❑ Swiss Army knife or similar
❑ scissors
❑ sewing kit
❑ spare batteries
❑ journal and pen
❑ Ziploc bags
❑ garbage bags
❑ travel alarm
❑ security pouch (see Documents, pages 19–20)
❑ guidebook/maps
❑ phrase book and/or small dictionary
❑ flashlight/bike headlamp
❑ small daypack
❑ extra passport photos
❑ automobile club card (see ANWB, pages 30–31)
❑ If you picnic, add basic utensils such as knife/fork/spoon set, plastic plate and cup.

Camping Gear

If you are camping, decide how much equipment you will need. Little more than a tent and sleeping bag are absolutely necessary. Beyond that you face the classic cyclist's dilemma—the tradeoff between comfort and weight. Ask yourself exactly what kind of camping you really want to do. How self-sufficient do you want to be? Will you cook for yourself every day, or will you eat out most of the time? Start with the bare minimum you feel you can survive with. If you find you need more, it is not difficult to find camping supply shops in Europe. The following is a basic list of camping supplies.
❑ tent
❑ sleeping bag
❑ insulated sleeping mat
❑ flashlight (or headlamp)
❑ stove*
❑ matches or lighter
❑ small cooking pot
❑ plate, cup, knife/fork/spoon set
❑ can opener & corkscrew
❑ dishcloth, scourer, detergent

---

* Make sure your stove is compatible with canisters available in Europe. GAZ brand is the most widespread. The gas canister, or any other type of fuel, can not be taken on the plane.

3.
Country Information

WHICH IS correct, the Netherlands or Holland? The correct name is the Netherlands, but both are generally accepted. It seems today that the two are used interchangeably. In fact, Holland refers to two of the provinces on the western side of the country, namely North Holland and South Holland. The Dutch name for the country is Nederland, which means "low land."

The stereotypical view of the Netherlands is that of windmills, tulips, wooden clogs, and canals. Yes, these symbols do exist, but the Netherlands is more than these cute images. The country is one of the most progressive countries in Europe, both culturally and socially. The Dutch government subsidizes several types of educational, artistic and social programs resulting in a well-educated population with an awareness of their background and the value of historical monuments and architecture. The country is rich in museums, galleries and exhibitions.

The Dutch have been battling the sea for centuries. Much of the country is below sea level, and prone to flooding. The windmills are not just symbols for the tourist. In earlier days these behemoths were used to drain lakes and keep the newly reclaimed land (polders) dry. They were strategically placed along canals and were the difference between swamp and fertile, usable land. Today many working windmills have been retired, and most are kept as beautiful and graceful antiquities, or for demonstrations, but all in all the romance and utility of the classic windmills have been replaced with modern sleek aerodynamic windmills, or pumps. Some windmills were also used to grind grains; some are still in use. Another feat of Dutch engineering is the Afsluitdijk, the 30-kilometer dike that turned the saltwater Zuiderzee into a fresh water lake, allowing for a great deal of land reclamation.

Tourist Information Office (VVV)

The VVV, or Tourist Information Office, will become your most cherished resource while in the Netherlands. You will become accustomed to searching out the VVV (pronounced like a cross between Vay Vay Vay and Fay Fay Fay) when arriving in a new town. The VVV symbol is clearly designated as three white Vs in a triangular format on a royal blue background, but often the international "i" symbol is also used. The offices are usually centrally located, sometimes in a building with historic significance. You will be amazed how widespread the locations of the VVV offices are, finding them in tiny towns where you would least expect one.

The VVVs provides sightseeing information, and free literature, but they also sell books and maps, reserve accommodation (sometimes for a small fee), and can assist with directions and local information. Each VVV has an official guide to their town or region. For example, the VVV Maastricht has a guide to Maastricht and surroundings (€1.50), plus a guide to the province, *VVV Gids Limburg* (€4).

Several VVVs offer independent bike tour packages. The VVV pre-books your lodging, transfers your luggage (you carry only your lunch and personal items during the day) and provides you with daily maps, itinerary and sightseeing. Some examples of VVV bike packages are VVV Central Holland (www. vvvhollandsmidden.nl), VVV South Holland (www.vvvzhz.nl) and VVV Texel (www. texel.net), and VVV Borger-Odoorn (www. tref.nl/ borger-odoorn/vvv). For other cycling packages see page 46.

Touring Club Offices (ANWB)

Another excellent resource is the ANWB, or Royal Dutch Touring Club (www. anwb.nl, Dutch only). This is the equivalent of the American AAA or British RAC. Membership to your country's automobile association entitles you to use their services, which includes everything from selling books and outstanding maps (used in the route section), to travel accessories and cycling gear, as well as free maps and other literature. Take your local association card for identification.

Museum Card

VVVs and most museums sell the Museum Jaar Kaart (Museum Year Card), one of the best bargains in the Netherlands. If you intend to visit at least a half dozen museums during your stay, especially some of the expensive ones like the Van Gogh Museum in Amsterdam (entry €9), then consider purchasing the Museum Jaar Kaart. It is good for entry, or discounted entry, into about 400 museums throughout the country, and is valid for one year from issue date. Some literature indicates you need a passport photo; no longer required (since 2004). The card costs €25 plus a once only administration fee of €4.95. Adult admission prices for museums vary from €2 to €9.

ANWB stands for *Algemene Nederlandsche Wielrijders Bond*, which translates to General Dutch Cyclist's Association. The ANWB existed well before the car, and at its inception over 130 years ago, was a cyclist's touring club. Today it caters to both motorists and cyclists.

The ANWB is also under contract with the state to provide the signposting around the country, both for general traffic and for cyclists. The latter category includes the red and white directional bicycle signs, various route signs, and the little ANWB *paddestoelen* ("mushrooms")—knee-high directional signs for cyclists and hikers that look like large mushrooms (see page 10).

Money Matters

The unit of currency is the Euro (€), as in most of the EU. At the time of writing €1 was about US $0.80. The Euro is divided into 100 cents, with bills of €500, €200, €100, €50, €20, €10 and €5, and coins of €2 and €1, and Eurocent coins of 50c, 20c, 10c, 5c, and 1c.

Confirm rates and commissions at banks and exchange places before exchanging as they vary for both travelers' checks and cash. Banks are open Monday through Friday 9 a.m. to 4 p.m. or 5 p.m. Be sure to change money for the weekend. Some exchange places are open longer hours and on weekends, but don't rely on this outside the big cities. You can also change money at most post offices and some hotels. GWK has exchange offices at most railway stations and are open daily until 6 p.m. or 7 p.m. ATM card rates are usually reasonable, but expect a fee for each transaction when you get home.

Credit cards are not widely used in family-owned small shops (including bike shops), small hotels, pensions, bed & breakfasts, and many campgrounds. Larger hotels and stores accept credit cards. Supermarkets don't usually accept credit cards, and acceptance in restaurants varies.

Business Hours

The Dutch love their weekend, and shops (including supermarkets) begin closing anytime after lunch on Saturday, and many do not re-open until Monday at 1 p.m. To compensate for this, shops in some towns are open late on either Thursday or Friday evenings. Most shops open from 9 a.m. to 5 p.m. or 6 p.m., but some larger chain supermarkets in bigger towns open until 8 p.m. In small towns, shops may be closed one weekday afternoon, usually Wednesdays.

Museums and monuments are normally open from 10 a.m. until 5 p.m., but many are closed on Mondays.

The VVV and ANWB usually maintain regular business hours. Most VVVs are closed on Sunday.

Telephones

The country code for the Netherlands is 31. To call from the US, you have to dial 011-31, followed by the area code minus the zero, and the local number. To call home from Holland, you have to dial 00, followed by the country code (1 for the US and Canada, 44 for England), the area code (minus the 0 in the case of England), and the local number.

It is almost impossible to find coin-operated public phones; most take only phone cards, and sometimes credit cards. Phone cards are available at train stations, post offices, supermarkets, tobacconists/newsstands and some VVV offices.

There are two major phone companies, KPN and Telfort. The ubiquitous lime green phone booths only take KPN phone cards; the blue Telfort phones only accept Telfort cards. All phones inside railway stations are operated by Telfort; KPN phones are outside.

International calling instructions are usually printed in phone booths in English. Before leaving home check rates and access phone numbers for your international phone carrier. Most hotels have a surcharge for phone calls.

If you have a cell (mobile) phone, make sure your phone is compatible with the European systems. If you have a GSM tri-band phone, in most cases, all you need is to purchase a Dutch SIM card to install in the phone and a prepaid phone card. You can buy both cards at the airport upon arrival, in "phone" shops, some railway station kiosks, and supermarkets.

Internet Access

Internet cafés are commonplace throughout the country in cities and most sizable towns. Often internet access is available in hotels, hostels, some VVVs and public libraries. Fees vary, from €0.60 to €1 for 15 minutes to €2 to €4 per hour. Throughout this book, internet access is listed in overnight towns where available.

Post Offices

Post offices are open Mondays through Fridays from 8:30 a.m. to 5 p.m.; some are also open Saturdays from 8:30 a.m. until noon. Larger post offices offer *poste restante* (i.e., mail-holding service at the post office) and currency exchange. Mail boxes have two slots: to send mail out of the country, put it in the slot marked *"Overige."*

Public Holidays & Events

On official public holidays, shops and businesses are closed; however, some museums and restaurants will be open.

Major Public Holidays:
❏ January 1 (New Year's Day)
❏ Easter (Good Friday, Easter Sunday and Easter Monday)
❏ Ascension Day
❏ Whit Sunday and Whit Monday (Whitsun is 40 days after Easter)
❏ Koninginnedag (Queen's Day, 30 April, see boxed text "Orange Day" below)
❏ December 25 (Christmas Day) and December 26 (Boxing Day)

Unofficial Holidays

Two unofficial holidays are "Remembrance Days" and even though neither of these days are official holidays, some shops and services may be closed. Both days are associated with World War II: May 4 is a memorial day honoring those who died, and May 5 acknowledges Liberation Day.

Carnival (Mardi Gras), the week prior to Ash Wednesday, is celebrated only in the predominantly Catholic provinces of Gelderland, North Brabant and Limburg.

Special Events

At any given time, local events and festivals take place throughout the country.

Cycling Events

National Cycling Day (Landelijke Fietsdag): second Saturday in May

Races and cycling events throughout the country with around 200 specially signed cycling routes of varying lengths. (www.holland.com, Dutch only)

Windmill Days

Nationale Molendag, or National Windmill Day, is the second Saturday in May. On that day, all the country's windmills are open to the public with special activities.

Orange Day

If you plan to be in the Netherlands on 30 April, and want to blend in, make sure you have something orange to wear. It is Koninginnedag (Queen's Day), the official birthday of Queen Juliana (the mother of Queen Beatrix, the current queen). Everyone will be decked out in orange, stemming from the royal family's lineage, the House of Orange. The country celebrates with parades, street markets, music and other festivities. Amsterdam becomes the site of a huge party, street market and general frivolity, and if you enjoy crowds, join in, otherwise steer clear until the party's over!

There is also a *Zaanstreek Molendag*, or Zaan Region Windmill Day, which falls on the last Saturday of September, with free admission to many of the mills in the area around Zaandam (see page 207).

Cheese markets
❑ Alkmaar: Traditional cheese market with cheese porters in their guild costumes. Fridays, mid-April to mid-September, 10 a.m. to noon (see page 74).
❑ Edam: The cheeses are brought in small cheese boats and traded at the market. Wednesdays, July and August, 9 a.m. to noon (see page 71).
❑ Gouda: Traditional market, starting with the age-old custom of taking the cheese to the Waag for weighing. Thursdays (see page 187).

Flower Parades
❑ Bulb District Flower Parade: first Saturday after 19th April.
   Magnificently-decorated floats leave Noordwijk to arrive in the evening, illuminated, in Haarlem via Sassenheim, Lisse, Hillegom and Bennebroek (see page 202).
❑ Aalsmeer Flower Parade: first Saturday in September.
   Procession from Aalsmeer, through Amstelveen and Amsterdam, concluding in the evening in Aalsmeer, the floats illuminated (see Aalsmeer, page 52).

Language

The official language is Dutch.

Friesland is a bilingual province. Everybody speaks Dutch, and about 75% of the population speak Friesian (*Fryske*), an ancient Germanic language. Road signs in Friesland are in both languages.

When the language genes were handed out, it seems that the Dutch won the lottery. The linguistic ability of the Dutch is quite astonishing. Apart from their own language, most people speak English like a native speaker, plus many are proficient in German and/or French. You will easily get by with English in the Netherlands, but a sure way to bring a smile to a Dutch person's face is to be able to use some basic Dutch (see Glossary, pages 284–286). You may want to carry a small dictionary or phrase book for that menu item that is eluding you or the sign that may be important to translate.

One peculiarity about Dutch place names is the combination of the two letters "ij" to represent one single letter of the Dutch alphabet, roughly the equivalent of "y." They are really one letter, and when used at the beginning of a place name, they are both capitalized.

4.

Food & Lodging

EVERY DAY you face the questions of where to sleep and where, and what, to eat. For some people, flexibility is paramount, and they try to make those decisions daily as the need arises. For others, it is something that is planned in advance.

Accommodations

The Netherlands has a range of lodging choices, and your own level of comfort and budget will determine where you rest your head each night. Throughout the

There are several hotels and B&Bs along this canal in Middelburg.

routes, accommodations such as hotels, bed & breakfasts (B&Bs), hostels and campgrounds are listed for the towns where the daily trips start and finish. The Netherlands Board of Tourism (www.holland.com) has extensive accommodation information in all categories. En route, VVVs will make reservations, often for a small fee of €2 or €3.

You can reserve anything from hotels to campgrounds in advance, either by phone, fax, or E-mail. Extensive accommodation listings are available from tourist offices, guidebooks, and on the Internet.

If you prefer to choose your lodging on a day-to-day basis, there are certain things to bear in mind. You must arrive early enough to locate lodging before rooms fill up and to seek the advice of the tourist office before it closes, and try to avoid busy tourist times and local festivals, when towns can be crowded and rooms scarce.

Hotels and Pensions

In hotels and *pensions* (small, family-run establishments), you will often have the option of a private or a shared bathroom. Be sure to ask about this when checking in or making the reservation. Also check whether breakfast is included—it is in most cases. In the route section, hotel and pension prices always include breakfast, unless otherwise indicated. Don't be afraid to ask to see the room, and ask whether there is a place off the street to keep your bike overnight. All hotels and pensions listed in the route section have a safe place to store your bike overnight.

Many cities have a lodging tax of about €1 to €2 per person per night. Prices listed in the book do not include this tax.

For online reservations, try the comprehensive www.hotelres.nl or the more limited www.hotels-holland.com.

Bed & Breakfasts

Bed & Breakfasts (B&Bs) are private homes offering a friendly atmosphere and a cultural experience. They are often an excellent value. Breakfast is included, and there is usually a place for your bike in the backyard, garage, or shed.

In Dutch, Bed & Breakfast is *Logie met Ontbijt*, and in Friesland, in the regional Fries language, it is *Bed en Brochje*.

Throughout the routes, B&B availability is indicated. As this form of lodging is often seasonal, and family-run, please check ahead to avoid disappointment. In towns where there are numerous B&Bs, check with local VVVs for current information. They will provide directions as well as book the room for you.

Vrienden op de Fiets

Vrienden op de Fiets, or "Friends of the Bicycle" (www. vriendenopdefiets.nl), is a unique organization that is truly bicycle-friendly. For a €10 membership fee, you can stay in any one of 2,100 private homes in the Netherlands and Belgium. The price is €16 per person, per night, including breakfast. You have to call your hosts to reserve a room at least 24 hours in advance. This program is restricted to cyclists and walkers. The hosts are often cyclists themselves, and happy to share their knowledge of the area. Locations range from cities to villages, and from city apartments to farmhouses in the country.

Hostels

Hostelling International (www.hihostels.com) provides economy-lodging for people of all ages. They operate some 30 official hostels in the Netherlands under the name Stayokay (www.stayokay.com). In Dutch, the word for (Youth) Hostel is *Jeugdherberg*, used generically to refer to all hostels.

To stay in a hostel, you don't *have* to be a member: non-members can stay by paying a small supplement, or join the first time you stay. Most hostels have gender-separated dormitory rooms with shared bathrooms, but some also have family rooms for families, couples, or small groups traveling together. Many require you to bring a sheet sleeping bag, while the blankets are provided; some have curfews. Hostels often provide meals and some have members' kitchens where you can prepare your own meals. In this book hostels convenient to the routes are listed.

Some are unofficial hostels, not affiliated with Hostelling International, and some of those do not maintain the same standards as "official" Hostelling International/Stayokay hostels. Whether official or not, the overnight charge varies between €15 and €25 per person for a dorm-bed, usually including a basic breakfast.

Camping

With official campgrounds in the Netherlands numbering over 2,000, campers are never far from a place to put their tent. If you are camping, plan for the extra weight of the camping equipment, which may slow your daily pace. In Dutch, the word

At the farm/mini-camping D'n Bobbel near Oirschot, you can either pitch your own tent or stay in one of these gypsy caravans.

camping is used both for the activity and for campgrounds. Although many campgrounds are open all year, some are only open from mid-April until sometime in October.

Facilities in campgrounds vary. You will always find shower/toilet facilities, and in many cases amenities such as a small shop, restaurant, swimming pool, and laundry facilities. In addition to larger campgrounds, there are small private campgrounds, or *mini-campings*. In summer, you can try "*camping bij de boer*" (camping on the farm). Campgrounds usually charge about €3 to €5 per tent, plus about the same again for each person.

Some campgrounds also have basic wooden huts, with a couple of bunk beds, a gas burner for cooking, and a place for your bicycle. All you need is your sleeping bag. Known as *trekkershutten*, these huts cost about €32 per night and sleep up to four people. Be forewarned: these huts are popular and require reservations during the summer months and on weekends. There are more than 300 *trekkershutten* locations throughout the Netherlands (www.trekkershutten.nl).

More rustic is *natuurcamping* (www.natuurkampeerterreinen.nl), an association of Dutch campgrounds in forest settings and other natural areas. A membership fee is required. *Het Groene Boekje* (the green booklet, €9), is available at ANWB offices and includes both the membership and a list of these campgrounds.

Facilities vary for smaller campgrounds. All have toilets, and most have showers (some *natuurcamping* sites may not have showers), some have a communal room with tables and chairs, and often a fridge. The amenities that these smaller campgrounds do not provide are more than compensated by ambiance.

For listings of campgrounds, you are referred to any of a number of camping guides available at ANWB and VVV offices, In addition to *Het Groene Boekje*, mentioned before, there are *Kleine Campings* (€8.95) and *Trekkershut Guide* (€2).

At times, you will come across signs along the road directing you to small, private campgrounds not listed in brochures and books. You can also ask at the local VVV.

In Enkhuizen—a historic Zuiderzee port city—you can find accommodation close to the scenic harbor.

Eating

As a cyclist, you owe it to yourself to eat regular, healthy meals. You will have no problem satisfying your appetite in the Netherlands, with cuisines from around the world, as well as local specialties.

The Dutch begin their day with a hearty breakfast (*ontbijt*), consisting of several varieties of bread, butter, jam, cheese, ham, a boiled egg, and coffee or tea. Typically, this type of breakfast is served in hotels, hostels, and B&Bs.

For picnics and supplies, bakeries, cheese shops, delicatessens, and supermarkets abound. There are also outdoor markets, many of which sell fresh produce and local products and offer great atmosphere. Supermarkets chains include Albert Heijn, De Boer, Aldi and Edah.

A great picnic snack available at most bakeries is a *broodje*, a bread roll sandwich with a generous serving of cheese, ham, roastbeef, or a spicy satay filling served warm. As well as individually owned bakeries, you can find Bakker Bart (www.bakkerbart.nl), a bakery chain with branches throughout the country.

Dutch Specialties

Dutch food itself is basic and substantial. Dutch dairy products including cheeses such as Gouda, Edam, and *Leidse kaas* (spiced with cummin seeds), are excellent. Fish specialties include mussels (*mosselen*), herring (*haring*), mackerel (*makreel*) and eel (*paling*). Traditional Dutch dishes include a thick pea soup (*erwtensoep*), a dish called *stamppot* (potatoes mashed with vegetables and served with smoked sausage), *hutspot*, (similar to stamppot but with carrots, onions and braised meat), and cheese fondue (*kaas fondue*). *Pannekoeken* are large crepes, served with savory or sweet accompaniments; they make a generous

"Rijsttafel": An Indonesian Feast

Partaking in a *rijsttafel*, whch literally translates as "rice table," you will be treated to a table full of Indonesian delicacies and taste sensations. The *rijsttafel* consists of rice and accompanying dishes: satay, curried meats, fish, chicken, gado-gado (a vegetable salad with peanut sauce), vegetables, eggs, coconut, peanuts, plus condiments, sauces, and sambals (chilli sauces). Be prepared; some of the dishes can be quite spicy.

A good *rijsttafel* costs around €20 to €25, and every visitor should experience this feast at least once. A few words of advice: come hungry, there is a lot of food, and guaranteed you will finish your meal bloated and with a smile on your face. You can also order many of these dishes individually.

All over the Netherlands there are Indonesian (*Indisch*) restaurants, but you will also see a Chinese-Indonesian (*Chinees-Indisch*) combination. The most authentic *rijsttafel* will be served in the *Indisch* restaurants.

"Gezellig"

There is no real translation for the Dutch word *gezellig*. Use any of the following words to describe a *gezellig* experience: congenial, warm, friendly, cozy, comfortable. *Gezellig* can be used to describe the pleasant atmosphere in a *bruin café*, a lovely meal with friends, or the warm reception at a B&B.

meal. For desert or a sweet snack, there are sweet mini-pancakes (*poffertjes*), and the ubiquitous *stroopwafels* (thin hard waffles with a caramel syrup filling).

From the days when the Dutch colonized Indonesia, they have developed a taste for Indonesian cuisine, and this has almost become the Dutch national food. For a veritable Indonesian feast, try *rijsttafel* (see boxed text on page 39), or try a combination plate —either *nasi rames*, a plate of fried rice topped with several of the items that are served with rijsttafel, or *bami rames*, the same thing with fried noodles instead of rice.

The Dutch brew a good strong cup of coffee. Meeting for coffee with friends is a favorite pastime. You will see ubiquitous signs advertising *Koffie is Klaar* (coffee is ready), *Koffie en Gebak* (coffee and pie–either made with apple (*appelgebak*) or another seasonal fruit). This is a nice afternoon treat at an outdoor café. If you like, you can ask for it *met slagroom* (with whipped cream). On the alcoholic side, try one of the varieties of Dutch beer, such as Heineken, Amstel, Oranjeboom, and Grolsch, and *jenever* (Dutch gin).

Restaurants sometimes serve lunch, and open for dinner around 5:30 p.m. Bars serve snack food. *Eetcafés* (similar to a pub) are good value and serve a variety of meals from snacks to a full menu. They usually open at noon and close the kitchen around 9 p.m., but stay open later for drinks. *Grand cafés* are similar to *eetcafés*, serving alcoholic and non-alcoholic drinks and meals, unlike cafés which serve coffee, tea, and cakes as well as alcoholic and non-alcoholic drinks. Wherever you eat, look for the *dagschotel* (daily special), often a local specialty or seasonal dish.

Typically Dutch are the *Bruine cafés*, or "brown cafes," with walls that are usually stained brown from years of smoke; newer ones simply paint their walls brown. Older cafés, with warm wooden interiors, are cozy and exude a *gezellig* atmosphere and are a great place for drinks. (See boxed text above for an explanation of the word "*gezellig*.")

5

Facts on Cycling in the Netherlands

CYCLING is way of life in the Netherlands. In this vibrant bicycle culture, the cyclist is the norm not the exception! The Netherlands has a population of 16 million who between them own 12 million bicycles. Every day, at least a quarter of them hop on their bikes for one reason or another—to ride to work, to shop, to visit a friend, or go to the beach. Annually, they cycle a total of 12.5 billion km, or 7.8 billion miles.

In this small country, about 300 km (188 miles) north to south at its longest, and 200 km (125 miles) east to west at its widest, there are 18,000 km (11,250 miles) of bicycle paths.

Bicycle Shops

The Netherlands is probably the easiest country in the world to find a bicycle shop. Virtually every city, town and village has one; there are more than 5,000 shops in this small country. Cycling through towns, you will be amazed to see so many bicycle shops. Most shops do repairs and carry parts, and many rent bikes.

Throughout the route descriptions in Chapters 6 through 14, bicycle shops are listed, but you can also check with the VVV or ANWB. If you need a bike shop, look under *Fiets* in the telephone book. Although most bike shops are individually owned, Halfords (www.halfords.nl, Dutch only) has over 130 full-service bike shops throughout the country. Like most other shops, bike shops are closed from Saturday afternoon until midday on Monday.

If you need repairs during the weekend, try a railway station bicycle shop, most of which are open 7 days a week.

Dutch bicycle shops often have an incredible selection of bicycle accessories, ranging from clothing to panniers, bells, and racks. If you couldn't find the right accessories back home, you're sure to find them once you arrive in Holland.

Bicycle Rental

Throughout the country, many bicycle shops rent bicycles, including over 100 railway station bike shops (*Rijwielshop/Fietspoint*). You can find railway station bike shops on the Dutch Railways, Nederlandse Spoorwagen (NS) website (www.ns.nl) by selecting "English," then "Facilities per Station," then enter the station name. If bicycle rental is available, it will be listed, with a phone number. In popular tourist areas and at peak tourist times, it is advisable to reserve ahead.

Railway stations rent the basic Dutch bikes. These practical and very solid bikes usually come with a rack and a lock. Rental prices are approximately €7 daily and €35 weekly, with a small discount if you have a train ticket. If you would like more variety, such as a mountain bike or a tandem, your best bet is a bicycle shop offering *Fietsverhuur* (bicycle rental). Some railway stations also rent tandems. Wherever you rent, you will have to leave a deposit of between €50 and €100.

Transporting Your Bicycle By Train

The Dutch Railways booklet *Fiets en Trein* (bike and train) has all the information regarding transporting your bicycle on the train, both within the country and internationally. It's only available in Dutch, but here's the essential information contained in it:

Some trains only have capacity for four or five bikes, and in summer the capacity may be filled, especially on weekends, which means you may have to wait for the next train.

Bikes are not allowed on the train during weekday rush hour—between 6:30 a.m. and 9 a.m., and between 4.30 p.m. and 6 p.m. There are no restrictions on weekends, public holidays, and during July and August.

You have to purchase a ticket for the bike at the same time as you purchase your own ticket. A bike ticket, called *dagkaart fiets*, costs €6 and is valid for the entire day of purchase, no matter what the length of your journey or how many trips you make. Load and unload your bike into a special bicycle carriage, denoted with a bicycle logo next to, or above, the door. The bicycle area has pull-down seats, so you can sit next to your bike. You have to remove your panniers and secure or hold your bike to immobilize it, so it doesn't fall during the journey. Folding bikes (provided they are folded) can travel on trains free and are not restricted to the special bicycle carriage.

A similar procedure applies for international travel, but many international trains do not take bicycles—check ahead to avoid disappointment. For international travel, in most cases, you will need a ticket and a reservation for both you and your bike. Some trains have a separate luggage compartment for bicycles, in which case you hand your bike to the conductor at the luggage carriage, without panniers, handlebar bags etc, and retrieve it at your destination. But be quick, because at most stations, trains don't stop for very long.

Transporting Your Bicycle By Ferry

Dutch ferries come in all shapes and sizes. They are integrated in the road system, because Dutch have determined that they are more cost-effective than building hundreds of bridges (although there are lots of bridges too). Some are tiny, and transport only bicycles and pedestrians, others are large enough to carry cars as well. The largest ferries are the ones that run between the mainland and the Wadden Islands.

Although some ferries are free, usually you will be charged a nominal fee on small ferries, which run on demand (they leave when they have a few passengers). Sometimes they will take you across on your own. Tickets are required on the large ferries, which run on set schedules. Try to keep small change handy if you will be riding on a route using a small ferry.

Bicycle Security

In general people are honest, and Europe is typically safe. But unfortunately a few warnings should be heeded.

In big cities, it is not safe to leave your bike locked on the street, day or night. Bicycle theft in larger cities is rampant, and if you've brought your own bike from home, it will stand out from the solid Dutch leviathans, and could be tempting to the would-be thief. If you have a rental bike then it is less conspicuous, but still be sure to lock it and remove all valuables.

Never leave panniers unattended on the bike. You are carrying your personal belongings and if camping, your "home" and your bed. If you are visiting a city for a long period of time, use either the *fietsenstalling* (see "Bicycle Parking," page 44), or check into your accommodation or campground, leave the bike there, and walk around on foot. Small towns and villages are much safer, and it should be safe to leave unloaded bikes locked while shopping, wandering around or visiting a museum. If you are traveling with another person, use two locks and lock the bikes together, as well as onto a rack, tree, pole or something immovable. If traveling alone, two locks are advisable. Or use *fietsenstalling*, if available.

Use your own discretion, but never leave bikes locked up when loaded unless you can watch them from a restaurant, café or through the bakery window. Also, remember to take off your bicycle computer and handlebar bag when you leave your bike. Never leave your passport, money etc. on the bike unattended; carry them on your person in a money pouch or belt. (If two people are traveling together, and all you need is a brief visit to a bakery, or supermarket, it is sometimes quicker to have one person run in, while the other waits with the bikes.)

These words may sound like the voice of doom, but remember that old saying: better safe than sorry. You don't want your trip spoiled because you left temptation in somebody's way.

Bicycle Parking

There are two types of bicycle parking. The first is the ubiquitous bicycle rack found outside supermarkets, shops, restaurants, at bus stops, outside the VVV and anywhere you might need to leave your bike. These racks appear in various forms, as freestanding racks, concrete slots in the pavement, small covered shelters, or metal attachments connected to the side of buildings. Lock your bike up when you leave it, and do not leave valuables on your bike.

The other type of parking is called a *fietsenstalling* (bicycle storage). These are like parking garages for bikes and are found in many cities and towns. They are usually privately owned, and for a small fee your bicycle will be parked in its own spot and watched by an attendant. These are great if you are coming into a city or town for the day and want to sightsee on foot for several hours. The other place where you can almost always find a *fietsenstalling* is the town's main railway station, where the standard fee for the day is €1.10. You can check with the VVV for *fietsenstalling* locations when you enter a town.

Bicycle Paths

It will not take long before you recognize the word *fietspad* (bicycle path). A standard *fietspad* sign is a blue circle with a white bicycle in the center. In the Netherlands, approximately 18,000 km of bicycle paths crisscross the country, making it a pleasure to cycle safely and comfortably. The majority of them are smooth and well-maintained.

Finding your way on Dutch bike paths is not difficult. There are numerous bicycle route signs. The directional signs specifically for cyclists are white signs with red lettering giving the town's name and distance with a little red bicycle symbol (see photo on page 10). The tip of these signs is shaped to a point indicating the direction. These will be located at turns or intersections. Sometimes these signs are green instead of red, denoting alternative scenic routes. There are also a number of bicycle route signs provided by the ANWB. These include regional route signs taking you on scenic loops or to points of local interest. Maps of these routes are available from VVV and ANWB offices in the area. (see below)

There is also a system of longer routes, called LF Routes (*Landelijke Fietsroutes*). This network covers more than 6,000 km. An LF network map and books covering these routes, for example *LF1: Noordzeeroute* (North Sea Route, see the Zeeland chapter, page 232), can also be purchased from VVV and ANWB offices. These routes are well marked with signs indicating the LF route number and name. Some of the routes in this book follow portions of these.

The ANWB also has series of routes, both long (*Lange fietsrondes*) and short (*Eendaagse fietsrondjes*). The longer routes cover large areas such as the *Zuiderzeeroute*, a signed 388 km route around the former Zuiderzee. The ANWB *Elfstedenroute* (11-cities route) is the basis for the route described in the Friesland chapter. The short routes, of which there are hundreds, are designed as day rides, often on a theme, and are usually somewhere between 30 km and 50 km. Both the long and the short routes are posted with hexagonal signs.

A recent introduction to the route system is the *Fietsnetwerk*, based on the so-called *Knooppunt* system of interconnected junctions (see boxed text below).

One type of signpost easily missed by those not used to them is the ANWB *paddestoel* (mushroom). These are 4-sided, knee-high markers roughly in the shape of a mushroom (see photo on page 10). These are specifically for hikers and cyclists, have directional information, and each one is numbered and referenced on the applicable ANWB/VVV map. Regular ANWB signposts for general use are also numbered and indicated on ANWB/ VVV maps. The number is usually at eye level on the post supporting the sign.

Cycle paths are important to the Dutch. Therefore when a *fietspad* crosses a freeway or major intersection, instead of forcing the cyclist to deal with the traffic obstacles, there will usually be a tunnel under the roadway, or a special bridge or overpass that the cyclist can use. In the case of a roundabout, there are special lanes for the cyclist around the edge, marked by broken white lines. Large bridges crossing a canal or river usually also have a bike path or a bicycle lane.

In rural areas there are often no cycle paths on quiet farm roads, and here cyclists use the road, staying close to the right, or on the right shoulder. If you do need to ride on a road, drivers are very aware of cyclists, and usually treat cyclists with respect. Remember, the driver is probably a cyclist too!

There are several types of bike paths. Many run alongside the roadway, sometimes merely separated by a white line, others separated by a concrete ridge or a grass strip. Some are paved with special red paving bricks, or the the asphalt may be in a reddish color. Bicycle paths can be either one-way, two-way, bicycles only,

"Knooppunt" System

In the mid-1990s, Belgian Limburg created a new bicycle network (*fietsnetwerk*), based on the "*knooppunt*" system of interconnected nodes or junctions covering the entire region. The idea has been so successful that it was also adopted in the southern provinces of the Netherlands. The idea is to follow an interconnecting numeric system along roads, canals, and bike paths.

Signposts indicate not only the junctions themselves, but directions to all nearby points. Signposts along the routes indicate the number of the route and the next number to which you are cycling. It's a great system once have it worked out. The only drawback is that it is difficult to use without the designated *knooppunt* map for the area you are in. Along the way, you will find maps on a board at several of the major junctions; however, it will still be helpful to buy a map at a VVV or ANWB office.

In this book, you will use the *knooppunt* network in Limburg (both Belgian and Dutch), and in parts of the province of Noord Brabant. In the cue sheets, a *knooppunt* is indicated by the letter K followed by a number, such as sign " K54" (meaning to *knooppunt* No. 54). For "Knooppunt" signs, see photos on page 247.

or shared with pedestrians, mopeds, or equestrians. Many paths are shared with *bromfietsen* (mopeds). If you hear one, stay to the right side of the path, allowing the *bromfietser* (moped rider) to pass. Although they always have a bell or a horn, they expect the loud noise of the motor itself is warning enough for cyclists. Don't ignore them; they are going faster than you.

Many bicycle paths crisscross the countryside and take you away from the main roads. These make for the most idyllic cycling experience. Many go from village to village, and the distance is often shorter than it is on the main road. For the routes in this book, they are used whenever possible. They go alongside dikes and rivers, edge farmer's fields, go through forests and sand dunes, and along the coast. They are used by locals for commuting, and many are used for recreational purposes and have benches and picnic tables strategically placed.

Alongside rivers and canals, some bike paths are old towpaths, known as a *jaagpad*. Before the advent of motorized barges, these paths were used by the horses that pulled the floating loads. Today, these are often multi-purpose service roads, used by cyclists, pedestrians, and sometimes cars. You will also find many bicycle paths adjacent to, or on top of dikes.

Obstacles to watch out for while cycling are tram lines (in major cities) and train tracks, especially when wet. Always cross them at a right angle to avoid slip-

Bike & Barge Tours

Cycling offers a view of Dutch life, but another view is from the water. The lifelines of this land of rivers and canals resemble blue lacework on a map. Transport by water in the Netherlands is as commonplace as transport by road.

When most people think of barges, they think of a working vessel, transporting gravel, machinery, or lumber. However, nowadays barges have two identities: the waterway workhorse and that of a floating hotel. For the latter, think small: a dozen or so cabins, a cozy eating area, and an outside deck for surveying the scenery. With about two dozen bikes on board, you have the makings of a bike and barge trip.

The group cycles by day through ever-changing scenery, interesting towns, guided by an informative tour leader. There are no bags to carry (they stay on board). All you carry is your lunch and personal effects. Bikes and panniers are provided, or you can bring your own. Breakfast and dinner are served on board, and before departure each morning, generous offerings for a make-your-own picnic lunch are provided. At night the barge awaits at that evening's destination.

Bike and barge tours start at €100 per person per day. The Dutch company Cycletours (www. cycletours.com) operates about eight different boats. Book directly with Cycletours, or through one of their US representatives, such as Pack & Pedal Europe (www.tripsite.com) or Van Gogh Tours (www.vangoghtours. com). Another Dutch company offering bike and barge tours is HAT Tours (www. hat-tours.com). US-based Bike & Barge Holland (www. bikebarge.com) offers 14- day tours.

ping or getting the front wheel caught in them. In rural areas, watch for cattle grids, and cattle themselves. Rural paths often pass through grazing areas

There are some places where bicycles are forbidden: on freeways, on sidewalks, and in pedestrian zones.

Some Basic Rules for Bicycle Paths

1. When a bicycle path is provided, it is compulsory to use it. Even where the road surface seems to be smoother, you are required to stay on the bike path.

2. Adhere to basic traffic rules. Overtake on the left, don't block the path, and if you need to stop, pull over to the side in order to keep the path clear.

3. In the Netherlands each bike must be fitted with a bell. This is essential for overtaking. Front and rear lights are also required.

4. Be aware of signs such as *Fietsers Oversteken* (Cyclists Cross Over) which indicates the bicycle path is ending on the side you are on and you have to cross the road to continue on the other side. The sign *Einde Fietspad* means the bike path ends. Finally, *Doorgaand Verkeer* means through traffic.

5. Only ride two abreast if it is not hindering other traffic on the path. Try to ride single file if bicycle traffic is heavy, if it is a two-way bicycle path, or if you know someone is about to overtake.

6. Give way to traffic from the right. Unless it is otherwise marked, always assume cars have the right of way when a bike path crosses a road. in addition to the traditional triangular yield sign, there are usually white triangles painted on the path or the roadway indicating whether you or the cars should yield. Drivers tend to have a great deal of respect for cyclists, but always err on the side of caution.

The windmills of Kinderdijk, the largest concentration of windmills in Holland.

7.   Always signal your intention to turn with an outstretched right or left arm,
     and when on a road, bicycles are considered *langzaam verkeer*,
     slow-moving vehicles, which have to give way to motorized vehicles both
     right and left.

Maps

Before you leave home, a good planning map is the Michelin map #715 *Neder-land/Pays-Bas* (1 : 400,000), but this map is not sufficiently detailed for cycling. Two Michelin maps in the 1 : 200,000 series cover the entire country and are the best cycling maps available outside the Netherlands. Michelin Map No. 531 *Noord-Nederland/Pays-Bas Nord (Amsterdam–Groningen)* covers the northern half of the country. Michelin Map No. 532 *Zuid-Nederland/Pays-Bas Sud (Rotter-dam– Apeldoorn–Maastricht)* covers the southern half of the country. Another useful map is Michelin Map No. 533, titled Nederland/Belgique (Brugge–Rotter-dam– Antwerpen). It covers the north of Belgium, the province of Dutch Limburg, and a portion of southern Netherlands. These 1 : 200,000 series maps provide a lot of valuable information for cyclists, including, distances, major inclines, scenic roads, unpaved roads, some bicycle paths, ferries, and tourist information.

Once you are in the Netherlands, you will find even more detailed maps at VVV and ANWB offices. For the routes in this book, maps from the ANWB/VVV *Toeristenkaart* series were used. Scaled at 1 : 100,000, these are ideal for cycling and are readily available for €7.95 per map. These maps are designed with the cyclist in mind and are beautifully clear. They show incredible detail, including bicycle paths, ANWB mushrooms and signposts with numbers, as well as tourist information such as location of windmills, bulb fields, campgrounds, hostels, castles, forests, sand dunes, and much more.

These maps either cover an entire province, or a section of the province. At the start of each route in this book, the maps used are indicated. The maps in the series are *Achterhoek, Drenthe, Flevoland, Oost Brabant, Friesland, Gelders Rivierengebied, Groningen, Limburg, Noord Holland, Zuid Holland, Twente/Salland, Veluwe, West Brabant,West Overijssel, Utrecht*, and *Zeeland*.

The *Zeeland, Oost* and *West Brabant*, and *Limburg* maps are also used to guide you through the portions of the routes into northern Belgium, and the *Lim-burg* map also covers the part of Germany described in one of the Limburg rides.

Many of the VVV and ANWB offices also produce their own individual maps. The ANWB has yet another series of 1 : 100,000 maps, and the VVV has a 1 : 50,000 scale series with even more detail. There are also other regional maps available from individual VVVs, highlighting cycle paths within their immediate area, and there are hundreds of regional ANWB day-ride maps.

6.

Amsterdam and Environs

AMSTERDAM is a city for everyone. It is cosmopolitan, yet quaint. It is a city of history, yet it is progressive. It is dotted with busy squares and gathering places, yet has quiet canal promenades and parks. It is a city of culture, housing some of the world's great museums, yet it is a city where the bicycle reigns. At the same time, it's easy to escape the city's hustle and bustle on short bike rides to delightful rural destinations just a short distance from Amsterdam. The first part of this chapter, will be your guide to the city itself, while the second part offers some scenic bike routes outside the city.

What to See in Amsterdam

A good way to get a different perspective of the city is to take a canal boat. The Canal Bus (Tel. 020 623 9886, www.canal.nl) departs opposite the central station and operates three routes, with 14 stops offering access to major attractions. Another option also departing opposite the central station, the Amsterdam Museumboot (Tel. 020 530 1090, www.lovers.nl), makes a canal circuit stopping at several points, allowing you to get on and off near most major museums. The ticket also entitles you to discounts on museum entrance fees.

Museums

Amsterdam boasts some of the world's best museums. Top billing goes to the three museums around the Museumplein (Museum Square). The striking Neo-Renaissance Rijksmuseum (National Museum, www.rijksmuseum.nl, open daily) houses a fine collection of Northern European paintings, especially Dutch masters. This 150-room museum is closed for renovation until 2008, but the Phillips wing has selected works on display, including Rembrandt's The Night Watch. Across the Museumplein is the Van Gogh Museum (www.vangoghmuseum.nl, open daily), with its superb permanent collection of hundreds of his paintings and drawings. Next door, the Stedelijk Museum (Municipal Museum, www.stedelijk.nl) has a collection of contemporary art. Unfortunately, it too is closed for renovation until until 2008. Until then, temporary exhibits can be found on the 2nd and 3rd floors of the Central Station Post Office building, Oosterdokskade 5 (open daily).

The Amsterdam Historisch Museum (Amsterdam Museum of History, Kalverstraat 92, www.ahm.nl, open daily) has exhibits about the history of the city. The Tropenmuseum (Museum of the Tropics, Linnaeusstraat 2, www. tropenmuseum. nl, open daily), originally devoted to the cultures of Holland's former colonies in the East and West Indies, now focuses on peoples and cultures of developing countries. The Joods Historisch Museum (Jewish History Museum, Daniel Meijerplein 2-4, www.jhm.nl, open daily) traces the history of Jewish people in the Netherlands, and the impact the Holocaust had on Amsterdam's Jewish community.

Amsterdam by Bike

Cycling in Amsterdam is easy. The city is level, and there are lots of bike paths. Pick up the *Stadsplattegrond voor Fietsers in Amsterdam*, a detailed map of Amsterdam and environs specifically for cyclists, with features such as recommended cycling routes and bike rental and repair locations (€3.90, at VVV locations, the ANWB, and some bike shops and bookstores).

Several companies offer guided bike tours of the city and outskirts. Yellow Bike Tours, Nieuwezijds Kolk 29 (Tel. 020 620 6940, www.yellowbike.nl) operates city bike tours (€17) from April to October, plus a day tour to Waterland (€22.50). Mike's Bikes, Kerkstraat 134 (www.mikesbikeamsterdam.com. Tel. 020 622 7970), runs lively bike tours (€22) of the city and rural areas south, daily and year-round. Mike's Bikes also has a night tour departing at 7 p.m. Both companies offer bike rental; reservations are recommended.

With three locations, MacBike (www.macbike.nl) is Amsterdam's largest bike rental outfit. Most convenient is their location at Centraal Station, where they not only have rentals, but also a *fietsenstalling* and a repair shop. Their other locations are Mr. Visserplein 2 and Weteringsschans 2. Daily rentals range from €6.50 to €9.75 plus insurance and €50 deposit (open daily, 9 a.m. to 5:45 p.m.). For independent cyclists, MacBike has mapped out five different tours of the city and surroundings (€1 each).

Bicycle Security Note:

Do not ever leave your bicycle unattended, even locked, day or night in Amsterdam. Bike theft is rampant.

Across the road is the Portuguese Synagogue (closed Saturdays). When built in 1675, it was the largest in world, and the interior is still intact. The Verzetsmuseum (Resistance Museum, Plantage Kerklaan 61, www. verzetsmuseum.org, open daily) tells the story of resistance fighters during World War II.

Other Sights

One of Amsterdam's most visited houses is the Anne Frankhuis at Prinsengracht 267 (www.annefrank.nl, open daily). The famous Dutch Jewish girl lived in hiding with her family and wrote her diary in the attic of this house. Plan to stand in line in the summer months. Another well-known residence is the Rembrandthuis at Jodenbreestraat 4 (www.rembrandthuis.nl, open daily), the home of 17th-century Dutch artist Rembrandt van Rijn. Etchings and furniture are on view.

The most famous square in Amsterdam is the Damplein (Dam Square), the site of the original dam that crossed the Amstel River. On the square is the Koninklijk Paleis (Royal Palace), now used for official functions, the Nieuwe Kerk (New Church), constructed around 1500, and the National Monument, erected in 1956 in honor of those who perished in World War II.

Behind the palace and a few blocks west are the Westermarkt and the Westerkerk (West Church). The church's 85 m (275 ft) tower is the highest in the city. Climb it (summer only) for a view over the city. Rembrandt is buried here. A little further west is the Jordaan, the Bohemian quarter.

A lively area is the Muntplein (Mint Square), with the impressive 15th-century Munttoren (Mint Tower) where coins were once minted. The structure remains from one of the old city wall gates.

If beer interests you, tour the Heineken Brewery, Stadhouderskade 78 (www. heinekenexperience.com, closed Mondays).

For tranquillity, the beguinage (Begijnhof) is a haven in the city. The tiny houses and garden were established in the 14th century. The house at No. 34, the

Typical view of an Amsterdam canal.

oldest preserved wooden house in Amsterdam, dates to 1475. Also visit the relaxing 120-acre Vondelpark, with its outdoor concerts and performances in the summer.

Street Markets

Street markets abound in Amsterdam. Waterlooplein is known for its flea market. Albert Cuypstraat (between Van Woustraat and Ferdinand Bolstraat) is home to the Albert Cuyp Markt, the city's largest street market. Saturdays you'll find the Bird Market on the Noorderplein. The Bloemenmarkt (Flower Market) is a daily occurrence on the Singel canal. A bit further afield, on the outskirts of Amsterdam, is the Aalsmeer Flower Auction (www.vba.nl, 7:30 a.m. to 11:00 a.m., weekdays only), a huge warehouse complex with flowers as far as the eye can see.

At Night

At night, Amsterdam sparkles with lamplit canals. Visit the "street of seven bridges," at the intersection of Reguliersgracht and Herengracht, just south of Rembrandtsplein. There are some good restaurants in this area. Wander down Utrechtsestraat, with its intimate restaurants and unusual shops. Nightfall also awakens the Red Light District. Be careful here, as pickpockets stalk the area.

Information

The three VVV tourist information offices in Amsterdam (Tel. 0900 400 4040, €0.55 per minute, www.visitamsterdam.nl) are incredibly busy. One is at Stations-

Bicycle Shops & Bicycle Parking

Amsterdam has over 100 bicycle shops. To find a bicycle shop in the telephone book, look under "Fiets."

Centrally located, Amsterdam central station's bike shop is run by Mac Bike (see boxed text "Amsterdam by Bike"). It is outside and downstairs (Tel. 020 624 8391). All MacBike repair facilities are open 9 a.m. to 5:45 p.m. daily. MacBike has two other repair locations: Mr. Visserplein 2, near Waterlooplein (Tel. 020 620 0985) and Marnixstraat 220 (Tel. 020 626 6964).

In Amsterdam, never leave your bike on the street, locked or unlocked. There are several secure attended *fietsenstalling* (bicycle parking facilities). MacBike operates a *fietsenstalling* at the central station, open 5:30 a.m. to 12:45 a.m. Amsterdam Locker has four guarded bike parking facilities in Amsterdam: Rokin 111, Singel 457, Binnengasthuisstraat 9, and Weteringschans 4A (near Leidseplein). All are open seven days per week. The Rokin and Leidseplein locations are open 24 hours per day; the other two are open 8 a.m. to 10 p.m. and, except the Rokin location, have repair facilities.

plein 10 across from the central station, the second is inside the central station (upstairs, platform 2), and the third is at Leidesplein 1. The VVV in the station is open until 8 p.m. daily (5 p.m. on Sunday); the others close at 5 p.m.

The ANWB office is at Museumplein 5 (Tel. 020 673 0844, www. anwb.nl). The ANWB sells travel books, maps, and travel supplies.

For maps and guidebooks, as well as books and magazines in English, head to the American Book Center, Kalverstraat 185 (Tel. 020 625 5537, www. abc.nl) or Waterstone's at Kalverstraat 152 (Tel. 020 638 3821).

For internet access, Easy Internet (www.easyeverything.com) has three Amsterdam locations: Damrak 33, Reguliersbreestraat 22, and Leidsestraat 24, open 9 a.m. to 10 p.m., Leidsestraat until 7 p.m.

Where to Stay

Amsterdam has lodgings to suit every budget. The VVV can assist with reservations, but you may want to pre-book. All the lodgings listed below have a secure space for bicycles. If you book elsewhere, be sure to ask if they have a place for your bicycle.

Hotels:

The small, bike-friendly Van Ostade Bicycle Hotel, on Van Ostadestraat (Tel. 020 679 3452, www.bicyclehotel.com) has a garage for bikes and rents bikes for €5 per day. Rooms with a shower cost around €110 and those without are €70. Prices quoted are for singles or doubles and include free internet access. Triples are available.

One of the best deals in Amsterdam is the Hotel van Onna, Bloemgracht 102/104/108 (Tel. 020 626 5801). Located in the Jordaan, it occupies three canal houses that have been converted into a charming 41-room hotel, complete with bicycle shed in the backyard. Price is €41 per person.

Between the Museumplein and Leidseplein, the 12-room Uptown Hotel (Tel. 020 428 3125, www.uptown.nl), in an 18th-century house, has singles for €75, doubles from €90. Reception is up a narrow flight of stairs, and you'll have to carry your bike up there to reach the courtyard.

On Singel 462, the historic Hotel Agora (Tel. 020 627 2200, www. hotelagora.nl) dates to 1735. Singles are €100, doubles start at €118, and triples and quadruples are also available.

Tucked behind the Dam square on Nes 5–23 is the Rho Hotel, its lobby is a former art-deco theatre built in 1908 (Tel. 020 620 7371, www.rhohotel.com). Singles are €95, doubles are €145, and triples are €175.

The elegant Hotel Schiller, Rembrandtsplein 26–36 (Tel. 020 554 0700, www.nh-hotels.com), built in 1912, houses 350 paintings of the Schiller collection. Single rooms begin at €90 and doubles at €100. Breakfast is €16 extra.

Hostels: The two Stayokay hostels (www.stayokay.com) offer bike parking. The centrally located 170-bed Stadsdoelen Hostel at Kloveniersburgwal 97 (Tel. 020 624 6832) has dorm rooms (with breakfast) for €22.50. The large 536-bed Vondelpark Hostel, Zandpad 5 (Tel. 020 589 8996) has dorm rooms (with breakfast) for €23, doubles for €77, and quadruples for €112.

One "unofficial" hostel that offers a secure place for bicycles is Bob's Youth Hostel, Nieuwezijds Voorburgwal 92 (Tel. 020 623 0063, www.bobsyouthhostel.nl), with dorm rooms including breakfast for €18, 2-person apartments for €70, 3-person appartments for €80. Another hostel is the large 500-bed Hans Brinker Hotel at Kerkstraat 136-138 (Tel. 020 622 0687, www.hans-brinker.com) near Leidseplein. Dorms are €21, single rooms are €52, doubles are €70, and triples are €90; all include breakfast.

Camping: The closest camping is Camping Vliegenbos, Meeuwenlaan 138 (Tel. 020 636 8855, www.vliegenbos.com), north of Amsterdam. Take the IJ ferry, after which it's a 5-minute bike ride. Open April through September. On an island in the IJmeer, east of Amsterdam, Camping Zeeburg, Zuider IJdijk 20 (Tel. 020 694 4430, www.campingzeeburg.nl), is open year-round. Further out near Weesp (southeast) is Camping Gaasper, Loosdrechtdreef 7 (Tel. 020 696 73 26, www.gaaspercamping.nl, mid-March to November 1).

Where to Eat

For Dutch food, De Eettuin, 2E Tuinwaarsstraat 10, in the Jordaan (Tel. 020 623 7706, www.eettuin.nl, open from 5:30 p.m.), has an interesting menu and a salad bar. Southeast of the Museumplein, Hobbema at Hobbemakade 63 (Tel. 020 671 1263) serves up reasonably priced Dutch specialties nightly, except Sundays. Both Dutch and international dishes can be found all day at Eetcafé de Staalmeesters, Kloveniersburgwal 127 (Tel. 020 623 4218).

Near the Anne Frankhuis, at Prinsengracht 191, the Pancake Bakery (Tel. 020 625 1333) serves no less than 60 types of pancakes, plus omelettes. Meneer Pannekoek, near the Dam Square at Raadhuisstraat 6 (Tel. 020 627 8500), offers pancakes, pasta, salads, and sandwiches.

Close to the Rijksmuseum, at P.C. Hooftstraat 2,7 is Sama Sebo (Tel. 020 662 81 46, www.samasebo.com, open for lunch and dinner, closed Sundays), one of Amsterdam's oldest and best Indonesian restaurants. Try the *rijsttafel* or one of their 30 other dishes. At Utrechtsestraat 63, Tujuh Maret (Tel. 020 427 9865) serves excellent Indonesian food all day, Tuesdays through Saturdays.

Stroll down Utrechtsestraat and you will find Tibetan food at Tashi Deleg at No. 65; Indonesian cuisine at Tujuh Maret (see above), as well as next door at Tempo Doeloe and at Soenda Kelapa, a few doors down. Quartier Latin at No. 49 and Vosges (www.vosges.com) at No. 51 offer French fare. You will find vegetarian meals at Golden Temple Restaurant at No. 126.

For casual dining, head to the Vroom & Dreesmann department store's restaurant, La Place (enter from Kalverstraat or Rokin near Muntplein), open daily, 9 a.m. to 8 p.m. Beautifully presented, the self-service array will whet anyone's appetite.

Amsterdam has several cozy "brown cafés" (see Chapter 4, page 40), many dating back several centuries. The truly *gezellig* Café 't Smalle in the Jordaan at Egelantiersgracht 12 opened in 1786. Facing the Westerkerk, Café Kalkhoven, Prinsengracht 283, dates from 1670, and behind the Nieuwe Kerk, De Drie Fleschen, at Gravenstraat 18, dates from 1650. At Spui 18, Hoppe has been in operation for 300 years.

Schiphol Airport

When you arrive at Schiphol Airport, you can travel to Amsterdam either by train or by bike.

The railway station for the Nederlandse Spoorwegen (NS) is downstairs in Terminal 3. Buy your ticket and the *dagkaart fiets* (see page 42) for your bike at the train station on the arrival level. As you board the train, look for the bike carriage indicated by the bicycle symbol. Trains run between 5:30 a.m. and midnight. There are four to five trains per hour to Amsterdam's central station; the trip takes about 20 minutes.

Schiphol to Amsterdam or Haarlem

Total Distance:	13.2 km (to Amsterdam)
Duration:	1 hour
Terrain:	Level
Maps:	*Stadsplattegrond voor Fietsers in Amsterdam* (see boxed text "Amsterdam by Bike"), or any other good map of Amsterdam and environs that shows Schiphol
Start/Finish:	Schiphol Airport/Amsterdam
Access:	Schiphol Airport, Terminal 3

Most international arrivals come into Terminal 3. From the Arrivals level go to the end of the terminal where the car rental companies are located. Go out the door and turn right. Begin by going left on the service road opposite the Sheraton.

The route takes you from Terminal 3, going left along a service road. At 0.5 km, you pass a *fietsenstalling* (bicycle parking); the red paved path is the start of the bike path. This path weaves you out of the airport area, then through a bike tunnel. Follow signs to Badhoevedorp and Amsterdam. Cycle along a farm road until Badhoevedorp.

At 4.4 km, cross Schipholweg and continue straight to Amsterdam. If you are going to Haarlem, go left and follow the Haarlem bike signs for 11 km. It's not a particularly interesting ride to Haarlem, as you follow Schipholweg (N232). Approaching Haarlem, you will see signs pointing to the Centrum.

En route to Amsterdam, you will spot your first Dutch windmill (6.4 km), Molen van Sloten, with an interesting exhibit and a cheese maker next door (open daily). Continue past the windmill and join the bike path (on Plesmanlaan) along

Yellow Bike Tours offers guided bike tours in and around Amsterdam, using their own yellow bicycles.

the Slotervaart (canal). At 10.3 km, just after going under the freeway, turn left onto Westlandgracht and cycle along the canal of the same name.

Enter the Vondelpark (11.4 km), cycling 2.0 km through the park. Follow the signs to the Centrum (city center). At 13.5 km, you are in the southwest of Amsterdam Centrum. At the Vondelpark gates, there are signs directing you to Centraal Station (central station) and the Leidseplein/Tourist Information.

Cue Sheet

| 0.0 | Start | Schiphol, Terminal 3 |
| | | go left on the service road |

Map 6.1. Rides to and from Schiphol Airport, and Amstel River Day Trip.

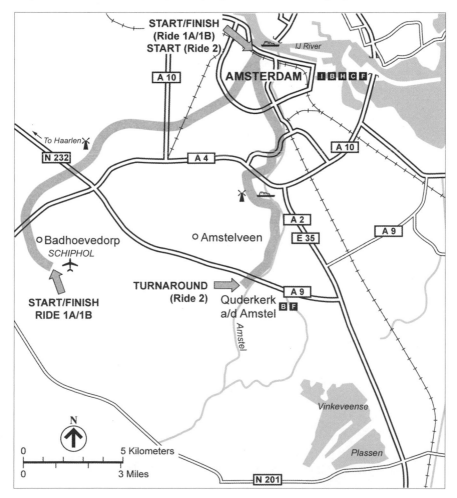

0.5	R	red paved bike path
0.8	R	sign "Badhoevedorp, Amsterdam"
0.9	L	sign "Badhoevedorp, Amsterdam"
1.5	CS	bike tunnel
2.3	L	sign "Badhoevedorp, Amsterdam"
2.7	R	sign "Badhoevedorp, Amsterdam," unmarked farm road
3.2	CS	sign "Badhoevedorp, Amsterdam," Sloterweg
3.9	SS L	tiled roof of Julian's farm
4.4	CS	sign "Amsterdam," Sloterweg, T-Badhoevedorp
4.4	L	sign "Haarlem," option (see text)
5.8	R	Nieuwe Meerdijk (no street sign) along canal
6.3	L	over bridge, sign "Centrum, Amsterdam-Zuid," Plesmanlaan
6.4	SS L	Molen Van Sloten (windmill)
10.3	L !	Westlandgracht (along canal)
10.7	R	Theophile de Bockstraat
11.4	CS	enter the Vondelpark, sign "Centrum via park"
12.4	VR	sign "Centrum"
13.5	End	Vondelpark gates (on Stadhouderskade)

From Amsterdam to Schiphol

Total Distance:	13.2 km
Duration:	1 hour
Terrain:	Level
Maps:	*Stadsplattegrond voor Fietsers in Amsterdam* (see boxed text "Amsterdam by Bike"), or any other good map of Amsterdam and environs that shows Schiphol
Start/Finish:	Amsterdam/Schiphol Airport
Access:	Amsterdam, Vondelpark gates

The route starts on the bike path through the Vondelpark, following signs for Badhoevedorp. Ride 2.0 km through the park. Exit at the far end of the park and cross the road onto Schinkelhaven (2 km). After the turn at 3.1 km, the Slotervaart (canal) will be on your right until Molen Van Sloten, the start of Badhoevedorp.

Go through Badhoevedorp on Sloterweg, cross Schipholweg, and continue on the bike path on the left side of Sloterweg. At this point you can already see the airport terminal across the fields. Sloterweg narrows to a farm road (10.5 km). At ANWB post # 9258, turn left. Follow the signs "Terminal'" through the bike tunnel and to the terminal itself.

If you are riding to Schiphol to catch a flight, be sure to allow enough time in case you get lost or have a mechanical problem that would cause you to miss your plane. Also, plan an extra hour for purchasing and packing a bike box, plus the two hours required for pre-departure check-in.

Cue Sheet

0.0	Start	Vondelpark gates (on Stadhouderskade) go SW through the Vondelpark
2.0	CS	exit the Vondelpark, sign "Badhoevedorp," Schinkelhaven/ Theophile de Bockstraat
2.7	L	Westlandgracht
3.1	R	Heemstedestraat/Plesmanlaan (canal on R)
7.2	SS R	Molen Van Sloten (windmill)
7.3	R	Nieuwe Meerdijk (along canal), T-Badhoevedorp
7.8	L	Sloterweg
9.1	CS	Sloterweg (cross Schipholweg), sign "Schiphol Centrum"
9.7	SS R	tiled roof of Julian's Farm
10.5	CS	unmarked farm road, sign "Schiphol"
11.0	L !	#9258, sign "Schiphol"
11.4	R	sign "Terminal"
11.7	CS	bike tunnel
12.9	L	sign "Terminal"
13.2	L	sign "Terminal/Plaza"
13.4	R	(15 m) L, sign "Terminal"
13.6	End	Terminal 3

Amstel River Day Trip

Total Distance:	22.6 km
Duration:	3 to 4 hours
Highlights:	Magere Brug, peaceful cycling along the Amstel River, windmill De Rieker, cheese farm and clog maker, Oudekerk a/d Amstel
Terrain:	Level
Maps:	*Stadsplattegrond voor Fietsers in Amsterdam* (see boxed text "Amsterdam by Bike"), or any other good map of Amsterdam and environs that shows Ouderkerk
Start/Finish:	Amsterdam/Amsterdam
Access:	Amsterdam central station or Waterlooplein. If renting bikes, MacBike has locations at both the central station and Waterlooplein.

Just ten minutes by bike, south along the Amstel River, takes you to a rural area that you won't believe is just a few kilometers outside one of the great cities of the world.

For details of this ride from Amsterdam to Ouderkerk a/d Amstel, see Day 1 of the South Holland Ride (pages 177–180). The ride starts at either the central station or the Waterlooplein. Because the distances in the cue sheet are calculated from the central station, you need to deduct 1.6 km if you start at Waterlooplein instead.

You can go all the way to Ouderkerk a/d Amstel, or you can shorten the ride by crossing the Amstel with the *pontveer* (ferry) opposite the Molen De Rieker. This ride can be done any time of year, but the ferry (50 cents) only operates from April through September, 10 a.m. to 6 p.m. daily.

Once in Ouderkerk, you can cycle back on the other side of the river, passing a windmill 700 m after leaving Ouderkerk. Cross a pedestrian/bike bridge 6.0 km after Ouderkerk. 600 m further, follow the sign left to the Centrum, then veer left through a complex of modern buildings. This brings you to Weesperzijde, where you continue straight, keeping the Amstel River on your left. Continue to the Waterlooplein and turn left to the station.

For map and cue sheet, see page177–180 South Holland Ride, Day 1.

Lakes & Rivers Day Trip

Total Distance:	40.6 km
Duration:	1 day
Highlights:	Bergse Pad, the lake area, cycling alongside the Vecht, villages of Nigtevecht, Vreeland, and Kortenhoef
Terrain:	Level
Maps:	Michelin 532 Zuid-Nederland/Pays-Bas Sud, ANWB/VVV Toeristenkaart Noord Holland
Start/Finish:	Hilversum/Hilversum
Access:	Trains leave Amsterdam four times per hour for the 25-minute journey. Some trains require a change in Weesp.

Begin in Hilversum, the seat of Dutch radio and and TV media. Leaving town, you will notice the many old villas converted into studios and offices. Cruise down 's-Gravelandse Weg. At 3.0 km, turn toward Spanderswoud woods.

Continue on Herenweg past farmland until the turn at 8.2 km onto Bergse Pad, which looks like a private path. This tiny path of hard-packed dirt across the Ankeveense Plassen (lakes) is devoted to walkers and cyclists. At 10.2 km, turn toward Weesp and watch for birds as you cycle along the water's edge; birding details can be found on the board at Spiegelplas (12.0 km).

After crossing the N253 (13.6 km), be aware that you are sharing Eilandsweg with the occasional car. Soon, the gorgeous Vecht River will be on your right, and you will see the picturesque village of Nigtevecht across the river. Should you wish to visit Nigtevecht, a six-passenger pedestrian/bike ferry (free) operates weekdays (7:30 a.m. to 8:30 a.m., noon to 1:30 p.m., and 3:30 p.m. to 5:30 p.m.), and weekends (noon to 5:30 p.m.).

Tranquil cycling along the Bergse Pad (Lakes and Rivers Day Trip).

By taking the boat, you can also cycle the alternate route on the west bank of the Vecht. This option takes you through quiet farmland and past three windmills.

If you are staying on the east bank, continue with the Vecht on your left. The turn (17.2 km) to Nederhorst den Berg comes right after the windmill on the opposite bank; the house on the corner displays the street sign Torenweg. In Nederhorst den Berg, note the church (18.1 km) perched on a mound, the *berg* (mountain) from which the town takes its name. At 18.5 km, the castle *Kasteel de Nederhorst* is now a recording studio.

The route follows the Vecht River to the village of Vreeland. A worthwhile stop is Pancake House Noord Brabant at Breedstraat 8 (closed Mondays, and Tuesdays October through March), which serves over 60 types of Dutch pancakes.

Map 6.3. Lakes and Rivers Day Trip.

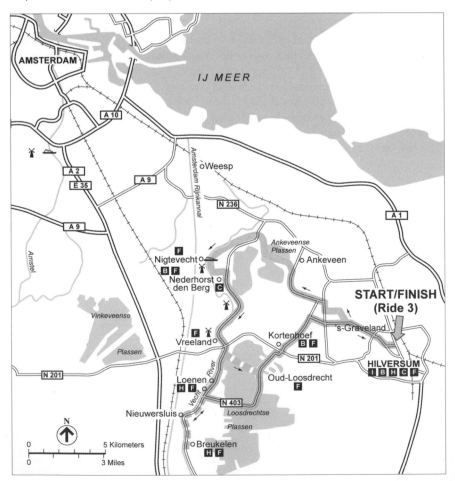

Note: If you want to shorten the route, turn left onto Alambertskade (23.2 km). It hard to find, as the sign is behind you. Once you are on Alambertskade, go through two gates, one at each end. It is 2.5 km to the other side. Then turn left and rejoin the route at cue 30.8 km.

Continue with more idyllic Vecht River cycling on the side trip to Breukelen (after which Brooklyn, New York was named). Stately homes line the canal.

From Loenen, the bike path follows the N403 across the lake to Oud-Loosdrecht. Continue along the lake, then beside a peaceful canal. Cross the N201 to old Kortenhoef, a ribbon village. The last 5 km returns to Hilversum on 's-Gravelandse Weg, flanked by woods. Follow Melkpad back to the station.

Cue Sheet

0.0	Start	Hilversum Railway Station go W on Stationsstraatsign "'s-Graveland"
0.2	RA CS	Melkpad
0.8	R	sign "'s-Graveland" 's-Gravelandse Weg
3.0	R	sign "Spanderswoud," Erfgooiersroute sign
3.1	VL	Oude Meentweg
4.4	L	sign "'s-Graveland & Nederhorst den Berg," Ankeveensepad
5.7	CS	Herenweg ir. Ankeveen and Nederhorst den Berg
7.6	VR	follow the main road sign "Ankeveen"
8.2	L !	Bergse Pad, sign "Nederhorst den Berg" #4082
10.1	L	cross little bridge
10.2	R	sign "Weesp" #7331, Googpad
12.0	SS L	bird watching at Spiegelplas
12.4	L	sign "Nederhorst den Berg," N253, #7623
13.6	R	cross N253
13.7	R	sign "Nigtevecht" Eilandsweg
15.4	CS	Nigtevecht ferry
15.4	SS L	(or alternate route) T-Nigtevecht
17.2	L !	Torenweg (sign on house)
18.1	SS L	church, T-Nederhorst den Berg
18.2	R	sign "Vreeland & Loenen, Slotlaan"
18.5	SS /r	Kasteel de Nederhorst (private castle)

19.0	R	sign "Vreeland," Overmeersweg
19.4	R	Vreelandseweg sign ""Vreeland & Loenen"
20.5	R	over bridge/Sluis Hemeltje sign "Vreeland
20.6	R	Bergseweg (ahead 50 m)
22.6	CS	sign "Loenen," Lindengracht (corner Breedstraat), T-Vreeland
22.9	R	sign "Loenen," Boslaan
23.2	ST L !	or **alternate route** via Alambertskade (see note on p. 63)
25.6	CS	T-Loenen, at Brugstraat
25.9	L	dir. "Loosdrecht & Hilversum," Bloklaan/N403
25.9	ST CS	RT = 8 km Breukelen
29.8	L	sign "Kortenhoef" Horndijk
30.8	CS	Moleneind
32.4	R	N201 dir. Hilversum
32.6	L	(cross N201) Kortenhoefsedijk
33.0	CS	church, T-Kortenhoef
35.1	R	Kerklaan/ 's-Gravelandse Weg
39.7	L	Melkpad/Stationsstraat
40.5	L	Stationsplein
40.6	End	Hilversum Railway Station

Alternate Route via Nichtevecht ferry:

15.4	-	Nigtevecht (CS 20 m)
15.4	L	sign "Vreeland & Loenen," Dorpsstraat (at church)
15.6	VL	Dorpsstraat
15.9	L	bridge over Amsterdam-Rijnkanaal
16.0	L	Vreelandseweg
22.6	SS	Molen De Ruiter
22.7	VL	sign "Loenen"
23.0	VL	Duinkerken
23.1	L	bridge/Breedstraat, sign "Loenen"
23.2	R	rejoin route (Lindengracht corner Breedstraat,) sign "Loenen"

Waterland Day Trip

Total Distance:	36.4 km to 56.7 km (depending on route choice)
Duration:	1 day
Highlights:	Durgerdam, coastal and canal cycling, island of Marken, Edam, Monnickendam, Broek in Waterland
Terrain:	Level
Maps:	Michelin 531 Noord-Nederland/Pays-Bas Nord, ANWB/VVV Toeristenkaart Noord Holland
Start/Finish:	Amsterdam/Amsterdam
Access:	IJ ferry north (behind) the Amsterdam central station

Map 6.3. Waterland Day Trip.

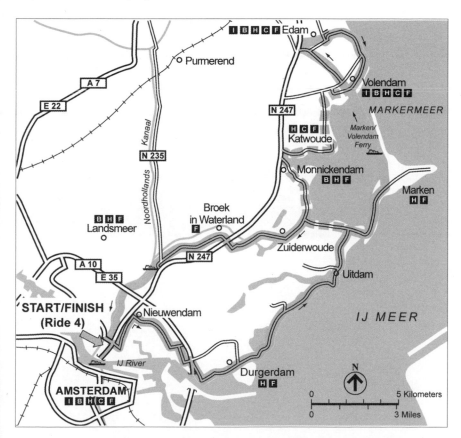

A two-minute ferry ride across the IJ River transports you to a watery wonderland surprisingly close to Amsterdam. If time permits, take the causeway to the island of Marken, where you can hop on another ferry to Volendam and Edam; or head straight to the fishing port of Monnickendam, then inland to Broek in Waterland.

This ride combines the first and last days of the tour of North Holland route described in Chapter 7. The first part, from Amsterdam to Edam (see page 68), offers two options: one via the island of Marken, the other via Monnickendam along the coast.

Returning from Edam, follow Day 6 (see page 98), which takes you through Monnickendam and Broek in Waterland, then along the Noordhollands Kanaal back to Amsterdam.

If you don't want to go all the way from Amsterdam to Edam, shorten the route by turning left to Monnickendam (18.0 km), then turning left at 20.1 km to Broek in Waterland. To return to Amsterdam, follow the directions from 15.1 km on Day 6 of the Edam to Amsterdam route (see page 100).

For map and cue sheet, see Chapter 7, page 68–71 and 98–100.

Cycling past traditional houses on the island of Marken (Waterland Day Trip or Day 1 of tour of North Holland).

7.

North Holland & Texel

THE PROVINCE of North Holland covers the area north of Amsterdam, stretching up to the island of Texel. It is bounded by the North Sea on the west, and the freshwater IJsselmeer and Markermeer on the east. Cutting through the province is the Noordzee Kanaal, and the IJ River. South of these are the cities of Amsterdam, Haarlem, and Hilversum, plus Schiphol Airport. This area is more densely populated than the area to the north, but it retains areas of bucolic bliss.

The ride in this chapter covers the area north of Amsterdam. For cycling in the superb lake region in the southeast, see the "Lakes & Rivers Ride" (page 61). The area south of Amsterdam is covered on the first and last days of the "Witches, Windmills, and West Coast Ride" (page 176).

Tour of North Holland

Total Distance:	276.5 km (or 347.8 km with Texel)
Duration:	6 days (or 8 days with Texel) (see page 82)
Highlights:	Island of Marken, Edam, windmills at Schermerhorn, Alkmaar's cheese market and cheese museum, tulip fields near Alkmaar, coastal dunes, island of Texel, the Aflsuitdijk (optional), Enkhuizen, the Zuiderzee Museum (in Enkhuizen)
Terrain:	Level
When to Go:	The best time to ride is between late April and late September. Tulips bloom in late April/early May in North

Holland, and hyacinths on Texel in mid- to late April. The most crowded months are July and August, when the Dutch take their summer vacations.

Maps:	Michelin 531 Noord-Nederland/Pays-Bas Nord, ANWB/VVV Toeristenkaart Noord Holland
Start/Finish:	Amsterdam/Amsterdam
Access:	This ride can start or conclude in Amsterdam, Alkmaar, Den Helder, Enkhuizen, or Hoorn. If you choose to go to the island of Texel only, take the train from Amsterdam to Den Helder, then the ferry to Texel (see "Southern Texel Route," page 84)
Connecting routes:	Connect to Friesland's Elfstedenroute either by cycling across the Aflsuitdjjk from Den Oever to Zurich and cycling 6.0 km to Makkum (see page 114), or by taking the ferry from Enkhuizen to Stavoren, where you can pick up the route on Day 2 of the ride (see page 109).

North Holland is primarily level and easy to cycle. You will follow some beautiful coastline and meander through sand dunes, and cycle beside colorful bulb fields. Visit the picturesque "cheese towns" of Edam and Alkmaar, and the historically interesting towns of Hoorn and Enkhuizen. Enkhuizen's Zuiderzee Museum is definitely worth a visit. As an option, you may cross one of the world's great engineering feats, the Afsluitdijk.

Day 1: Amsterdam to Edam (25.3 or 33.3 km)

Take a quick ferry ride across the IJ River and take a coastal ride mostly atop a dike to Marken. The route will take you through the village of Nieuwendam. At 1.9 km, there is a huge roundabout, which requires careful navigation to locate Nieuwendammerdijk. The route then follows the Markermeer coast through several villages. The first is Durgerdam, a pretty village of wooden houses lining the water. After Durgerdam, the bike path goes up onto the dike, where you overlook the Markermeer. The lakes to the left, formerly peat bogs, are home to many bird colonies. Pass through tiny Uitdam, built on the dike.

At 18.0 km, go right to Marken or left to Monnickendam. Unless the boat isn't running (see page 69), you should definitely head to Marken. For the alternate route, stay on the dike until Monnickendam, then cycle beside the dike to Volendam. (You will cycle most of this on Day 6 in the opposite direction). This option adds 8 km to the ride to Edam.

Marken, once an island, is now joined to the mainland by a causeway built in 1957. Although Marken gets its share of tourists, it still maintains a certain charm, with its traditional green and black wooden houses built on stilts and its small, picturesque harbor. Visit the Marken Museum, Kerkbuurt 44 (open daily, Easter through November), for a glimpse of Marken lifestyle.

At the harbor, the Marken Express is a 30-minute ferry ride across the water to Volendam. (The cost is €4 per adult and €1 per bike. It departs every 30 to 45 minutes until 6 p.m., April through October.) Volendam is larger than Marken, and has swarms of tourists. As a result, there are lots of seafood restaurants, cafés, and souvenir shops lining the harbor.

Leave Volendam on Zeestraat; look for ANWB signpost #2396. Cycle along the canal the 3 kilometers to the delightful cheese town of Edam.

Cue Sheet

From behind the Centraal Station, go west 120 m on De Ruijterkade. Take the IJ ferry (IJveer) across the river.

| 0.0 | Start | from the IJ ferry, go N along the Noordhollands Kanaal |
| 0.2 | L | LF7b Buiksloterweg |

Map 7.1. Tour of North Holland, Days 1 & 2, and Dunes Day Trip.

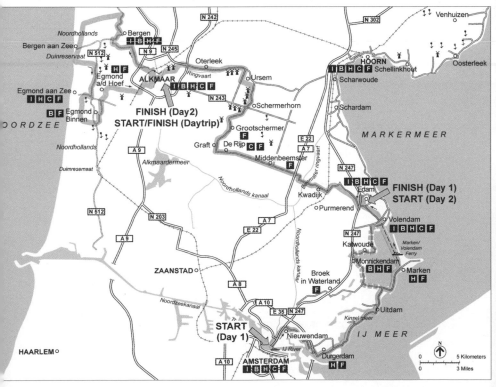

69

0.3	VR	LF7b Buiksloterweg sign "Edam and Volendam"
0.9	R	over canal, sign "Marken and Vliegbos"
1.0	L	Adelaarsweg, sign "Marken and Vliegbos"
1.9	RA R !	Meeuwenlaan, sign "Marken," T-Nieuwendam
2.0	R	Nieuwendammerdijk, sign "Marken"
4.0	CS	bike path, sign "Durgerdam and Marken"
4.2	R	bike path onto Schellingwouderdijk, sign "Durgerdam, Marken"
7.2	L	Durgerdammerdijk, T-Durgerdam
8.5	CS	onto Uitdammerdijk bike path
9.0	SS	birdwatching at Waterland-Oost
15.8	CS	bike path becomes road, T-Uitdam
18.0	R	sign "Marken"
21.8	L	Beatrixbrug, T-Marken
21.9	L	sign "Haven/Havenmeester"
22.1	L	sign "Marken Express," harbor/ferry
22.1	L	along harbor, T-Volendam
22.3	R !	Zeestraat #2396
25.0	R	sign "Centrum," Burg. Versteeghsingel
25.1	L	Baanstraat, sign "VVV"
25.3	End	Damplein, VVV Edam

Alternate Route via Monickendam:

18.0	L	N518, sign "Monnickendam"
20.1	L	sign "Broek in Waterland and Zuiderwoude"*
22.4	RA R	Zuideinde, sign "Volendam and Edam"
22.8	CS	harbor, T-Monnickendam
22.9	R	Noordeinde
23.4	CS	over bridge, sign "Katwoude"
24.0	R	sign "Volendam and Edam"
24.0	SS L	Irene Hoeve (see page 98)

24.5	SS L	Jacobs Hoeve (see page 98)
29.2	R	sign "Volendam and Edam," Zuiderzeeroute sign
30.3	L !	Zeestraat #2396, T-"Volendam"
33.0	R	sign "Centrum," Burg. Versteeghsingel
33.1	L	Baanstraat, sign "VVV"
33.3	End	Damplein, VVV Edam

* This cue (20.1 km) is for Waterland Day Trip only, see page 66.

Edam

Edam has remained relatively unspoiled. Stand on the Damplein for a view of the Speeltoren, the remnant of a 15th-century church, which has one of the oldest carillons in the country. Cross to the Edams Museum at Damplein 8 (closed Mondays, open April through October), in Edam's oldest house, built in 1530. Visit the Waag (Weigh House) on the Kaasmarkt, where a market is held on Wednesday mornings. In July and August, there is also a cheese market on Wednesday mornings (www.edammerkaasmarkt.nl). The 15th-century Grote Kerk, or Nicholaaskerk, is famous for its stained glass. Although cheese is no longer made in Edam, there are cheese farms in the area (see Day 6).

Information:	VVV Edam is in the Stadhuis at Damplein 1 (Tel. 0299 315 125, www.vvv-edam.nl). Internet access is available at the library, Dijkgraaf Poschlaan 8 (Tel. 0299 368 080).
Bicycle Shop:	Ronald Schot, Grote Kerkstraat 7-9 (Tel. 0299 372 155, www.ronaldschot.nl), operates a full-service bike shop with rentals.
Where to Stay:	Across from the VVV, Damhotel (Tel. 0299 371 766, www.damhotel.nl) has singles for €55 and doubles for €90. Hotel-Restaurant De Fortuna, Spuistraat 1-7 (Tel. 0299 371 671, www.fortuna-edam.nl), is a collection of five renovated 17th-century houses on a pretty canal. When reserving, mention you have a bike. Singles are from €62.50 and doubles are from €87.50. The four-room Pension-Café De Harmonie at Voorhaven 94 (Tel. 0299 371 664, www.harmonie-edam.nl) is €70 for a double. The VVV has a list of B&Bs.
	Camping Strandbad, Zeevangszeedijk 7A (Tel. 0299 371 994, www.campingstrandbad.nl), is right on the edge of the IJsselmeer.

If lodging in Edam is full, Volendam is an option. The VVV Volendam is at Zeestraat 37 (Tel. 0299 363 747, www.vvv-volendam.nl).

Where to Eat: Both the Hotel-Restaurant De Fortuna and the Damhotel have excellent restaurants. De Eeterij at Prinsenstraat 5 (Tel. 0299 371 630) has an interesting menu, but is closed Mondays and Tuesdays. Volendam, an easy 3-kilometer ride away, has many restaurants, especially on the harbor.

Day 2: Edam to Alkmaar (41.6 km)

Travel along pretty canals, through architecturally rich villages, and past several windmills en route to Alkmaar.

Leave Edam and cross the N247 toward Alkmaar and Kwadijk. Cross the bridge over the canal (5.2 km) and continue straight. Kwadijk is a linear village of almost 3 km, straddling Kwadijkerweg.

Enter Middenbeemster along a tree-lined road. The route takes you straight through town, but at the main intersection, the only one with a traffic light (11.0 km), turn right and ride about 200 m to see the lovely homes along the canal; then return and continue on the route.

At 16.0 km, you'll go up onto a dike, turn left, then almost immediately turn right across a small bridge to enter the town of De Rijp. Notice the great old houses on both sides of the narrow road, with their gabled roofs. In the center of town (16.7 km), you will see the Stadhuis, built in 1630, with the Waag on the ground floor. Turn left and visit the Gothic church, noted for its 17th-century stained glass windows. Visit the Museum In 't Houten Huis (Museum in the Wooden House) at Jan Boonplein 2 (open weekends only except in July and August), for a history of the town and area. For a different perspective, go left at the church and ride along the canal on Rechtestraat to view the backs of the houses.

Return to the center of town (16.7 km) and continue on the main street, turning right at 18.0 km. 100 m after the turn, the beautiful building on your right was formerly the Stadhuis of the separate village of Graft.

Just north of Grootschermer (22.0 km) is the Nic. Jonk Museum, Haviksdijkje 5 (www.beeldentuinnicjonk.nl, open Wednesdays through Sundays, May through November), with its sculpture garden, plus painting and ceramic gallery. The ride north from Grootschermer is on the Molendijk. At the intersection of N243, visit the middle of the three windmills, the Museummolen Schermerhorn (windmill museum, open daily, April 1 to October 31, 10 a.m. to 5 p.m.). See and learn about a working windmill. Tip: Avoid visiting the Museummolen on Friday afternoon when tour buses returning from the Alkmaar Cheese Market stop here.

At this intersection (24.3 km), *do not* follow the sign "Alkmaar 9 km" pointing left. Instead, continue north to Ursem, then follow windmill-lined dikes all the way to Alkmaar. At 36.0 km, turn right to go over the freeway. This tangled overpass requires several turns. Follow the LF15b route signs until you end up alongside a pleasant canal, a windmill ahead. At 37.5 km, turn right over the footbridge, continue into Alkmaar, pass five more windmills (39.0 km), cross the Noordhollandskanaal, and continue to the Waagplein, the focal point of the town.

Cue Sheet

0.0	Start	VVV Edam go E on Hoogstraat
0.2	R	Burg. Versteeghsingel
0.4	R	Singelweg
0.6	L	cross Singelweg, sign "Purmerend"
0.7	R	sign "Alkmaar," N247
0.9	L	sign "Alkmaar," Groot Westerbuiten
1.2	R	over bridge/along canal, sign "Kwadijk"
5.2	R	over bridge, sign "Kwadijk"
5.3	CS	sign "Alkmaar," Kwadijkerweg
8.5	R	Purmerenderweg
8.8	L	Rijperweg dir. "Middenbeemster"
11.0	SS R	houses, T-Middenbeemster
15.6	SS L	bulb fields
16.0	L	Westdijk
16.1	R	Oosteinde
16.7	SS L	T-De Rijp (center)
18.0	R	sign "Alkmaar & Schermerhorn," Raadhuisstraat
18.1	SS	Stadhuis, T-Graft
19.4	R	Meerdijk
21.0	R	sign "Alkmaar and Schermerhorn," Kopdammerdijk
21.1	L	't Kieftennest, T-Grootschermer
21.9	L	over bridge
22.0	R	sign "Schermerhorn," Molendijk
24.3	SS L	RT = 300 m, three windmills and the Museummolen
24.4	CS !	sign "Ursem," cross N243

27.5	L	Ursemmerweg
28.7	R	Rustenburgerweg
29.4	L	Noord-Schermerdijk
30.2	SS	three windmills
32.6	L	Otterlekerweg
33.1	R	Korte Molenweg
36.0	R !	LF15b over N242 (4 x turn)
37.5	R	over bridge
37.8	CS	't Wuiver
38.1	R	Herenweg
38.8	L	sign "Centrum," Molenkade
40.2	L	Frieseweg
41.0	VL	over Noordhollands Kanaal, sign "Centrum"
41.1	R	Kanaalkade
41.3	L !	Voordam
41.5	R	over canal (to Waagplein)
41.5	L/end	(20 m) Waagplein, VVV Alkmaar ahead

Alkmaar

Alkmaar is best known for its traditional cheese market, Friday mornings in the summer. Held on the Waagplein, the spectacle showcases the cheese carriers, who transport brightly colored sleds piled with cheeses from the auction ring to the Waag. Today, the market is kept alive for tourists.

Among the highlights is the 14th-century Waag, with the Kaasmuseum (cheese museum, www.kaasmuseum.nl, closed Sundays, April through October) located inside. Also noteworthy are the 16th-century Vismarkt (fish market), the Grote Kerk, the Stadhuis, and an 18th-century windmill, the Molen Van Piet, Clarissenbuurt 4 (www.molenvanpiet.nl, open Fridays and Saturdays, July through September), still in use as a flour mill. Other museums in town include the Stedelijk Museum, the Nationaal Bier Museum (National Beer Museum), and the Hans Brinker Museum.

Information: VVV Alkmaar, Waagplein 2 (Tel. 072 511 4284, www.vvvalkmaar.nl) is in the Waag. ANWB Alkmaar is at Noorderkade 134 (Tel. 072 511 9041). Internet café Het Communicatiepark, is at Koorstraat 33-35 (Tel. 072 514

3035). Internet access is available at the centrally located library, Gasthuisstraat 2 (Tel. 072 515 6644).

Bicycle Shops: The huge bike shop, Paul Harder Fiets, is on Laat 49 (Tel. 072 511 2488, www.paulharder.nl). At the railway station is Fietspoint Stoop, Stationsweg 43 (Tel. 072 511 7907), which rents bikes.

Where to Stay: Lodging in Alkmaar is in short supply, but Bergen, 6 km further, has an abundance of hotels and B&Bs (see Day 3).

The only reasonably priced hotel in Alkmaar that has a place for bikes is Hotel Stad en Land, Stationsweg 92-94 (Tel. 072 512 3911), near the station. Singles are €52.50 and doubles are €75.

The other option is one of about a dozen of B&Bs in town, which the VVV will reserve for a small fee.

There is no hostel in Alkmaar. The closest is Stayokay Hostel Egmond, Herenweg 118 (Tel. 072 506 2269, www.stayokay.com/egmond), between Egmond Binnen and Egmond a/d Hoef, about 8 km west of Alkmaar.

Camping Alkmaar, Bergerweg 201 (Tel. 072 511 6924), is west of Alkmaar on the way to Bergen, and is open April to mid-September.

Where to Eat: There are several restaurants around the Waag. On Mient, there is an Indonesian restaurant, and across the road is an Italian restaurant. On Ritsevoort, there is a cluster of restaurants, including an Argentinian steakhouse and a French bistro. For Dutch fare, try Hof van Alkmaar, Hof van Sonoy 1 (Tel. 072 512 1222, closed Mondays), in an old almshouse.

Dunes Day Trip (37.8 km)

Total Distance: 37.8 km

Duration: 4 to 5 hours

Highlights: Bergen, Noordhollands Duinreservaat (sand dunes), bulb fields (in the spring)

Terrain: Mainly level, sometimes gently undulating

Maps: ANWB/VVV Touristenkaart Noord Holland

Start/Finish: Alkmaar/Alkmaar or Bergen/Bergen

Access: This is a circuit ride, starting and ending in Alkmaar. It can also begin and end in Bergen. The first 6 km from Alkmaar to Bergen is the same as the start of Day 3 (see page 78).

A short ride to the art town of Bergen brings you to the edge of the Noordhollands Duinreservaat (North Holland Dune Reserve), a protected area of rolling sand dunes. If you are cycling in mid-April or early May, you will see the bulb fields in bloom in the area around Egmond a/d Hoef and Egmond Binnen. You will enter the Noordhollands Duinreservaat at 8.4 km. Your daycard (purchased at the automated ticket machine for €1.10 per adult) is good for repeated entries.

You have the choice of numerous bicycle paths in the reserve, and you can create your own route by following the numbered ANWB mushrooms. This route explores only one option that takes you north-south through the reserve, entering and leaving a few times.

The reserve area between Bergen and Bergen aan Zee offers lovely cycling through a mix of pine and oak forests, punctuated with open heath. After Bergen aan Zee (14.2 km), join the signed LF1a (Noordzeeroute), heading south and riding through 4 kilometers of rolling sand dunes.

Around 18.7 km, the views are everything you'd expect from a Dutch landscape: windmills, cows, and tulip fields.

The last part of the ride follows several small canals, goes through Heiloo, and at 32.9 km, you will enter a cool forest, through which you will ride for about 2 km before turning north on Kennemerstraatweg back to Alkmaar. Turn left at the windmill (36.4 km), keeping the canal on your right until the turn onto Geesterweg (37.3 km) back to the station.

Cue Sheet

0.0	Start	Alkmaar Railway Station/Fietspoint Stoop
0.0		go SW on Stationsweg, sign "Bergen"
0.2	R	Bergerweg
1.0	R	Oude Hoeverweg
1.1	L	Johan Wagenaarkade
1.6	VR	LF7b Bergerweg/N510
3.7	RA L	sign "Bergen aan Zee," Nesdijk
5.1	R	sign "Bergen aan Zee," Meerweg
5.5	SS R	thatched roof house
5.6	R	Studler van Surcklaan
5.9	L	Ruinelaan
6.2	R	Dorpsstraat (20 m), L Kerkstraat

6.4	CS	VVV Bergen, T-Bergen
6.7	CS	Breelaan
7.5	CS	cross Duinweg
8.4	L	#22908, sign "Bergen aan Zee and Egmond"
8.4	-	enter Noordhollands Duinreservaat
9.3	L	#22907, sign "Bergen aan Zee"
10.3	R	#22906, sign "Bergen aan Zee," Helmweg
12.1	R	#22911, sign "Bergen aan Zee," Korteweg
12.6	VL	#20975, Verspyckweg
13.1	L	LF1a #22912, Elzenlaan
13.5	R	LF1a #22913
14.1	VL	parking area, T-Bergen aan Zee
14.2	VL	LF1a, sign "Egmond," Parkweg
14.6	R	LF1a, sign "Egmond," re-enter Noordhollands Duinreservaat
18.4	R	LF1a, sign "Egmond a/d Hoef and Egmond Binnen," N511
20.4	R	LF1a Nachtegalenpad
21.4	R	LF1a
21.6	L	sign "Egmond Binnen"
22.6	R	LF1a #24218, re-enter Noordhollands Duinreservaat
24.5	L	N#22884, sign "Egmond Binnen," Middenweg
25.0	R	#22885, sign "Egmond Binnen"
25.6	CS	cross N512
25.8	CS	Abdijlaan, T-Egmond Binnen
26.0	L	sign "Alkmaar," Krijt
26.3	R	sign "Alkmaar," Doelen
26.8	L	Hoge Dijk
28.3	CS	Heilooer Zeeweg
28.3	CS	sign "Alkmaar"
29.2	R	Zomerdijkje, sign "Alkmaar"

30.0	R	bike path
31.9	CS	cross Belieslaan
32.3	L	LF15a De Dors
32.4	R	LF15a Belieslaan
32.9	L	LF 15a Westerweg (along railway tracks)
33.8	R	LF15a Kuillaan
34.3	L	Kennemerstraatweg
36.4	L	at windmill/Varnebroek/Kennemersingel
37.3	L	Geesterweg
37.6	R	Stationsweg
37.8	End	Alkmaar Railway Station

Day 3: Alkmaar to Den Helder (55.6 km)

Riding from Alkmaar to Den Helder is a real coastal experience. The Schoorlse dunes are a roller-coaster ride through the hilly grass-topped sandy mounds. The route follows two stunning sections of sea wall; one just after Camperduin, the other just before the Texel ferry in Den Helder. If it's springtime, the bike path high above the N502 affords spectacular views of the bulb fields.

The first stop of the day is Bergen, reached by going along the Nesdijk (3.7 km), through a forest, and past several eye-catching thatched cottages (5.5 km to 5.7 km).

Bergen (6.4 km) is a lively resort and artists' town with several galleries stemming from the Bergen School of Art. In Bergen and beach towns in the vicinity, there is an abundance of hotels, B&Bs, and restaurants. Here, you are on the edge of the Noordhollands Duinreservaat (see "Dunes Day Trip," page 75).

If you choose to stay in Bergen instead of Alkmaar, the VVV, Plein 1 (Tel. 072 581 3100, www.vvvnoordzeekust.nl), can reserve hotels and B&Bs. Het Witte Huis, Ruinelaan 15 (Tel. 072 581 2530), has singles for €50.00 and doubles starting at €77.50. With a lovely porch, Hotel 1900, Russenweg 3-5 (Tel. 072 581 2771, info@hotel1900.com), has singles from €45 and doubles from €64. The closest campgrounds are the three in Schoorl (10.6 km). There are VVV offices in Schoorl, Bergen aan Zee, and Egmond aan Zee. Bergen's bicycle shop, Busker, is at Kerkstraat 1 (Tel. 072 589 5196).

From Bergen, follow the signs north to Schoorl. From Schoorl, continue through the forest and enter the Schoorlse Dune Area (11.3 km). Follow the route toward Camperduin and Hargen, clearly marked by the ANWB mushrooms (some of which are not indicated on the Noord Holland map). At 13.0 km, continue straight to the right of the café. You can access the beach at 15.7 km and 17.5 km.

At 20.2 km, you reach Camperduin, nothing more than a few restaurants and a hotel. From here, the route follows the LF1b (Noordzeeroute) to Den Helder. At the *Strandvonder* statue, turn right for a magnificent 6 km ride on the sea wall (dike) beside the North Sea.

At 26.2 km (just north of Petten) the bike path (partly hard-packed dirt) goes through the hilliest dunes of the day. At 29.6 km, the route exits the dunes to a bike path alongside the N502. After Callantsoog (35.5 km), the bike path climbs to above the road. If you are here in spring, you will overlook tulip fields.

At 47.4 km, you'll see an ANWB mushroom pointing to Den Helder and the Texel ferry. Following the route directly to the ferry will take you along the coast; going directly to Den Helder takes you through the town itself.

To go to Texel, continue to the ferry terminal, following the bicycle signs and the sign *"Voetgangers en fietsers bestemming Texel"* (Pedestrians and cyclists destination Texel). Only round trip tickets are sold, and cost €4 per adult and €2.70 per bike. The ferry crosses in 25 minutes, leaving once an hour, and operates until about 9 p.m. (Tel. 0222 369 691, www.teso.nl).

(For cycling directions from the ferry to Den Burg, see "Den Burg," page 82.)

If you decide to stay in Den Helder instead of going to Texel, the VVV office is at Bernhardplein 18 (Tel. 0223 625 544, www. vvvkopvannoordholland.nl). The ANWB office is at Spoorstraat 64 (Tel. 0223 614 802). There is a bike shop at the station (Tel. 0223 619 227). Den Helder is a naval base and has a Marine Museum covering the history of the Dutch navy. Even if you didn't plan to visit Texel, it would be more fun spending the night there, in Den Burg, rather than in Den Helder, so consider hopping on the ferry and cycling the 5.9 km to Den Burg.

Cue Sheet

0.0	Start	Alkmaar Railway Station/Fietspoint Stoop go SW on Stationsweg, sign "Bergen"
0.2	R	Bergerweg
1.0	R	Oude Hoeverweg
1.1	L	Johan Wagenaarkade
1.6	VR	LF7b Bergerweg/N510
3.7	RA L	sign "Bergen aan Zee," Nesdijk
5.1	R	sign "Bergen aan Zee," Meerweg
5.5	SS R	thatched roof houses
5.6	R	Studler van Surcklaan
5.9	L	Ruinelaan
6.2	R	Dorpsstraat (20 m), L Kerkstraat
6.4	CS	VVV Bergen, T-Bergen

Map 7.2. Tour of North Holland, Day 3.

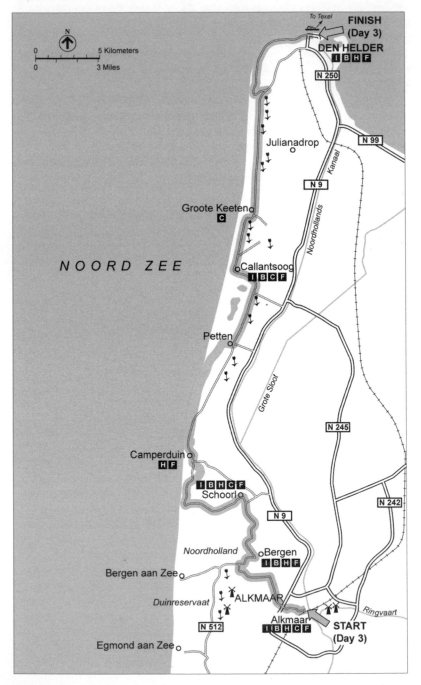

6.7	CS	Breelaan
7.5	R	sign "Schoorl," Duinweg
8.0	CS	cross road, LF7b, sign "Schoorl"
8.6	CS	LF7b #22917, sign "Schoorl," Postweg
9.4	L	LF7b #22920, sign "Schoorl," Duinweg
10.4	CS	sign "Schoorl Centrum"
10.6	-	T-Schoorl, VVV 50 m on R
10.6	L	LF7b, sign "Groet"
10.7	L	bike path through forest
11.3	L	LF7b, sign "Hargen aan Zee," Schoorlse Zeeweg
13.0	CS !	#20567, sign "Hargen," Café de Berenkuil
15.7	R	#20597, sign "Camperduin and Hargen" (L to beach)
17.5	R	#22928, sign "Camperduin and Hargen" (CS to beach)
19.0	CS	#20899, sign "Camperduin and Hargen," Harger Zeeweg
20.2	L !	LF1b #20900, T-Camperduin
20.3	R	along sea dike (*Strandvonder* statue)
26.1	CS	LF1b (gravel 20 m)
26.2	L	LF1b bike path through dunes
26.6	L	LF1b #25245, sign "Den Helder and Callantsoog"
26.7	R	LF1b #25246, sign "Den Helder and Callantsoog"
28.9	R	LF1b #25247, sign "Den Helder and Callantsoog"
29.6	L	LF1b/N502, bulb fields on L
35.5	CS	LF1b T-Callantsoog (restaurant area on tiny street)
35.6	R	LF1b Kerkplein/N502
36.3	CS	LF1b/N502
39.1	VL	LF1b, bike path above N502
41.8	CS	LF1b/N502
43.3	R	LF1b (30 m), L LF1b
44.4	CS	LF1b #20300/62420, R (60 m) #20301

47.4	L !	LF1b #12537/20792 (sign "Texel," L) (sign "Den Helder," R)
48.5	L	LF1b #21080, sign "Boot Texel", Grafelijkheidsweg
49.9	L	LF1b N#21244, sign "Boot Texel"
50.0	R	LF1b #21230
55.1	R	to ferry following, signs "Boot Texel"
55.6	End	"Ingang Rijwielen" (Bicycle Entrance), Texel ferry

Texel

Texel (pronounced TESSel) is the largest of the Wadden islands. It is 24 km long and 9 km wide and has 135 km of bicycle paths. The island is mainly rural. Den Burg is the main settlement. In the south, the quaint village of Den Hoorn has a maritime atmosphere, and north of Den Burg are the pretty villages of De Waal, Oosterend, and De Cocksdorp.

Bird lovers will revel in the ample opportunities to view birdlife; Texel's dunes and freshwater lakes are breeding grounds and nesting places for over 300 species. Nature lovers will want to visit EcoMare (see "Northern Texel Route").

There are two suggested rides on Texel. The first is a short ride offering a taste of the southern part of the island. The second is a longer route going all the way to the lighthouse at the northern tip. For walkers, Texel has several trails in the dunes and nature reserves.

Den Burg

Den Burg, Texel's capital, is roughly in the center of the island. It has hotels, B&Bs, a hostel, and camping. Lodging can also be found in Den Hoorn, De Waal, De Cocksdorp, and De Koog. Campgrounds are scattered all over the island. There are 10 regular campgrounds and an astounding 28 farms offering *camping bij de boer*.

To cycle to Den Burg, go straight from the ferry; after 100 m, turn left toward Den Burg, and after another 400 m, turn right onto the N501. Continue on the bike path along the N501 until 5.9 km, then turn right on Emmalaan.

Information: The VVV, at Emmalaan 66 (Tel. 0222 314 741, www.texel. net), has lots of information on Texel, including a map with two bike routes (€1.50), a booklet with four bike routes and 24 walking trails (€3.50), and *Bird-watching on Texel* (€3.50) in English. Ask for the free booklet *Echt Texels Produkt* (www.echttexelsprodukt.nl), which describes 34 local farms, producers, and purveyors of Texel products open for visits.

During opening hours, there is one terminal for internet access at the VVV. The other option is Den Burg's library, Drijverstraat 7 (Tel. 0222 312 743).

Bicycle Shops: There at least two dozen bicycle shops and rental facilities in Den Burg, De Koog, De Cocksdorp, Den Hoorn, Oosterend, Oudeschild, and the ferry terminal (see "Southern Route"). In the center of Den Burg is the bike shop F. Zegel, Parkstraat 14 (Tel. 0222 312 150).

Where to Stay: In the center, the cozy Hotel-Café De Smulpot, Binnen-burg 5 (Tel. 0222 312 756, www.desmulpot.nl), has singles for €62 and doubles for €100. North of the center, Hotel Koogerend, Koogerstraat 94 (Tel. 0222 313 301, www.fletcher.nl), has singles from €35 and doubles from €70. On Emmalaan 6 is Hotel-Brasserie Den Burg (Tel. 0222 312 106, www.hoteldenburg.nl). Also ask the VVV about B&Bs.

In a rural setting 2 km east of Den Burg is Stayokay Hostel Panorama, Schansweg 7 (Tel. 0222 315 441, www.stayokay.com/texel).

The VVV has an excellent brochure, *Camping Texel*, listing all of the island's campgrounds. Most of the large campgrounds are to the west and north of Den Burg, the closest being De Koorn-aar, Grensweg 388 (Tel. 0222 312 931, www.koorn-aar.nl), west of Den Burg. En route to De Waal (see "Northern Texel Route") is *Mini-Camping bij de Boer*, Family Snoey-Bakker, Waalderweg 120 (Tel. 0222 312 468), 3 km from Den Burg.

Where to Eat: Both Hotel-Café De Smulpot and Hotel-Brasserie Den Burg (see "Where to Stay") have restaurants. Tasty meals can be had at both Spijslokaal Het Schoutenhuys, Groeneplaats 14 (Tel. 0222 312 041, closed Mondays and Tuesdays) and Eetcafé De Bruintje Beer, Stenenplaats 2 (Tel. 0222 320 164). For Asian fare head to Restaurant Azië, Groeneplaats 12 (Tel. 0222 313 833), and for pizza, Pizzeria Venezia, Kogerstraat 7 (Tel. 0222 312 570).

Lamb is a specialty on Texel, and is available at many restaurants on the island.

Southern Texel Route (24.8 km)

Total Distance:	24.8 km
Duration:	3 hours
Highlights:	Forests, sand dunes, birdwatching, Den Hoorn, bike path along the Prins Hendrikpolder dike, Maritime and Beachcombers Museum, Texel Brewery, bulb fields (in spring)
Terrain:	Level
When to Go:	The best time to ride is between mid-April and September. Crowds are thickest in July and August. Most campgrounds don't open until Easter and close around end September. Bulb fields bloom for two to three weeks starting in mid-April.
Maps:	Michelin 531 Noord-Nederland/Pays-Bas, ANWB/VVV Touristenkaart Noord Holland, Texel Cycling Map (available from VVV Texel)
Start/Finish:	Den Burg/Den Burg (or ferry landing)
Access:	Cycle (see "Tour of North Holland," Days 1, 2, and 3) or take the train to Den Helder; then take the ferry to Texel.
Connections:	In the summer months there is a ferry to the adjacent island of Vlieland, then another ferry to the island of Terschelling. From Terschelling, one ferry goes to Harlingen (Day 3 of Friesland's "Elfstedenroute"), and another to Ameland.

This is a lovely circuit ride that gives a glimpse of the island if you have limited time. For someone taking the train to Den Helder, spending the day on Texel is a great option, as the route can start and finish at the ferry. You can rent a bike at Fietsverhuur Veerhaven Texel, Pontweg 2 (Tel. 0222 319 588)

After leaving Den Burg, just before the forest begins at 3.4 km, stop at Catherinahoeve, a working farm and restaurant, Rozendijk 17 (Tel. 0222 312 156, www.catharinahoeve-texel.nl). The forest continues for about 3 km, then opens up into farmland. At 8.5 km, turn right to the western dunes; turning left takes you into the pretty village of Den Hoorn.

At mushroom #21900 (10.8 km) go straight to the dunes, as well as to the lakes of De Geul and Petten, home to many birds. From here, the route swings back to the ferry past several brightly colored bulb fields.

After 't Hoorntje (14.4 km), veer right onto a bike path alongside the Prins Hendrikpolder dike. Although it is tempting to ride atop the dike next to the water, signs indicate it is "at your own risk" due to the sloping path and tides. Follow the bicycle path alongside the grassy dike for 3 km.

When you reach Oudeschild (19.3 km), the set of steps to the right allows you to climb up and view the sea from the top of the dike. Wind through the narrow streets with quaint old houses to the Maritiem and Jutters Museum (Maritime and Beachcombers Museum, www.texelsmaritiem.nl, closed Sundays and Mondays).

Halfway between Oudeschild and Den Burg is the island's brewery, Texelse Bierbrouwerij, Schilderweg 214B (Tel. 0222 313 229, www. texelse-speciaalbier. nl, open Tuesday, Wednesday, and Saturday afternoons, March through October, call to reserve a tour).

Cue Sheet

0.0	Start	VVV Den Burg go W on Emmalaan
0.2	R	N501
2.3	L	Rozendijk, sign "Straasenbossen and Fonteinsol"
3.4	CS	#23850 cross over (forest begins)
3.4	SS L	Catharinahoeve
4.7	L	#23840/03854, sign "Den Hoorn"
4.8	R	#20724
7.4	CS	#23856
8.4	R	unmarked
8.5	L	#21434 Klif/Herenstraat
8.5	SS R	sign "Loosmanduin," dune area
9.2	R	Kerkstraat (50 m), R Stolpweg, T-Den Hoorn
9.3	R	#21898, sign "De Mok, De Geul, and Petten"
9.5	L	#21899, sign "De Mok, De Geul, and Petten," Mokweg
10.8	L	#21900 sign "'t Hoorntje," Molwerk
10.8	SS CS	sign "De Geul," dune area

Half a shed?

As you cycle around Texel, especially the southern half of the island, you can't help but notice the odd looking structures that look like half a shed in the sheep pastures. These *schapenboeten* are used for hay and feed storage, not as housing for the hardy Texel sheep which remain outside all year. However, they do protect the sheep from prevailing westerly winds that blow across Texel; on windy days, the sheep huddle along the sheltered east face.

12.3	R	#21902, sign "'t Hoorntje"
13.0	L	sign "'t Hoorntje," Molwerk
13.2	CS	cross N501, sign "'t Hoorntje"
13.6	CS	sign "Oudeschild" (at ferry)
13.8	L	Dageraad
14.0	VR	Noorderhaaks/Landsdiep (along dike), T-'t Hoorntje
14.4	VL !	onto road, VR bike path along dike
15.0	CS	bike path along dike
17.8	R	Redoute
19.3	SS R	steps
19.3	L	De Ruytestraat, T-Oudeschild
19.5	R	De Ruytestraat
20.4	SS L	Maritiem and Juttersmuseum and windmill
20.5	L	sign "Den Burg," Heemskerckweg
21.0	L	sign "Den Burg," Schilderweg
24.0	L	dir. "Den Helder," Emmalaan
24.8	End	VVV Den Burg

Northern Texel Route (46.5 km)

Total Distance:	46.5 km
Duration:	1 day
Highlights:	Oosterend, cycling the eastern sea dike, Eierlandse Dunes, birdwatching, De Slufter, EcoMare.
Terrain:	Level
When to Go:	See "Southern Texel Route"
Maps:	See "Southern Texel Route"
Start/Finish:	Den Burg/Den Burg
Access:	See "Southern Texel Route"
Connections:	See "Southern Texel route"

The first stop is the tiny village of De Waal, which hasn't changed much in the last century. Texel's agricultural past can be found in the Agrarisch en Wagenmuseum (Tel. 0222 312 951, closed Sunday mornings and Mondays, open Easter through September). Continue to Oosterend, a somewhat larger village that still retains the old Dutch charm of yesteryear. Note the traditional Texel houses with dark green aprons and white trim, and the restored 12th-century church, the oldest church on the island.

From Oosterend, cycle to the Lancasterdijk, which protects the east side. Stop to watch birds at the small lake, Wagejot; then take the side trip to the tiny hamlet of Oost. Pass the very scenic Het Noorden windmill, used to keep the polder drained. Continue cycling along the dike until 16.9 km, where you have to carry your bike down 15 steps, and continue cycling on the side of the dike near the water. The level area to the right is De Schorren, a protected breeding ground for birds.

De Cocksdorp, the island's northernmost village, sits on the edge of the Eijerlandse Polder. De Cocksdorp has lodging and restaurants on the main street, Kikkerstraat. Continue on past the lighthouse (no entry). From ANWB mushroom #21447, cycle on a 4 km bike path through the Eijerlandse Dunes.

Climb the steps (29.2 km) for a fabulous view over De Slufter, created when the sand dike broke in 1858. The result is a unique wetland influenced by the tides. In July and August, purple wildflowers, sea lavender, cover the area. Two kilometers further is De Muy, a marshy breeding ground for many bird species. Guided walks are available through EcoMare.

Pass through De Koog, developed as the island's tourist town in the early 20th century, and cycle through the forest to EcoMare, Ruyslaan 92 (Tel. 0222 317 741, www.ecomare.nl). Set in the dunes, EcoMare is a sanctuary for birds and seals, a natural history museum, and an information center dedicated to the nature of Texel, the Wadden islands and the North Sea.

More forest paths lead to open farmlands and back to Den Burg.

Cue Sheet

0.0	Start	VVV Den Burg go NE on Emmalaan
0.7	CS	Bernhardlaan
1.6	R	Waalderstraat
2.1	R	Georgiëweg/Waalderweg
3.0	CS	Camping bij de Boer, Fam. Snoey-Bakker
3.6	L	Bomendiek, sign "De Waal"
3.9	CS	(at church) Hogereind, T-DeWaal
4.0	SS R	Agrarisch en Wegenmuseum

4.3	L	Waalderweg/Oosterenderweg
7.7	R	Oosterenderweg/Mulderstraat
8.3	R	Bijenkorfweg (30 m), R Peperstraat

Map 7.3. Texel—Southern & Northern Routes.

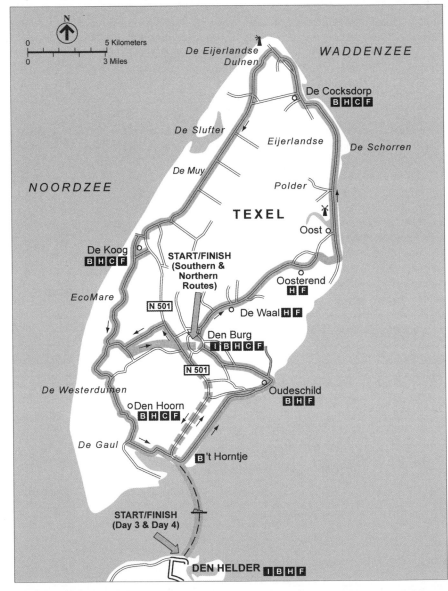

8.4	L	Kerkstraat, T-Oosterend
8.5	L	Oesterstraat
8.6	L	Achtertune
9.5	R	Oostkaap
10.4	L	Lancasterdijk
12.5	ST L	RT = 1.5 km Oost
12.5	VR	onto dike
12.9	SS L	Molen Het Noorden (windmill)
14.5	CS	through gate
16.9	VR !	onto dike, 15 steps
19.4	VL	off dike
19.7	R	Stengweg
20.2	ST L	RT = 500 m, T-De Cocksdorp
20.2	CS	Stengweg
20.8	VR	(onto dijk) Volharding
22.5	CS	Stengweg
22.9	L	#21447, sign "De Koog"
22.9	SS	*vuurtoren* (lighthouse)
25.5	CS	#21446
29.2	SS R	De Slufter steps
32.9	R	Ruigendijk, sign "De Koog"
34.7	L	#20274, Badweg
34.8	R	Dorpsstraat, T-De Koog
35.9	R	Schumakersweg
36.4	L	Bosrandweg (at 36.9, into forest)
37.5	R	Pelikaanweg
38.1	R	Ruijslaan, sign "EcoMare"
38.7	SS R	#20020/62423, EcoMare
39.4	VR	#20284 forest path
41.0	VL	#20342, sign "Den Burg"

42.1	VR	(10 m) CS #23840/03854, (10 m) L
42.2	CS	cross Rozendijk onto Bakkenweg
43.1	L	Westerweg
45.8	R	N501
46.3	L	Emmalaan
46.5	End	VVV Den Burg

Day 4: Den Helder to Enkhuizen (77.9 km)

This a long day, but the cycling is easy, as the first half of the route passes through two huge polders. The route traverses North Holland from west to east. Finish the day alongside the IJsselmeer, passing through Medemblik, and on into Enkhuizen. If the distance is too great, Medemblik is a suitable overnight option.

From the ferry terminal, follow the signs to Leeuwarden and Alkmaar. If you wish to go into town, turn right at 1.5 km and go about 500 m to the center. The route itself turns left and skirts the city along the waterfront.

The next 5 km are on a bike path beside the N250. At 7.3 km, turn right (just before a Bethlehem service station) and take the overpass to join the N99. At 8.0 km follow the bike path along the N99 over the Noordhollandskanaal, using the Duinroute sign as a cue.

Bulb fields start at 8.9 km; the town of Breezand is surrounded by them. At 13.2 km, cycle along a canal into the town of Anna Paulowna, which is also the name of the polder surrounding it. At the town's center (16.5 km), across from the church, is a delightful polder garden, Poldertuin (open April and May only).

Cross the Oude Veer, and soon pick up LF10a route signs. Cross the locks (28.1 km) and notice that the water level is higher on the left, Amstelmeer, than on the right. Follow the dike along the south of the lake to De Haukes. At 29.1 km, turn left rather than follow the LF10a sign.

At 31.6 km, the route turns to the right. If you are leaving the route here to head across the Afsluitdijk to Friesland, turn right to Hippolytushoef on Koningin Julianalaan. Cycle for 600 m through a forest; a bike tunnel takes you under the N99. In 100 m, turn left on Koogerweg. After another 100 m, turn left onto Koningstraat. After another 100 m, turn right onto Nieuwstraat. Another 200 m will take you to the Kerkplein (Church Square), where LF10a signs lead you out of town toward Den Oever, which is 7 km east. Follow the LF10a route to Den Oever through the charming towns of Stroe and Oosterland.

Den Oever is tiny. The VVV is at Oostkade 3 (Tel. 0227 512 972, www. kopvannoordholland.nl). There are two hotels, a B&B, a campground, some restaurants, and a supermarket.

From 31.6 km, the route continues through rural landscape studded with tulip fields. Cross the A7 and ride along the edge of the forest until 37.6 km, where you turn southeast along the Hoge Kwelvaart canal for 6 km. Look for bulb fields to your left.

At 47.2 km, turn right onto Zuiderdijkweg, the dike along the IJsselmeer. The wind whips across the level Wieringermeer Polder, where 49,000 acres were reclaimed in the late 1920s. The IJsselmeer remains hidden from view by the dike until after Medemblik. You'll pass rows of modern windmills on your right.

At 54.1 km, the large building on the right as you enter Medemblik is Gemaal Lely, an important pumping station for the polder. Medemblik is one of the oldest towns in the Netherlands, its main focus being the yacht harbor. A few sights of note are: the Bakery Museum (near the VVV), Nieuwstraat 8 (www. deoudebakkerij.nl, closed Mondays), the Steam Engine Museum, Oosterdijk 4 (www.stoommachinemuseum.nl, closed Mondays), the castle, Kasteel Radboud, Oudevaartsgat 8 (Tel. 0227 541 960, open daily, May 1 to September 15), and the Stadhuis (55.1 km). The tiny VVV, Kaasmarkt 1 (Tel. 0227 542 852, www. vvvmedemblik.nl), has been relegated to the back of the post office. Medemblik has two hotels, a B&B, several restaurants, and a bike shop, Leo Smit, at Almereweg 41A (Tel. 0227 541 200).

Leaving Medemblik, turn left (55.7 km) following the harbor around to the left; then go up a narrow street onto the dike (the castle will be on your left). This dike, one of the most scenic portions of the route, is higher than the houses for much of the way. You will have fabulous IJsselmeer views to the left, and bird's eye views of houses, farms, and villages to the right, most of the way to Enkhuizen.

Cue Sheet

0.0	Start	Den Helder ferry terminal go N on bike path, sign "Centrum"
0.8	L	sign "Leeuwarden and Alkmaar," Duinroute, Westerstraat
1.5	L	sign "Leeuwarden and Alkmaar," Binnenhaven/N250
7.2	CS	sign "Breezand, Leeuwarden, and Alkmaar," under N99

Crossing the Afsluitdijk

This 30 kilometer long dike was built in 1932 to close off the IJsselmeer from the sea. At the beginning of the dike is a statue to Lely, the engineer who designed it. At 6 km from Den Oever, there is a monument to the completion of the dike. The tower, which affords a panorama over the IJsselmeer and the Waddenzee, has the inscription "A living nation builds for its future."

If you are cycling the Afsluitdijk, be prepared to do the full 30 km. With the wind at your back, it's an easy ride. Facing a stiff wind, it can be a long trip. Because prevailing winds are from the southwest, your best chance of the wind at your back is if you ride from west to east. (Note: To connect to Friesland's Elfstedenroute, Day 3, cycle 7 km south from the Afsluitdijk to Makkum.)

7.3	R !	sign "Breezand," Touwslagersweg
8.0	U	follow bike path along N99 (over Noordhollandskanaal), Duinroute
8.9	R	Duinroute, Schorweg
9.5	L	Duinroute, J.C. Leeuwweg
10.2	R	Burg. Lovinkstraat
10.9	CS	over railway tracks, T-Breezand
11.9	L	cross canal on white footbridge (30 m) R
13.2	L	Molenvaart
13.3	R	over bridge to other side, Molenvaart
16.5	CS	T-Anna Paulowna

Map 7.4. Tour of North Holland, Day 4.

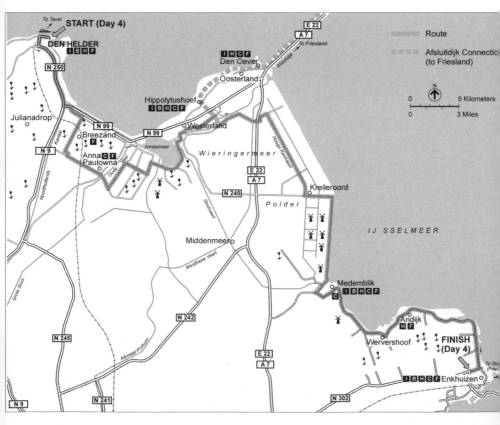

16.5	SS L	Poldertuin
16.7	CS	cross Hoge Oude Veer/Kerkweg
17.9	L	Veerweg
20.3	R	LF10a Kruisweg
22.4	L	LF10a Lotweg
23.5	R	LF10a Oosthoekweg
28.1	CS	over locks
28.6	R	LF10a De Haukes
29.1	L !	unmarked, do not follow LF10a
29.2	R	Hoelmerkruisweg
30.3	R	LF10a Westerklief
31.6	R	Zuiderkoogweg
31.6	ST L	Hippolytushoef/Afsluitdijk (option to Friesland)
32.6	L	after footbridge, Wieringerrandweg
34.7	VR	Hippolytushoef
36.4	L	Friesweg
36.5	R	over A7
36.6	L	Sluitgatweg
37.6	R	Oosterkwelweg
43.1	VR	over bridge
43.2	L	Kreileroord (other side of canal)
45.1	L	Oosterterpweg, T-Kreileroord
47.2	R	Zuiderdijkweg (dike along IJsselmeer)
54.1	SS R	Gemaal Lely
54.2	VR	follow road
54.6	L	Medemblikkerweg
54.7	L	sign "Centrum and Enkhuizen," Oude Haven
55.1	R	Nieuwstraat (at the Stadhuis)
55.5	CS	VVV Kaasmarkt, T-Medenblik
55.6	CS	over bridge

55.7	L !	Pekelharinghaven/Oudevaartsgat
55.7	SS L	Kasteel Radboud
56.1	R	(up onto) Oosterdijk
56.2	R	Oosterdijk
56.9	R	(50 m) L, sign "Enkhuizen and Wavershoof"
57.7	R	along IJsselmeer
57.8	SS R	Stoommachine Museum (Steam Engine Musuem)
60.0	CS	Onderdijk
61.0	L	dir. "Enkhuizen & Andijk"
62.4	L	cross road and onto dike
64.8	R	continue on dike
65.0	R	onto bike path on adjacent dike
68.0	CS	T-Andijk
76.2	R	Immerhornweg
76.7	R	to the station and VVV, Donkerlaantje
76.8	L	to the station and VVV, Prins Bernhardlaan (at edge of park)
77.0	R	(10 m) L over footbridge, Sybrandsplein
77.1	L	(10 m) R to the station and VVV, Van Bleiswijkstraat
77.7	R	Stationsweg
77.9	End	VVV Enkhuizen (on L) and the Enkhuizen Railway Station (on R)

Enkhuizen

Enkhuizen is the gem of the former Zuiderzee. This delightful port town oozes charm and has some interesting sights, such as the Dromedarius Tower with its carillon and view from the top, the Stadhuis, the old gevangenis (jail), and the main attraction of the town, The Zuiderzee Museum.

The Zuiderzee Museum, Wierdijk 12-22 (Tel. 0228 351 111, www.zuiderzeemuseum.nl), is actually two museums, the Binnenmuseum (Indoor Musuem) and the Buitenmuseum (Outdoor Museum). The Buitenmuseum (open daily, April through October) has actual houses, workshops, and other buildings from the Zuiderzee vicinity. (The Zuiderzee became the freshwater IJsselmeer in 1932, when that area of water was cut off from the sea by the Afsluitdijk.) The

Binnenmuseum (open daily, year-round) has maritime exhibits and memorabilia housed in the 300-year-old Dutch East India Company warehouse.

Information:	VVV Enkhuizen, Tussen Twee Havens 1 (Tel. 0228 313 164, www.vvv-enkhuizen.nl), is across the road from the railway station.
	If you are taking the boat to Stavoren to join the Elfstedenroute in Friesland, Rederij V & O (www.veerboot.info) runs two or three boats daily, depending on the season. One-way adult fare is €7.80 and bikes are €4. Tickets can be purchased at the VVV.
Bicycle Shops:	Dekker Tweewielers is at Nieuwstraat 2 (Tel. 0228 312 961); a second location is at Westerstraat 222 (Tel. 0228 312 490).
Where to Stay:	Enkhuizen has several hotels and B&Bs, all conveniently listed on the VVV door.
	The prize of Enkhuizen hotels is Hotel Recuerdos, Westerstraat 217A (Tel. 0228 562 469, www.recuerdos.nl). The lovely old house is small, so book ahead; singles are €55 and doubles are €80 for the first night, but are discounted for multiple nights. Het Wapen van Enkhuizen, Breedstraat 59 (Tel. 0228 313 434, www.hollandhotels.nl/hetwapenvanenkhuizen), has singles from €47 and doubles from €61. On a quiet backstreet, the Apartment-Hotel Driebanen, Driebanen 59 (Tel. 0228 316 381, www.hoteldriebanen.com), has singles from €57 and doubles from €81, plus €1.40 per bike.
	Camping Enkhuizer Zand, Kooizandweg 4 (Tel. 0228 317 289), near the Zuiderzee Museum, is open April through September.
Where to Eat:	At the VVV, pick up the free booklet *Culinair Enkhuizen* (www.culinairenkhuizen.nl) for a listing of two dozen restaurants. Restaurant De Boei, Havenweg 5, serves excellent fish, an Enkhuizen specialty. For upscale dining, try De Admiraal, next door at Havenweg 4.

Day 5: Enkhuizen to Edam (44.7 km)

Wind through the streets of Enkhuizen and leave through the Koepoort, built in 1649. Cycle through Bovenkarspel, the next town. At 3.9 km, you come to a tiny harbor, Broekerhaven, where you have to walk your bike around to the right over the locks. The route then goes onto the dike, with views of the Markermeer, traditional farmhouses, apple and pear orchards, and tulip fields. LF15b signs will keep you on track; always keep the water to your left. Oosterleek (11.6 km)is a charming typically Dutch village that makes for a nice diversion

If you're wondering about the cacophony as you approach 17.0 km, look down at the Vogel Broedplaats, a nesting area for hundreds of birds. Pass through Schellinkhout, where there is a waterfront park ideal for picnics. 800 m further is the thatched Schellinkhout windmill, contrsting with the modern windmills behind.

Enter Hoorn past the Oosterpoort (23.6 km)—the town's eastern gate built in 1578. Formerly a Zuiderzee seaport, Hoorn is now a port on the freshwater Markermeer. Many old buildings and mansions reflect the rich life of merchants and traders of bygone days. The Rode Steen, the picturesque central square (24.3 km), is surrounded by restaurants and shops. The 1609 Waag and the West Fries Museum (www.wfm.nl, open daily) are also on the Rode Steen. In the square's center is a statue of Jan Pieterszoon Coen, founder of the Dutch East India Company.

VVV Hoorn (24.9 km) is on Veemarkt 4, (Tel. 072 511 4284, www.vvvhoorn.nl). There are plenty of lodging and restaurant possibilities.

At 27.0 km, the road becomes busy, but at 29.0 km, you will ride alongside the dike again. Climb the steps at 30.6 km to the memorial of the storm of November 5, 1675, when water broke the banks of the Westerdijk and flooded the area.

Cue Sheet

0.0	Start	Enkhuizen Railway Station (cross road) go W
10 m	R	LF15b Parklaan/Admiraliteitsweg
0.5	R	LF15b Korte Tuinstraat
0.6	L	LF15b St. Jacobstraat (over footbridge)
0.7	R	LF15b Burgwal
0.9	L	Westerstraat
1.0	SS	Koepoort (old city gate)
2.7	L	LF15b Broekerhavenweg, T-Bovenkarspel
3.9	R !	LF15b Peperstraat (at Broekerhaven)
4.0	L	Zuiderdijk (under N506)
4.2	L	onto bike path along N506
4.6	L	onto dike
4.9	VL	bike path on dike
11.6	ST R	RT = 1 km Oosterleek

17.0	SS R	Vogel Broedplaats
20.2	SS R	Molen Schellinkhout
23.5	L	LF15b Kleine Oost/Grote Oost
23.6	SS R	Oosterpoort
24.3	R	Rode Steen/Kerkstraat, T-Hoorn

Map 7.5. Tour of North Holland, Day 5.

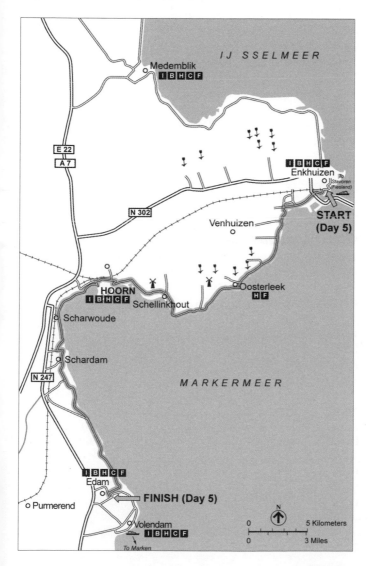

24.5	L	Gouw
24.6	L	Gedempte Turfhaven
24.9	CS	Breed
25.2	R	Westerdijk
27.0	L !	busy road, sign "Scharwoude"
30.6	SS L	steps/memorial
31.6	L	Schardam
32.0	CS	T-Schardam
35.6	SS L	Gemaal Warder steps/view
43.1	CS	Camping Strandbad
44.0	CS	Voorhaven
44.4	L	over footbridge (15 m), R Voorhaven
44.7	End	Damplein, VVV Edam (for information on Edam, see p. 71)

Day 6: Edam to Amsterdam (31.4 km)

From Edam to Volendam, ride along the dike. At Zuidpolder (1.6 km), it's tempting to ride atop the dike, but this path is for pedestrians (although local cyclists often ride it). From Volendam, follow the dike to Monnickendam. You have the opportunity to visit two cheese farms: Jacobs Hoeve (10.8 km) and Irene Hoeve (11.3 km).

Monnickendam's focal point is the picturesque harbor, where you'll find De Waag, the old weigh house built around 1600, which is now a restaurant. The 16th-century Speeltoren, the gracious bell tower in the center, still chimes on the quarter hour. Attractive gabled houses line the town's narrow streets.

Head south, continuing along the dike. At 15.1 km, leave the dike, turning inland to Zuiderwoude (16.5 km). From here to Broek in Waterland, cycle beside a lake and through pastoral landscape.

On the north side of the N247 (19.4 km), the route loops through Broek in Waterland and directs you to the Dutch Reformed Church, the pride of the village. Originally built in 1573 but burned by the Spanish, the church was rebuilt in 1628. Do take the time to visit it (open May through September, closed Sundays).

Continue by riding along the canals and tiny streets beyond the church. The canals of Broek in Waterland were the setting for the 1865 story *Hans Brinker, or The Silver Skates*.

The route out of Broek in Waterland follows the Broekermerdijk. At 24.1 km, go over the freeway and cross the Noordhollandskanaal by ferry at 24.7 km (operates daily, 7 a.m. to 7 p.m., 27 cents). Cycle along the Noordhollandskanaal back to the IJ ferry, and cross the IJ to Amsterdam.

Cue Sheet

0.0	Start	VVV Edam go E on Voorhaven
0.6	R	Oosterkade
0.7	L	sign "Volendam," Keetzijde
1.6	CS !	Zuidpolder (on road)
3.1	VL	Noordeinde (along dike)
4.7	CS	harbor/Marken Express
5.0	CS	Zuideinde
5.6	VL	sign "Monnickendam"
6.1	L	sign "Monnickendam"
10.8	SS R	Jacobs Hoeve

7.6. Tour of North Holland, Day 6.

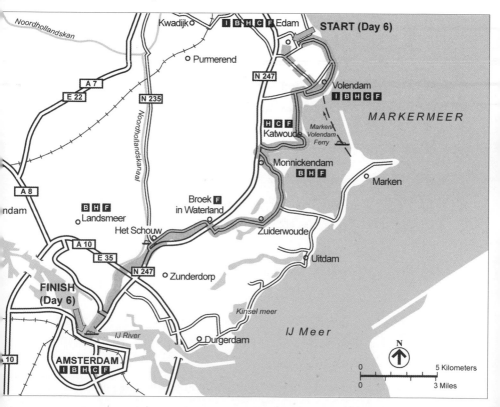

11.3	SS R	Irene Hoeve
11.3	L	N247, sign "Monnickendam"
11.4	CS	N247/bridge/Noordeinde
12.4	VL	Middendam/Haven, T-Monnickendam
12.5	CS	Haven/Zuideinde
12.8	RA L	N518, sign "Zuiderwoude," Waterlandse Zeedijk
14.2	CS	cross N518, bike path on other side
15.1	R !	sign "Broek in Waterland and Zuiderwoude"
16.5	R	sign "Broek in Waterland," T-Zuiderwoude
18.6	VR	Molengouw
19.0	VR	sign "Monnickendam," Zuideinde
19.1	CS	cross white footbridge
19.2	R	bike tunnel under N247
19.4	R	Havenrak (lake on L), T-Broek in Waterland
19.7	L	sign "Dorpshuis"
19.7	SS R	Dutch Reformed church
19.8	R	(after church) sign "Broeker Huis" (a school)
20.0	L	over bridge, immediate L to Roomeinde
20.2	L	past Dutch Reformed church
20.3	R	Havenrak (lake on R)
20.6	R	along N247, sign "Het Schouw and Amsterdam"
20.8	R	sign "Het Schouw and Amsterdam," Broekermerdijk
24.1	L	overpass N247 to N235
24.7	-	ferry on L
24.7	L	(other side) Kanaaldijk (along Noordhollandskanaal)
28.7	R	(50 m) L LF7a, sign "Centrum"
31.0	L	LF7a, sign "Station," Buiksloterweg
31.3	-	IJ ferry
31.3	L	De Ruijterkade
31.4	End	rear of the Centraal Station in Amsterdam

8.

Friesland

THE PROVINCE of Friesland is typified by its verdant green pastures dotted with characteristic black and white Friesian cows. Battling years of invasion by the sea, the resourceful Friesians took to building their villages, especially the churches, on *terpen* (man-made mounds to protect against floods). The Friesians are extremely proud of their province, and have their own language. Notice that town and road signs are both in Dutch and in Friesian (see language section, page 34). Friesians also have a reputation for being some of the most skillful skaters in the land.

Elfstedenroute (Tour of 11 Cities)

Total Distance:	252.1 km
Duration:	5 days
Highlights:	Friesian landscape, IJsselmeer coastline, Leeuwarden, Sneek, Sloten, Hindeloopen, Schaatsmuseum, Bolsward, Harlingen, Dokkum, Dokkumer Ee
Terrain:	Level
When to Go:	Mid-April to October.
Maps:	Michelin 531 Noord-Nederland/Pays-Bas Nord, ANWB/VVV *Toeristenkaart Friesland*, ANWB/VVV Elfstedenroute booklet with maps (Dutch only)

Start/Finish: Leeuwarden/ Leeuwarden

Access: Railways stations at: Leeuwarden, Sneek, Workum, Bolsward, Harlingen, Frankeker, Stavoren (by ferry from Enkhuizen or by rail), Makkum (from Afsluitdijk, "Tour of North Holland Ride")

Connections: "tour of North Holland" via the Afsluitdijk from Makkum, or ferry to Enkhuizen from Stavoren, "Megaliths, Memorial, and Mini-Venice" by rail to Groningen from Leeuwarden

The Elfstedenroute is a signed ANWB cycling route, allowing cyclists to experience the 11 towns of the famous winter event, the *Elfstedentocht*. It follows the signed route except at the start and end of each day, when it diverts to begin and end at the VVV. The circuit route begins and ends in Leeuwarden, but may be picked up at any point en route. Some of the longer stages can be shortened; alternate overnight towns have been suggested.

Leeuwarden

Leeuwarden, the capital of Friesland, is a much underrated and undervisited city. It has a most agreeable center with historic areas, canals, lovely parks, and lots of quiet, architecturally interesting streets.

The two most well-known museums in Leeuwarden are the magnificent Museum Het Princessehof at Grote Kerkstraat 11 (www.princessehof.nl, open daily) and the Fries Museum at Turfmarkt 11 (www.friesmuseum.nl, closed Mondays). Museum Het Princessehof has one of the most comprehensive collections of ceramics in the world. The Fries Museum is devoted to the history of Friesland, with arts, crafts, costumes, and archaeological finds. The top floor, the Verzetsmuseum (Resistance Museum), outlines the activities of the Friesian resistance during World War II and the plight of Friesian Jews during the Holocaust.

The *Elfstedentocht:* A Winter Wonder

This 200-kilometer skating race, begun in 1909, connects 11 towns in Friesland. Weather conditions must be perfect: the race can commence only when the entire route on canals has ice at least 15 cm (6 in) thick. The last race was held in 1997, and before that, in 1986. When it does happen, the *Elfstedentocht* committee organizes the event in record time. The Dutch declare a day off, and the whole country watches the event, in person or on television. 16,000 skaters take part in the race. The winning time in 1997 was 6 hours, 49 minutes.

The *Elfstedentocht* is now more than a skating race. In the spring there is an 11-cities bicycle race, which attracts over 15,000 participants and is 230 kilometers long. The 11 towns are Leeuwarden, Sneek, IJlst, Sloten, Stavoren, Hindeloopen, Workum, Bolsward, Harlingen, Franeker, and Dokkum.

One of Leeuwarden's most famous citizens was Mata Hari, the World War I spy and exotic dancer. Her statue is on Korfmakersstraat where it meets Over de Kelders, and her house, now the Friesian Literature Museum on Grote Kerkstraat 212 (closed weekends) contains Mata Hari memorablia.

At the far end of Grote Kerkstraat is the Grote Kerk, or Jacob's Church. Also of interest is the huge, incomplete Gothic tower, Oldehove (closed Mondays). Near Oldehove, in the center of a traffic circle, is *Us Mem* (Our Mother), a statue of a cow representing Friesian prosperity.

Information:	VVV Leeuwarden is at Sophialaan 4 (Tel. 0900 202 4060, www.vvvleeuwarden.nl). The ANWB Office, Zaailand 112 (Tel. 058 213 3955), is in the same building as the library, which has internet access. There is also internet access at OXO (see "Where to Eat").
Bicycle Shops:	Fietspoint Leeuwarden Station, Stationsweg 3 (Tel. 058 213 9800), has rentals. Halfords is at Wirdumerdijk 45 (Tel. 058 213 2401).
Where to Stay:	Centrally located, with a very bike-friendly owner, Hotel 't Anker, Eewal 69-75 (Tel. 058 212 5216, www.hotelhetanker.nl), has singles for €26 and doubles for €47, with showers and toilets down the hall. With private facilities, singles are €55 and doubles are €65. The pricey Bilderburg Oranje Hotel, Stationsweg 4 (Tel. 058 212 6241, wwwbilderberg.nl), across from the station, has singles from €105, doubles from €135, and breakfast is €15 extra. There are several hotels on the outskirts of Leeuwarden.
	The VVV can book one of the half dozen B&Bs in town.
	Camping Kleine Wielen, De Groene Ster 14 (0511 43 1660), open April to end September, is 6 km east by a lake near the N355.
Where to Eat:	On Nieuwestad, Humphreys has interesting three-course menus for €18.95. Two good bets on Eewal are Spinoza Eetcafé at #50 (Tel. 058 212 9393, www.eetcafespinoza.nl), which has meat, fish, and vegetarian meals, and Spijslokal next door (Tel. 058 216 2214), which serves European cuisine. For pancakes on a boat, try 't Pannekoekschip, across from the VVV at Willemskade 63. OXO, Stationsweg 6 (Tel. 058 212 9013, closed Sundays), serves up meals alongside three computer terminals.

Day 1: Leeuwarden to Sneek (46.1 km)

Day 1 takes you to three of the 11 cities: Leeuwarden, IJlst, and Sneek. The first 4 kilometers are through the unexciting outskirts of Leeuwarden. You will see your first Elfstedenroute (ELF) sign at 0.4 km.

Shortly after Jellum, the circular side trip (8.2 km) takes you to Beers, a tiny hamlet huddled around the old village *poort* (gateway) built in the early 16th century. There is also a small church on a *terp*.

At 10.7 km, turn right and follow the bike path (using ELF route signs) onto Swettepaad. This takes you along an idyllic 4 km stretch along the small canal, the Sneekertrekvaart. At 17.2 km, just before going through the bike tunnel, you will see the first of many modern windmills that characterize the province.

At the turn to Easterwierrum (20.7 km), there is no ELF sign. At 24.7 km, Boazum is a 1000-year old village built on a *terp*. Turn right and ride 100 m to the 12th-century St.-Maartenskerk. Should you wish to visit the church, ring the bell, and within a few minutes a docent will arrive to let you in.

At 29.1 km, the route diverges, so do not follow the ELF sign. Instead, turn right to IJsbrechtum and follow Monumentenwei. The monument you see at 34.4 km is a war memorial.

The sign at 39.4 km welcomes you to IJlst. You will cross the first bridge at 40.7 km; stay on the left side of the canal. At 41.0 km, watch carefully for the turn onto Sudergoweg.

At 41.5 km, you turn onto Sneekerpad, a lovely bike path that cuts through farms and fields to Sneek, passing Molen De Rat (41.6 km), a thatched windmill (www.zwfriesland.nl/derat, open Fridays and Saturdays, May through September).

Carefully follow the signs through the outskirts of Sneek. At 44.8 km, you will see ELF signs in two directions. Turn left onto Lemmerweg toward Sneek. The other sign is for the *Sneekermeerronde* (see below). En route to the VVV and before turning left into the center, you pass the beautiful Waterpoort.

Cue Sheet

Note: The "ELF" abbreviation indicates an Elfstedenroute sign at a turn or significant juncture.

0.0	Start	Leeuwarden Railway Station go N on Sophialaan sign "Centrum"
0.1	RA L	Langemarktstraat
0.4	L	ELF Harlingertrekweg
1.4	L	ELF Heliconweg (over bridge)
1.5	R	ELF Snekertrekweg
1.8	VR	ELF Zwettestraat

2.3	R	ELF Jameswattstraat
2.7	R	ELF Newtonlaan
3.8	R	N31

Map 8.1. Friesland, Elfstedenroute, Day 1.

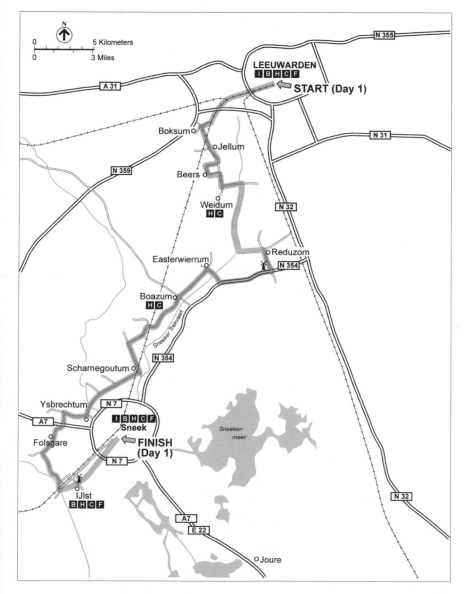

5.0	R	ELF cross railway tracks
5.7	L	Hegedyk, sign "Jellum," #843, T-Baksum
7.7	CS	T-Jellum
8.2	ST R	RT = 2.0 km T-Beers
9.4	L	ELF Delemawai T-Weidum
10.7	R	ELF turn onto Swettepaad
14.2	L	ELF farm road
15.7	R	ELF Overijsselse-Straatweg
17.2	R	ELF bike tunnel to N354
17.4	R	ELF N354
20.7	R	sign "Easterwierrum," De Dille #450
21.7	L	ELF Doarpsstrjitte, T-Easterwierrum
24.7	SS R	church, T-Boazum
25.6	VR	cross railway tracks
25.7	L	ELF Suderdyk #135
27.3	L	ELF Legedyk, sign "Scharnegoutum," #208
29.1	R !	at church, sign "IJsbrechtum," St. Maartensdyk
33.1	R	ELF (rejoin), sign "Folsgare," Epemawei, T-IJsbrechtum
34.4	L	ELF Monumentenwei
35.4	L	ELF Monumentenwei, T-Folsgare
37.0	L	ELF, sign "IJlst," Nessenwei
38.1	CS	T-Oosthem
39.1	R	ELF, sign "Heeg," Nijezil
39.4	L	ELF Yloostinslaan
40.1	R	ELF Stadslaan
40.7	L !	over first bridge only, T-IJlst
41.0	L !	ELF Sudergoweg
41.3	L	ELF Dassenboarch
41.5	R	ELF Sneekerpad
41.6	SS L	Molen De Rat (windmill)

43.3	R	ELF De Wieken
43.4	L	ELF Bovenas
43.5	R	ELF De Wieken (40 m), L ELF Molenkritte
43.9	L	ELF bike tunnel under N7
44.2	R	bike path/N7
44.3	L	ELF N7
44.8	L !	ELF, sign "Sneek," Lemmerweg
45.4	RA CS	Lemmerweg
45.8	L	Oude Koemarkt (right after the Waterpoort)
46.0	VR	Grote Kerkstraat (past the church)
46.1	R	Marktstraat
46.1	End	(15 m) VVV Sneek/ANWB

Sneek

Sneek (pronouned *snake*) is the water sport capital of Friesland. There are plenty of sailing and windsurfing schools in the area (ask the VVV). If you want to cycle around the Sneekermeer, there is a separate signed route *Elfstedenroute: Snee-kermeerronde* (44.0 km).

There are a few sights of note in Sneek, three of which you pass on your way to the VVV. The first, the striking 1613 twin-turreted Waterpoort, was the town's southern gateway. Next, on Grote Kerkstraat, is the Martinikerk, built in 1498 (open mid-June to mid-Sept, 2:30 p.m. to 5 p.m., evenings in July and August; closed Sundays). Across from the VVV, at Markstraat 15, is the ornate rococo Stadhuis (open weekdays from 2 p.m. to 4 p.m.). Also visit the Fries Scheepvaart Museum, Kleinzand 14 (open daily), with a collection of all things nautical.

Sneek is crowded during Sneekweek, an annual regatta in early August. Another busy week is in late July, when *skûtsjes* (old trading boats with a wide, flat-bottomed hull) take to the Friesian lakes.

| Information: | The VVV/ANWB share a location at Marktstraat 18 (Tel. 0515 414 096, www.vvvsneek.nl). Pick up a free brochure that includes a map and lodging, restaurant, and sightseeing information. Check e-mail at the VVV, where there is one terminal, or the library at Wijde Noorderhorne. |
| Bicycle Shop: | The most central bike shop, with rentals, is Twa Tsjillen, across from the library at Wijde Noorderhorne 8 (Tel. 0515 413 878). |

Where to Stay: Across from the VVV, Hotel-Restaurant De Wijnberg, Marktstraat 23 (Tel. 0515 412 421, www.hoteldewijnberg.nl), has singles from €54 and doubles from €78. Hotel-Restaurant Hanenburg, Wijde Noorderhorne 2 (Tel. 0515 412 570, www.hotelhanenburg.nl), offers singles for €50 and doubles for €65.

The free VVV brochure lists several B&Bs in Sneek.

The Stayokay hostel is about 2 km southeast of Sneek en route to the Sneekermeer, at Oude Oppenhuizerweg 20 (Tel. 0515 412 132, www.stayokay.com/sneek). There are several campgrounds in the area: De Potten at Offingwier (near the Sneekermeer), Hart van Friesland at Uitwellingerga, and De Domp, the closest to Sneek, at Domp 4 (Tel. 0515 412 559, April to late October).

Where to Eat: Both hotels listed have restaurants. Offering a traditional Fries menu is Onder de Linden at Marktstraat 30 (Tel. 0515 412 654). Several restaurants can be found along Wijde Noorderhorne and Grootzand and around Leeuwenburg, including the restaurant Van der Wal (Tel. 0515 413 863), at Leeuwenburg 11, with *dagschotels* (day menus) from €7.95.

Day 2: Sneek to Workum (75.6 km)

This is a long day, but the cycling is easy, with panoramic coastal vistas and typical Friesian pastoral scenes. You'll ride through cool forests, and visit four more Elfsteden towns: Sloten, Stavoren, Hindeloopen, and Workum. Should you wish to break this into two days, Sloten, Balk, Oudemirdum and Stavoren are overnight options.

Leaving Sneek, follow the busy N7, then a service road along the A7 for the first 4 kilometers. At 4.3 km, enter the village of Oppenhuizen, which melds into the adjacent village Uitwellingerga. At 6.6 km, the Elfstedenroute, sign is small, and the turn onto the bike path is easy to miss.

At 8.7 km, an overpass takes you over the A7; continue to the Langweer ferry. The small ferry (50 cents) runs daily, 7 a.m. to 9 p.m., but on Thursdays does not operate until noon. Soon after Langweer, you cycle beside a forested road for almost 3 kilometers, and through pastoral land to St.-Nicolaasga, dominated by its neo-Gothic church.

From St.-Nicolaasga, you will see the huge telecommunications tower in the distance, beckoning you to the intersection where you cross over the Prinses Margriet Kanaal. In tiny Tjerkgaast, note the church built on a *terp*.

With only 650 inhabitants, Sloten is the smallest of the 11 cities. There is a windmill located by the Lemsterpoort, and you can still walk on part of the old city wall. The VVV, Koestraat 44 (www.friesekust.nl), is open a couple of days a week and daily in July and August. There is one pension, Pension 't Brechje, Voorsteek 110 (Tel. 0514 531 2980), and several campgrounds. There are cafés and restaurants along Sloten's tree-lined canal.

Leaving Sloten, the route follows the Slotermeer, then turns toward Balk, a small town with a beautiful Stadhuis (at the corner, just before the turn at 33.7 km). From Balk, follow the canal. At 37.9 km, turn left onto a gorgeous tree-lined bike path for the 3 km to Oudemirdum.

Oudemirdum has a few hotels, some B&Bs, a few shops and restaurants, and at least five campgrounds within 2 km. It is in a woodsy setting, and is a popular recreation center. The VVV is at Brink 4 (Tel. 0514 571 414, www.friesekust.nl).

Leave Oudemirdum on a forested road that leads to a rather unique tribute. On your left (41.9 km) is a large empty frame with Friesian flag motif and a small, sign, "Friesian Farm." As you stand in front of it, you realize it is framing an actual farm in the background. On the left is a poem in Dutch, and on the right is the same poem in Friesian.

From here, go along a road with quintessential Friesian farmland on the right and magnificent IJsselmeer views on the left the entire way to Stavoren. Mirnser Klif (45.2 km), 200 m to the left, is a beach with a grassy picnic area and café. To the right is Het Rijsterbos, a forest with walking paths. At 48.0 km, stop and climb the steps at Vogelhut de Mok for a fabulous view over this protected natural area. High above, on Roode Klif (52.5 km), enjoy expansive views over the IJsselmeer to Stavoren from a cliff. The Realklif monument honors Friesians who defended their coast in 1345.

Cross the Johan Frisokanaal to enter Stavoren. The ferry to Enkhuizen leaves from Stavoren (see "Enkhuizen," page 95). The VVV is at the ferry terminal (Tel. 0514 681 616, www.friesekust.nl). The tiny hotel, De Vrouwe van Stavoren, Havenweg 1 (Tel. 0514 681 202, www.hotel-vrouwevanstavoren.nl), is ideally located on the harbor (singles from €42, doubles from €60). There is one B&B in town, plus a campground, Camping Sudemer, on the way in, on the right. The bicycle shop with rentals, P. Bakker, is at Smidstraat 14 (Tel. 0514 681 288).

From Stavoren, the route turns inland. At Molkwerum, where there are several campgrouds, you rejoin the coast. The dike obscures the IJsselmeer, but you can climb the steps for a view.

Hindeloopen, is a charming little town on the banks of the IJsselmeer, riddled with tiny canals and footbridges. The VVV is at Nieuwstad 26 (Tel. 0514 522 550, www.friesekust.nl), 100 m from the turn at 67.5 km. For lodging other than camping, head to Workum, where the options are far superior.

In days gone by, Hindeloopen was famous for its wooden painted furniture, examples of which can be seen in the Hidde Nijland Stichting Museum on Dijkweg 1 (Tel. 0514 521 420, open daily, March through October). Set aside time for the Schaats Museum (Skating Museum), Kleine Weide 1-3 (Tel. 0514 521 683, www.schaatsmuseum.nl, open daily), which has an amazing collection of memorabilia from the *Elfstedentocht*.

The ride to Workum is a great way to end the day. Begin on a bike path through lush pastures, sheep grazing all around; then cruise into Workum on a small road atop a dike.

Cue Sheet

0.0	Start	VVV Sneek go W (15 m) on Marktstraat
15 m	L	Grote Kerkstraat
0.1	VL	Oude Koemarkt
0.3	R	Lemmerweg
0.7	RA CS	go halfway through roundabout
1.2	L	ELF N7, sign "Joure"
1.7	R	bike path/N7
2.9	R	ELF A7, sign "Uitwellingerga"
4.3	L	ELF De Bou, T-Oppenhuizen
4.9	R	Noardein dir. "Uitwellingerga"
6.6	R !	ELF (small sign) bike path
8.6	L	ELF cross road
8.7	R	ELF Pontdijk (over A7)
10.9	CS	Langweer ferry
13.8	CS	T-Langweer
17.5	L	ELF N927 #5290
17.6	R	ELF cross N927, bike path
17.7	R	ELF #63634 bike path
18.9	R	unmarked
19.0	L	ELF Kerkstraat
19.5	VR	Gaastweg, T-St.-Nicolaasga
20.3	VL	unmarked road
21.0	L	ELF Noed
21.2	R	sign "Sloten"
22.5	VL	ELF upper bike path along N927
22.8	R	ELF cross the Prinses Margriet Kanaal

24.6	SS	church T-Tjerkgaast
27.0	L	ELF Van der Walplein
27.1	R	ELF Koestraat, T-Sloten
27.4	R	ELF Lyste Jerden
27.7	L	ELF Lyste Jerden
31.0	R	ELF Menno van Cohoornweg
31.9	VR	ELF Jachtlustweg
33.7	L	ELF Raadhuisstraat, T-Balk
35.8	R	R over canal, L along N359

8.2. Friesland, Elfstedenroute, Day 2.

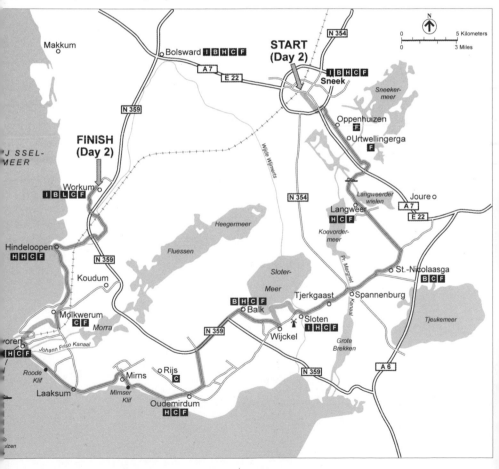

37.5	L	ELF over canal, R bike path
37.9	L	ELF Sminkewei
40.1	R	ELF Boegen, T-Oudemirdum
41.1	R	ELF Jan Schotanuswei, sign "Stavoren"
41.6	L	ELF Huningspaed
41.9	SS L	framed viewpoint
45.2	SS L/R	Mirnser Klif/Rijsterbos
47.2	L	ELF Wieldijk, sign "Stavoren"
48.0	SS L	Vogelhut De Mok
52.5	SS L	Reaklif (monument and view)
55.6	L	ELF Stadsfenne/Voorstraat
56.3	R	ELF Voorstraat
56.4	L	ELF Smidstraat, T-Stavoren
56.6	R	Stationsweg
57.6	L	Jurisdictie
57.8	R	Jurisdictie, sign "Hindeloopen"
58.1	CS	unmarked bike path
60.6	L	ELF De Wymerts #23944
61.2	L	ELF Hellingstrjitte, T-Molkwerum
61.8	R	ELF Sédyk
67.4	R	ELF Nieuwstad, T-Hindelopen
67.5	L	ELF Meenscharssteeg
67.6	L	unmarked
68.0	CS	ELF cross road, canal on left
68.7	L	ELF (10 m), R ELF, cross bridge, canal now on your right
69.8	R	ELF, sign "Workum"
70.3	L	ELF, sign "Workum," onto dike
74.6	VR	ELF Sylspaed/Sud/Noard
75.6	End	VVV Workum

Workum

Workum, a linear town, stretches for 2 km along the main street, Sud, turning into Noard at the Merk. The town's hub, the Merk, is where you'll find the 15th-century Stadhuis, the huge 16th-century Gothic St. Gertrudiskerk, the 17th-century Waag, and many other houses of architectural interest. The town was the home of Jopie Huisman, a junk collector and artist without formal training, whose most famous and brilliant works are paintings of old shoes, rags, worn clothing, and the like. A few doors down from the Merk is the Jopie Huisman Museum, devoted to his work (www.jopiehuismanmuseum.nl, open daily).

Information: VVV Workum is at Noard 5 (Tel. 0515 541 300, www.friesekust.nl). Head to the library, at the corner of Begine and Hearewei, to check e-mail (open Tuesdays, Wednesdays, and Fridays after 2 p.m.).

Bicycle Shop: Scheltma is at Sud 74 (Tel. 0515 541 678).

Where to Stay: In the center, Hotel De Gulden Leeuw, Merk 2 (Tel. 0515 542 341, hotel-de-guldenleeuw@planet.nl) has singles for €35 and doubles for €60. At Merk 3 is the unusual De Herberg van Oom Lammert en Tante Klaasje (Tel. 0515 541 370, www.oomlammertentanteklaasje.nl). Designed to represent bygone days, the rooms have beds built into the wall (*bedstee*). Singles are €40 and doubles are €70. There are four B&Bs in Workum.

On the IJsselmeer, the large Camping It Soal (Tel. 0515 541 443, www.itssoal.nl) is 3 km southwest of Workum and is open April through October. For mini-camping in Workum, go to Welgelegen, Lange Leane 11 (Tel. 0514 522 442, www.dewitte-welgelegen.nl).

Where to Eat: Most of the restaurants are around the Merk. Hotel De Gulden Leeuw (see above) has a good restaurant. Pizzeria Italia is at Merk 27 (Tel. 0515 540 999), and the upscale Bistro de Waegh is at Merk 18 (Tel. 0515 541 900). You can eat pancakes at De Wijmerts, at Noard 10 (0515 542 565), and Chinese food at Azie, Sud 98 (Tel. 0515 541 488).

Day 3: Workum to Harlingen (32.3 km)

Large, stately farmhouses, with elegant white swans on their roof posts are characteristic of Friesland. Fine examples can be seen as you cycle along the canal from Workum to Bolsward. At 9.9 km, a cluster of four farmhouses comprises the hamlet of Arkum, but blink, and you'll miss Arkum — even on a bike.

From Tjerkwerd, at ANWB mushroom #20135, cycle between two tiny canals surrounded by pastures to Bolsward. At 13.5 km, the route turns left. To go into Bolsward, turn right on Bargefenne Dijkstraat. Follow, signs to the Centrum, and in 400 m you will be rewarded with the sight of a most stunning Stadhuis. The Stadhuis, built in 1614, also houses the Oudeheidkamer (Antiquities Museum), with its silverware, costumes, and local artifacts. Also of interest is the Martinikerk, a large 15th-century Gothic church. To reach it, turn left at the Stadhuis onto Rijkstraat, which becomes Grote Dijlakker, and proceed 200 m.

VVV Bolsward, Marktplein 1 (Tel. 0515 572 727, www.bolsward.nl), is across from the Hotel De Wijnberg, Marktplein 5 (Tel. 0515 572 220), one of the two hotels in town. There are a couple of B&Bs, and the bike shop, Koopmans Twee-wielers, is at Grote Dijlakker 58 (Tel. 0515 572 717).

Leave Bolsward by heading west, crossing the N359, and following the bike path alongside the A7. At 16.3 km, turn right to Schettens and join farm roads to Witmarsum, skirting the town itself. At mushroom #25054 (50m from the turn at 19.6 km), a right turn leads to a monument to Menno Simonzoon (1496-1561). Born in Witmarsum, he became a priest and founded the Mennonite religion.

At 20.6 km, turn left for the side trip to Makkum. Continue straight on the main road, crossing the A7 about half way to Makkum. After 7.4 km, veer right into Makkum on D.S. van Trouwenlaan. In 400 m, go left at Kerkstraat, and left again after 100 m to the Markt. The VVV (www.friesekust.nl) is 100 m further.

Makkum is famous for ceramics. The Fries Aardewerkmuseum (Ceramics Museum, open daily) is located in the Waag, built in 1698, the lower floor of which also houses the VVV. The town has a couple of hotels, B&Bs, and several eateries.

Makkum is the closest point on this route to the Afsluitdijk, where it is possible to cross to North Holland (see boxed text "Afsluitdijk," page 91).

After your side trip to Makkum and rejoining the route at 20.6 km, pass through Arum on your way to Harlingen. Arum has two churches with unusual steeples, one at 23.9 km and the second at 24.3 km. The most interesting place in Arum is the Rock 'n Roll Museum (www.rockmuseum.nl).

Tiny Kimswerd, with only 640 inhabitants, is known as a "village of tradition", with houses dating from the last three centuries. Outside the church (27.1 km) is a statue of Greate Pier, a 15th-century freedom fighter.

Continue to the seaport of Harlingen. At 31.6 km, turn right. A short block brings you to the Zuiderhaven (South Harbor), one of two harbors in town. The other is Noorderhaven (North Harbor). Follow Zuiderhaven and turn right onto Grote Bredeplats (32.1 km), which becomes Voorstraat, and on to the VVV.

Cue Sheet

0.0	Start	VVV Workum
		go NE on Noard
0.5	R	ELF Dwarsnoard
0.8	L	Trekwei

Map 8.3. Elftstedenroute, Day 3

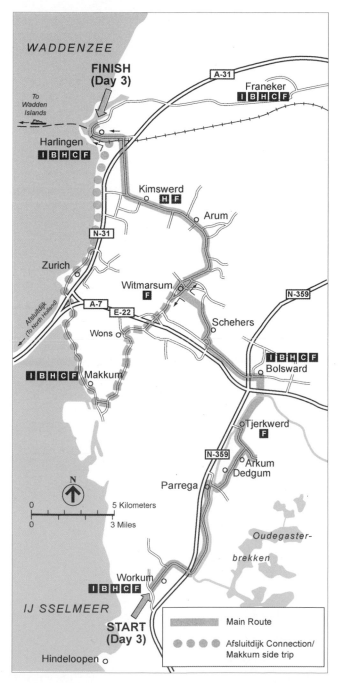

1.0	R	unmarked, sign "Bolsward"
1.4	L	onto bike path (1.6 km bike tunnel under N359)
1.8	L	ELF unmarked road
6.5	R	ELF Horstweg, T-Parrega
6.9	L	ELF Ysgumerweg
8.9	SS	T-Arkum
9.4	L	ELF Hemdijk, T-Tjerkwerd
10.8	L	ELF #20135 over canal (20 m), R onto bike path
13.0	CS	bike tunnel under A7
13.2	VR	unmarked
13.3	L	Oordje #20182
13.5	L	ELF Harlingerstraat/A7
13.5	ST R	RT = 800 m to T-Bolsward
16.3	R	ELF unmarked
16.4	L	ELF Van Osingaweg
16.9	R	ELF, sign "Witmarsum," Van Osingaweg, T-Schettens
19.6	L	ELF Easthimmerwei, sign "Harlingen"
19.6	ST R	(50 m) RT = 500 m Menno Simonzoon Monument
20.6	R	ELF Arumerweg, sign "Harlingen"
20.6	ST L	RT = 16.2 km, sign "Makkum"
23.9	SS	churches, T-Arum
24.0	SS L	Rock 'n Roll Museum
27.1	SS R	Greate Pier (Grote Pier)
28.6	SS	birdwatching area: Hegewiersterfjild
30.9	L	Stationsweg
31.3	R	over bridge, Rozengracht
31.6	R	Zuiderplein
31.7	L	Zuiderhaven
32.1	R	Grote Bredeplaats/Voorstraat
32.3	End	VVV Harlingen

Harlingen

Harlingen is a city for strolling, especially along the picturesque Noorderhaven. Voorstraat is the main shopping street, where you can find the elegant 18th-century Stadhuis and the Museum Het Hannemahuis, Voorstraat 56 (Tel. 0517 413 658, open April through September; closed Mondays; also closed on Sundays April through June), an 18th-century building with maritime exhibits.

Harlingen is also the jumping off point to the islands of Terschelling and Vlieland, with daily ferries to each island. These are two more of the Wadden islands (see "Texel," page 82). Vlieland is the more tranquil of the two; no cars are allowed, except for a few owned by residents. Either island is great for cycling, and both have hotels and campgrounds. Terschelling also has a youth hostel. There is a VVV on each island, plus bicycle shops that also have rentals.

Information:	VVV Harlingen is at Voorstraat 34 (Tel. 0517 417 222, www.vvv-harlingen.nl). The library at Voorstraat 52 has internet access.
Bicycle Shops:	Huizer is at Lanen 18 (Tel. 0517 412 201), and Kalksma is at Kleine Voorstraat 95 (Tel. 0517 412 208).
Where to Stay:	On pretty Noorderhaven, at #67, Hotel Anna Casparii (Tel. 0517 412 065, www.annacasparii.nl) has singles for €63 and doubles from €78. Hotel Het Heerenlogement, Franekereind 23 (Tel. 0517 415 846, www.heerenlogement.nl), has singles for €60 and doubles for €80. The VVV has a list of economically priced B&Bs and pensions.
	Camping De Zeehoeve, Westerzeedijk 45 (Tel. 0517 413 465, www.zeehoeve.nl), is 1 km south of town.
Where to Eat:	Both above-mentioned hotels have good restaurants. At Grote Bredeplats 35, Nooitgedagt (0517 434 211) is a trendy, cozy eatery. At Voorstraat 38, try De Gastronoom (Tel. 0517 412 172, www.de-gastronoom.nl). Go to De Byzantijn at Voorstraat 46 (Tel. 0517 413 066) for Greek food. Fish is a specialty in Harlingen, and De Tjotter, St. Jacobstraat 1 (0517 414 691, www.detjotter.nl), serves up tasty fish dishes in both their restaurant and casual fish bar.
	If you're looking for the epitome of a Dutch cheese shop, Homminga, at Voorstaat 21, has a fabulous array of cheeses. There is a lively market along Voorstraat on Saturday mornings.

Day 4: Harlingen to Dokkum (72.3 km)

This is a long day with few options for overnight lodging, other than in Franeker and a few B&Bs in villages en route. There are more options for campers. Allow time to stop at Franeker's planetarium and the *terp* at Hegebeintum.

The route initially follows the N390; the signage is poor out of Harlingen. The route turns toward the sea and onto a bike path (4.4 km) along a coastal dike. There is no Elfstedenroute sign where you turn right at 8.3 km; however, there is an LF10a sign.

Continue to Sexbierum and cycle through an area with several modern windmills before going under the A31 to Franeker. The Elfstedenroute to the center of Franeker is rather convoluted but is well-signed.

There are only two reasons to stop in Franeker. One is the splendid Stadhuis, and the second is the Planetarium. The 16th-century Stadhuis is on the Raadhuisplein. You can visit the council chambers on the main floor (closed weekends). Across the canal from the Stadhuis is the Planetarium (www.planetarium-friesland. nl, open daily May through September, closed Sundays and Mondays October through April). Now a museum, it was the home of Eise Eisinga, an 18th-century wool comber and self-educated astronomer. From 1774-1781, Eisinga created an ingenious and incredibly accurate planetarium on his living room ceiling.

The VVV is at Sint Martiniplantsoen 43 (Tel. 0900 540 0001, www. friesekust. nl). There are a couple of hotels and a campground in Franeker. The closest B&B is in Dongjum (19.6 km).

Leaving Franeker, continue straight on the bike path on the left side of the road (17.4 km). Soon, you arrive at Dongjum. At 19.8 km, there is a church and Commonwealth War Grave. The church is on a *terp*, typical of the area. En route you will pass more churches built on *terpen* in Boer, Ried, and Berlikum, the latter with an interesting dome (27.8 km).

St.-Annaparochie is a fairly ordinary town, but the church (32.9 km) is where Rembrandt married in 1634. A statue commemorates the event.

From here, you ride to Nij Altoenae alongside a tree-lined canal flanked with attractive old houses. At 35.0 km, turn right onto Oudebildtdijk. At Oude Bildtzijl (39.4 km), turn right and go along a tiny canal for 2 km. Continue along quiet farm roads to Marrum (50.0 km), where the now unused Marrum-West Nijkerk railway station is being restored. Ferwerd has a large 15th-century Gothic church (on a *terp*, of course), reachable by going left at Vrijtof (CS for 50 m at 51.9 km, then turn left through the archway).

The signs for VVV Ferwerd are confusing, as the VVV is 2.5 km out of town at Hegebeintum (54.4 km), the area's star attraction. Hegebeintum, the highest *terp* in the Netherlands (9 m above sea level), has a 12th-century church perched on top. The VVV/Visitor's Center (Tel. 0518 411 783, rekreaasje@planet.nl, closed Mondays), has displays of unearthed items (dating to 5 B.C) from *terp* excavations. Tours of the church are available (last tour is at 4 p.m.).

Continue to Holwerd, and then along the N356 and on to Dokkum, circling the city on the old ramparts.

Cue Sheet

0.0	Start	VVV Harlingen go W on Voorstraat
0.2	R	ELF Zuiderhaven
0.3	R	ELF Noorderhaven
0.6	L	ELF over canal to Biloltstraat
1.0	CS	bridge/Oude Ringmuur
1.1	L	ELF LF10a bike path along N390
4.2	R !	(unmarked) bike path toward sea
4.4	R	ELF LF10a along dike
8.3	R	LF10a
9.0	CS	ELF Liauckmaleane (gravel 400 m)
9.4	R !	(unmarked), sign "Sexbierum" and N393
9.7	L	ELF N393

8.4. Friesland Elfstedenroute, Days 4 and 5.

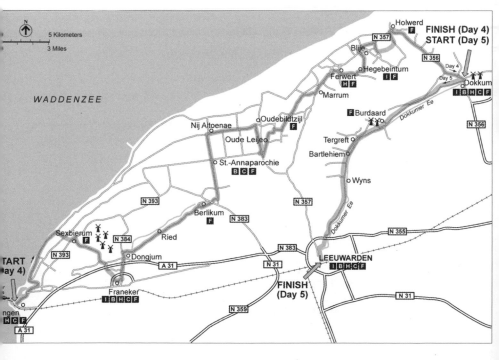

10.2	R	ELF Tsjerk Hoddesstrjitte dir. "Franeker"
10.4	CS	T-Sexbierum
12.7	VR	ELF bike path
14.2	R	ELF bike tunnel under A31
14.4	CS	ELF A31
15.2	R	CPM Rommestraat
15.3	R	ELF (10 m), L P.S. Gerbrandystraat
15.6	VL	ELF Rinze Werkhovenstraat
15.7	L	ELF Rients/Koppmansstraat/under N31
15.9	R	ELF Hottingastraat (along A31)
16.2	R	ELF (80 m), L ELF Burg. Juckemastraat
16.6	R	ELF along two canals
17.0	L	ELF Harlingerweg
17.1	L	sign "Centrum"
17.2	CS	ELF Voorstraat
17.2	ST R	RT = 800 m, T-Franeker, sign "sights"
17.4	CS !	ELF bike path on N384
18.0	RA CS	statue of stylized skaters (R in RA)
19.6	R	ELF Dorpsstraat, T-Dongjum
19.8	SS R	church on terp
27.8	ST L	RT = 200 m domed church, T-Berlikum
28.5	R	ELF Bitgumerdijk
28.9	L	ELF Hemmemawei
29.3	R	ELF bike path along road
32.5	CS	T-St.-Annaparochie
32.9	SS R	church and statue
32.9	CS	Stadhoudersweg, sign "Nij Altoenae"
35.0	R	ELF Oudebildtdijk, T-Nij Altoenae
39.4	R	ELF Leysterstreek, T-Oude Bildtzijl
41.5	L	ELF

41.6	L	ELF Oude Lejie
42.1	R	ELF Langedyk, T-Oude Leije
43.5	L	ELF unmarked road
45.7	R	ELF Roodschuursterlaan
46.0	L	ELF Hogeherenweg
48.0	L	(30 m) R Hogeherenweg
49.7	R	ELF
49.8	L	N357, T-Marrum
50.0	SS R	old station
51.3	R	ELF Marrumerweg
51.9	R	ELF Hegbeintumerdyk, T-Ferwerd
54.1	L	ELF Pypkedyk, sign "Hegbeintum"
54.4	SS	Hegbeintum, VVV Ferwerd
54.5	R	ELF Vogelzangsterweg
54.6	L	ELF Vogelzangsterweg
56.5	R	ELF LF10a Boatebuorren
57.2	L	ELF LF10a Hoofdstraat, T-Blije
57.3	R	ELF LF10a Farrewei
57.3	L	ELF LF10a Zwarteweg
58.0	R	ELF LF10a
58.1	L	ELF LF10a Horneweg
60.2	L	ELF LF10a Medwertwei
61.7	R	ELF N357
62.0	R	ELF Hegebuorren, T-Holwerd
62.2	L	ELF Waling/Dykstrastrjitte
62.3	R	ELF Stasjonwei, sign "Dokkum"
62.6	L	N356
70.0	R	ELF Voorstreek
70.2	VR	ELF beside Dokkumer Ee
70.5	L	De Helling (80 m), becomes Hellingpad

70.8	R	over bridge immediate R Westerbolwerk
71.9	L	ELF De Dam, sign "Binnenstad"
72.1	R	Grote Breedstraat
72.3	L/end	Boterstraat, VVV/ANWB Dokkum

Dokkum

Dokkum's old center is completely moated and easily circumnavigated by foot or bicycle along the *bolwerk* (ramparts). The big church in Dokkum, The St. Martinuskerk, is built on a mound erected to commemorate St. Boniface, an English missionary, and his 52 companions, all murdered here in 754. The Waag, built in 1752, Grote Breedstraat 1, is now a restaurant (De Waegh), and bears Dokkum's coat of arms. The museum, Het Admiraliteitshuis, is in the former Admiralty House at Diepswal 27, and has a collection of regional antiquities, items excavated from local burial mounds, and Friesian art (closed Sundays and Mondays, April through October).

Information:	The VVV/ANWB are housed together at Op de Frieze 13 (Tel. 0519 293 800, www.vvvdokkum.nl). Access the internet at the library, Brokmui 62, about 1 km east of the center.
Bike shops:	Haisma Tweewielers is at Woudweg 3 (Tel. 0519 292 467), and Halfords is at Grote Breedstraat 22 (Tel. 0519 221 100).
Where to Stay:	In the center, Hotel-Restaurant De Posthorn (Tel. 0519 293 500, www.hotel-deposthoorn.nl) at Diepswal 21 has a lovely position on the canal; singles are €60 and doubles are €80. Centrally located, Hotel-Café-Restaurant 't Raedhûs, Koningstraat 1 (Tel. 0519 294 082, www.raedhus.nl) has singles for €40 and doubles for €57. Across the

Above: Elfstedenroute signs guide you through the 230 km cycling route.
Left: Boazum, a traditional Friesian village.

Zuider-Bolwerk is Hotel Van der Meer, Woudweg 1 (Tel. 0519 292 380), where singles are €40 and doubles are €65.

There are several B&Bs in Dokkum. Addresses are available from the VVV and its website.

Camping Harddraverspark, Harddraversdijk 1A (Tel. 0519 294 445, April through October), is conveniently located in a park across the water from the Oosterbolwerk.

Where to Eat: All the above-mentioned hotels have restaurants. Other options include pizza and pasta at Pizzeria Romano, Koornstraat 8 (Tel. 0519 297 756, closed Mondays), and Chinese-Indonesian fare at Happy Wok on Hantumerweg 6 (Tel. 0519 292 308).

Day 5: Dokkum to Leeuwarden (25.8 km)

The route follows the Dokkumer Ee (river) back to Leeuwarden. This is the last section of both the cycle route and the official *Elfstedentocht*. The only difficult part about leaving Dokkum is the roundabout at 0.9 km. Be sure to take the street (unmarked) after going about three-quarters of the way around. The Dokkumer Ee will be on your left, and there are bicycle signs pointing to Voorstreek and Birdaard.

At 1.7 km, begin cycling on the *jaagpad*, the old towpath, with the Dokkumer Ee on your left. You arrive in Birdaard, a pretty village straddling the canal. The Molen De Zwaluw (9.9 km) is open Tuesdays through Saturdays, May 1 to October 1 (burdmolen@hetnet.nl). Leaving the village, you will cross a steep bridge, the first of four such bridges. You'll have to walk your bike over each bridge.

Leave the river for a short time at 12.4 km, returning to it at the hamlet of Bartleheim. Follow the river all the way back to Leeuwarden, the river on your left almost the entire way. At 25.4 km, you will see the Elfstedenroute sign, the first one you saw on Day 1; turn left toward the station.

Cue Sheet

0.0	Start	VVV Dokkum go SW across the Markt
90 m	L	Koningstraat
0.1	R	Hogepol
0.2	VR	Honspoort/bridge/Altenastreek
0.9	RA !	ELF, sign "Voorstreek and Birdaard"
1.0	L	ELF Betterwird, sign "Birdaard"
1.1	L	ELF Hendoweg

1.6	VL	ELF Eewal
1.7	VL	ELF to Dokkumer Ee (Jaagpad)
6.3	L	back to Dokkumer Ee
9.9	SS R	Molen De Zwaluw (windmill), T-Birdaard
10.6	CS !	high bridge
12.4	R	unmarked
12.5	L	ELF onto road
14.1	L	ELF Bartlehiem
14.4	R	bike path along Dokkumer Ee, T-Bartlehiem
14.5	CS !	high bridge
17.9	CS !	high bridge
19.1	CS !	high bridge
21.6	L	ELF
21.7	R	Dokkumer Trekwei
21.9	CS	IE Paad along Dokkumer Ee
22.3	L	unmarked along Dokkumer Ee
22.5	L	unmarked
22.9	CS	ELF bike tunnel under N355 Dokkumertrekweg
24.1	L	ELF Noordersingel
24.5	RA L	ELF at Us Mem statue (see page 103)
24.6	L	Harlingerstraatweg
24.7	R	ELF Pier Panderstraat/Westersingel
25.4	L	ELF Langemarktstraat, sign "Station"
25.7	VR	Sophialaan, sign "Station"
25.8	End	Leeuwarden Railway Station

9.
Groningen & Drenthe

THESE TWO provinces occupy the North-eastern part of the country. Groningen is in the northeastern corner, bordered to the north by the North Sea and to the east by Germany. This rural province is studded with churches built on *wierden* or *terpen* (mounds) as protection from flooding. The gem of the province is the city of Groningen.

Drenthe, the province south of Groningen, is a region of forests, peat bogs, heaths, lakes, and picturesque farms.

Drenthe is known as the "bicycle province." Winds are not as strong here, and numerous forests provide shelter and shady cycling. One of the country's biggest cycling events takes place here annually.

"Drenthe is so beautiful. It draws me and pleases me so very much that it would be better if I had never seen it."   *Vincent van Gogh, 1883*

Bicycles, bicycles, and more bicycles. This huge *fietsenstalling* (bicycle parking facility) is outside the railway station in Groningen.

Groningen & Drenthe Tour: Megaliths, Memorial, and Mini-Venice

Total Distance:	153.7 km
Duration:	3 days
Highlights:	Groningen, *hunebedden*, Orvelte, Kamp Westerbork, Dwingelderveld National Park, Giethoorn
Terrain:	Level
When to Go:	Visit any time from April through October. Most of the attractions are open all year; however, in villages like Dwingeloo and Giethoorn, several hotels and restaurants are closed from mid-October to mid- to late April.
Maps:	Michelin 531 Noord-Nederland/Pays-Bas Nord, ANWB/VVV Toeristenkaart Drenthe
Start/Finish:	Groningen/Meppel
Access:	Groningen/Meppel

Connecting routes: The Hanzeroute (Chapter 10) begins in Meppel. Join the Elfstedenroute (Friesland), one hour by train from Groningen to Leeuwarden.

This ride begins in the city of Groningen and soon enters the province of Drenthe. Each day offers amazing variety: explore ancient *hunebedden* (see boxed text below), cycle through picturesque villages, remember the tragedy of the Holocaust at Kamp Westerbork, and visit Dwingelderveld National Park. A tiny part of the ride goes into Overijssel and through the picturesque village of Giethoorn.

Mysterious Megaliths

Scattered along the Hondsrug Ridge in northwest Drenthe are the amazing *hunebedden*, groups of giant boulders that form prehistoric burial chambers dating to 3000 B.C. Drenthe is home to 53 of the country's 54 *hunebedden*; the 54th is in Groningen. Typically, a *hunebed* consists of a ring of upright boulders on which rests a capstone, forming a chamber. This was almost certainly covered with earth to form a mound. Excavations have revealed pottery and wooden vessels, some of which are displayed in museums in Assen, Borger, and Emmen.

No one knows for sure how these massive boulders, some weighing up to 20 tons, found their way here, but one theory is that they were transported by Ice Age glaciers from Scandinavia. It is not known how the people moved the boulders and placed the huge capstones.

Groningen

Groningen is a lively university town. It has a cosmopolitan feel, with trendy shops, restaurants, and cafés to suit every budget, plus plenty of cultural venues. The city suffered considerable damage during World War II. The restoration resulted in an interesting mix of old and new buildings. Groningen is a walking and cycling city, and the city center is relatively car-free.

Right across the road from the station, located on its own island in a canal is the Groninger Museum (www.groninger-museum.nl, closed Mondays except in July and August). It contains an Oriental porcelain collection, archaeological and historical exhibits, works from the Groninger De Ploeg School, and contemporary exhibits. Another interesting museum is the Noordelijk Scheepvaartmuseum, Brugstraat 24 (www.noordelijkscheepvaartmuseum.nl, closed Mondays), a maritime museum focusing on the history of Dutch shipping all the way back to the 6th century. For a view of the city, head to the 96 m (315 ft) high Martinitoren of the Martinikerk (open daily, April through November).

Information:	Groningen's VVV is at Grote Markt 25 (Tel. 0900 202 3050, www. vvvgroningen. nl), about 1 km from the station. (From the station, go right; in 200 m, turn left onto Herestraat and follow it to the Grote Markt). The ANWB is at Trompsingel 21 (Tel. 050 318 4345). The internet can be accessed at the library, Oude Boteringstraat 18 (Tel. 050 368 3683).
Bicycle Shops:	Rijwielshop VOF B. Kruis, Stationsplein 13 (Tel. 050 312 4714), is located outside the train station. In the center, Vincent van Ellen Tweewielers is at Oude Ebbingstraat 79 (Tel. 050 312 9800).
Where to Stay:	Hotel Friesland, Kleine Pelsterstraat 4 (Tel. 050 312 1307, www.hotelfriesland.nl), has simple singles for €28 and doubles for €48; showers and toilets are down the hall. The

One of the *hunebedden* (ancient megaliths) lining the route between Groningen and Borger.

trendy Martini Hotel, Gedempte Zuiderdiep 8 (Tel. 050 312 9919, www.martinihotel.nl), has singles from €69.50, doubles from €79.50, and breakfast is €7.50. The upscale Corps de Garde, Oude Boteringstraat 72-74 (Tel. 050 314 5437, www.corpsdegarde.nl), has singles for €96 and doubles for €110.

There are several B&Bs. Check with the VVV.

Simplon Jongerenhotel Youth Hotel, Boterdiep 72 (Tel. 050 313 5221, www.simplonjongerenhotel.nl), has both dorm rooms and regular rooms.

Stadspark Camping, Campinglaan 4 (Tel. 050 525 1624, www.stadscampings.nl), is about 3 km southwest of Groningen, and is open mid-March to mid-October.

Where to Eat: At Poelestraat 35, try Stadlander (Tel. 050 312 7191). At Shuitendiep 1017 is Pancake Ship (Tel. 050 312 0045, www.pannekoekschip.nl); Eetcafé 't Zwarte Schaap is at Shuitendiep 52 (Tel. 050 311 0691). Eetcafé d'Ouwe Brandweer, Gedempte Zuiderdiep 75 (Tel. 050 318 0323, www.ouwebrandweer.nl), is decorated in a fire brigade motif (brandweer means fire brigade). Just north of the center, De Kleine Moghul, Nieuwe Boteringstraat 62 (Tel. 050 318 8905) has reasonably priced Indian food to eat in or take out.

Day 1: Groningen to Borger (45.7 km)

This is "*Hunebed* Day." Spend the day cycling through pretty Drenthe countryside, stopping to explore intriguing *hunebedden* (see boxed text "Mysterious Megaliths," on page 126), some hidden in forests. Finish in Borger by visiting the country's largest megalith in the grounds of the National Hunebed Information Center.

Go east from the Groningen Railway Station, keeping the railway tracks on your right. At 1.1 km, go under the N46; the road curves left and the tracks will be on your left. Cycle beside a canal until the turn to Haren (3.3 km). Go through Haren; watch carefully for the turn at 6.9 km to Noordlaren and Onnen.

From Noordlaren, a short side trip leads to the first *hunebed* of the day. From opposite the 13th-century church (14.2 km), follow Kerkstraat west for 200 m to Zuidlaarderweg and then turn left. Note the windmill behind the houses across the road. Go 400 m south on Zuidlaarderweg, watching carefully for the *hunebed* sign. Turn right onto a narrow gravel bike path and continue for 600 m. The small *hunebed* is on your right, and has a capstone resting on five uprights. It is the only *hunebed* in the province of Groningen. Return to the church the way you came.

At 15.0 km, the huge campground on the left, Parc de Bloemert, gives access to the lake, Zuidlaardermeer.

Continue through Zuidlaren and ride until you go under the N34, where you cycle on a quiet road through farms; pass a cluster of thatched houses on your left (22.0 km). At 22.7 km, turn left into a thickly wooded forest laced with cycling and walking paths; look for two cute thatched cottages tucked between the trees (23.1 km). At 23.4 km, the mound with the protruding rock is a *grafheuvel* (ancient burial mound). Take a short side trip by turning right at 24.4 km; after 60 m there is a *hunebed* to your left. Continue further for 60 m to the Ontmantelde *hunebedden*, which look like mounds of dirt but are actually burial mounds.

It's easy to miss the Annen *hunebed* (25.7 km), on your right and at the corner 20 m after the roundabout. Unfortunately, it is missing some capstones.

Continue through Annen, curving right with the road, until the turn (27.2 km) to Gieten. Eexterweg takes you through open farmland, into a forest, and through Eext.

The Eexterhalte *hunebed* (33.5 km) is one of the biggest, yet one of the easiest to miss. Follow the small sign pointing left on the bike path. Cross the road, then go about 100 m to this huge, complete *hunebed* topped by six capstones and balanced on about 20 uprights.

Just after the Eexterhalte *hunebed*, go through the roundabout (33.7 km); the bike path is on the left. The next 5 km is lovely cycling through the dense forest Boswachterij Gieten.

En route to Borger, visit the twin Drouwen *hunebedden*. At Hotel Drouwen (42.4 km), a tiny sign on the other side of the road points right. Go 300 m; you can't miss the double *hunebedden* on the left. Back on Borgerweg, the mound with seven trees (44.4 km) is a *grafheuvel*. The side trip at 45.4 km takes you to the largest *hunebed* and the Information Center (see "Borger"). Go left (45.4 km) on Hunebedstraat, veer right after 450 m, and continue for 250 m. The *hunebed* and entrance to the Information Center are on your left. Return to Borgerweg (now called Hoofdstraat) and continue to the VVV.

Cue Sheet

0.0	Start	Groningen Railway Station go E (right) along the front of the station
0.5	CS	LF14a Lodewijkstraat (tracks on R)
1.1	R	Helperzoom, under N46, road curves left
3.3	R	LF14a bike path dir. "Haren," #14323
3.6	CS	bike path (LF14a turns)
4.3	CS	Kerklaan
5.7	R	Kerkstraat
6.0	L	Rijkstraatweg (at church), T-Haren

Map 9.1. Groningen & Drenthe Tour, Day 1.

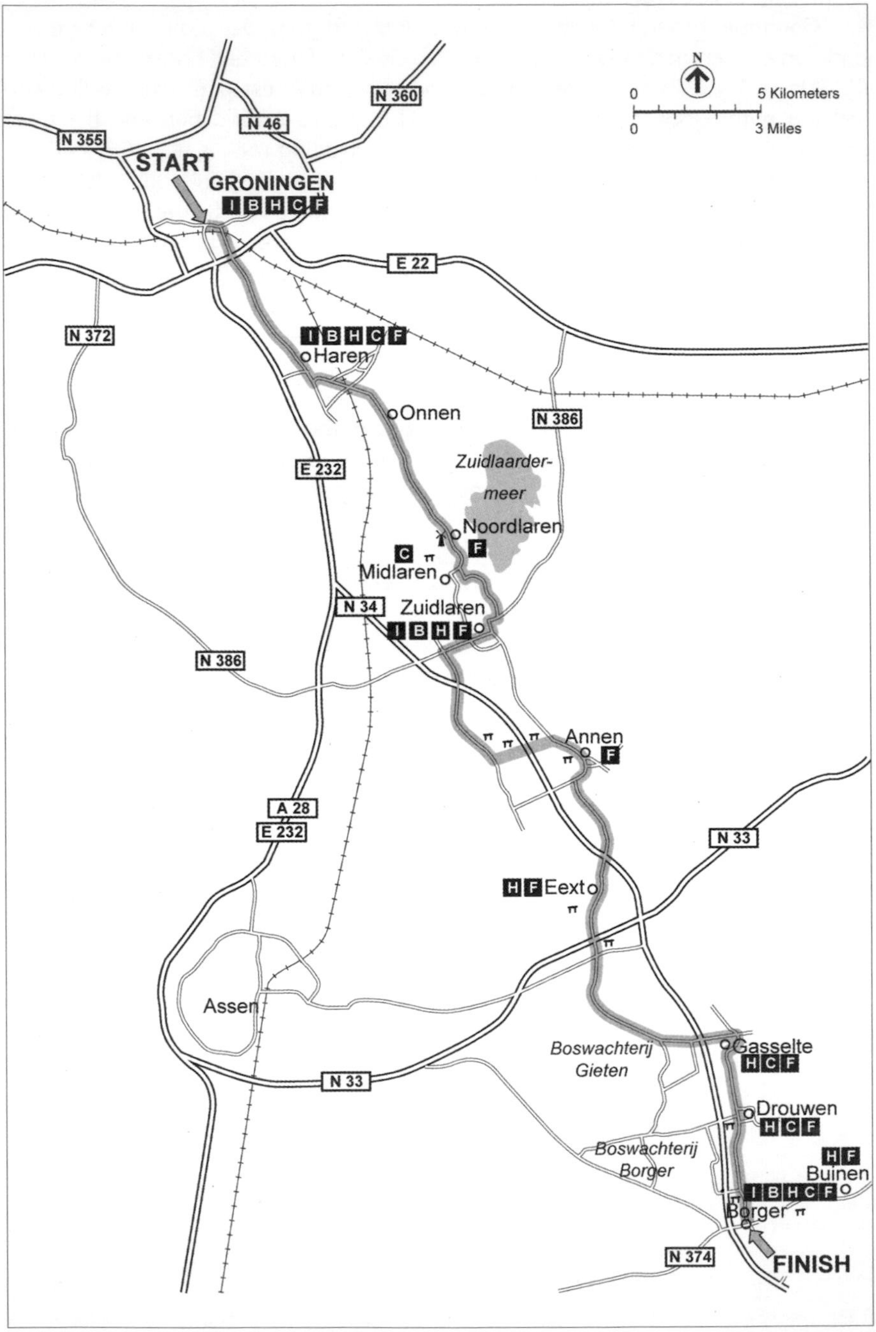

6.9	L !	Hertenlaan, sign "Noordlaren, Onnen"
8.0	CS	cross railway tracks, Paterswoldersmeer sign
8.1	R	sign "Noordlaren, Onnen, Paterswoldersmeer"
9.4	CS	T-Onnen
9.9	SS R	thatched farmhouse
14.2	CS	church, T-Noordlaren
14.2	ST R	RT = 2.4 km *hunebed*
15.0	SS L	Zuidlaardermeer (lake on left)
15.4	L	Zuidlaarderweg
17.6	R	dir. Gieten and Assen
17. 8	VL	Kerkbrink (sign "VVV, 1 km")
18.0	R	Stationsweg, T-Zuidlaren
18.6	CS	VVV Zuidlaren (on R)
19.6	L	Schipborgerweg
20.2	VR	Schipborgerweg
20.7	R	De Borg (under N34)
22.7	L	sign "Annen," Strubbenweg (enter forest)
23.4	VR	Strubbenweg
24.3	SS R	burial mound, #24348 Galgenberg
24.4	ST R	RT = 240 m *hunebedden* and burial mounds
24.9	CS	under N34
25.6	R	10 m
25.7	RA CS	Zuidlaarderweg
25.7	SS R !	20 m Annen *hunebed*
26.8	VR !	Brink, T-Annen
26.9	CS	dir. "Gieten" Kruisstraat
27.2	L	sign "Gieten," Eexterweg
31.2	CS	Kerkstraat, in Eext
31.4	VR	Stationsstraat (church on left)
32.9	CS	under N33

33.5	SS L !	Eexterhalte *hunebed* (left, short pathway)
33.7	RA CS	#20946, bike path on L
35.6	VL	Broomkroonpad, #21635
37.5		bike path curves R
37.8	L	LF14a sign (Restaurant Nije Hemelriek to R)
37.9	CS	#20160
38.8	R	LF14a #6610 (post)
39.2	L	LF14a #24856 sign "Drouwen"
39.6	CS	under N34
39.8	R	LF14a #24861 sign "Borger," Veldkampsweg
40.4	L	LF14a #24860 Sodemorsweg
40.7	R	#20988 Kerkstraat/Borgerweg/Hoofdstraat
42.4	ST R !	RT = 600 m (at Hotel Drouwen) #20935 to Drouwen Hunebed
44.4	SS L	burial mound
45.4	ST L	RT = 1.4 km to museum and biggest *hunebed*
45.8	RA CS	N374 (30 m), R Oude Brink
45.9	End	VVV Borger

Borger

Borger is home to the Netherlands' largest *hunebed*. It is 24 m (74 ft) long, with nine capstones, 26 uprights, and two endstones. Adjacent to it is the Nationaal Hunebedden Informatiecentrum, Bronnegerstraat 12 (Tel. 0599 236 374, open daily, closed January). Enter from Hunebedstraat (see side trip, 45.4 km). The museum has information about megalithic tombs, displays from excavations, and more.

Another *hunebed* within easy reach of Borger is toward Buinen. Cycle east on the N374 from the intersection with Hoofdstraat (in the center of Borger) for 1.2 km. The *hunebed* is on your right.

Information:	VVV Borger is at Grote Brink 2A (Tel. 0599 234 855, www.tref.nl/borger-odoorn/vvv. Computeroptimized, Torenlaan 13 (Tel. 0599 657 507), has internet access.
Bicycle Shop:	Borger's bike shop, Egberts, is on Hoofdstraat 63 (Tel. 0599 234 224).

Where to Stay: The modern Hotel Bieze-Borger, Hoofdstraat 21(Tel. 0599 234 321, info@hotel-bieze.nl), has singles for €47.50 and doubles for €72.50. Hotel-Pension Nathalia, Hoofdstraat 87 (Tel. 0599 234 791), charges €26 per person per night (€5 one-night surcharge). The Pension Molenerf, Torenlaan 18 (Tel. 0599 236 048, www.molenerf.com) charges €20 per person per night (€5 one-night surcharge).

Camping Hunzedal, De Drift 3 (Tel. 0599 234 698, www.hunzedal.nl), is about 1 km east of Borger (open April through October). There are two mini-campings on Strengenweg, about 2 km west of Borger.

Where to Eat: Hotel Bieze-Borger (see "Where to Stay") has a good restaurant. Across the road, 't Hunebed, Hoofdstraat 22 (Tel. 0599 234 256, www.hunebed.nl), serves pizza and Dutch food. D'Aole Restaurant, Kruisstraat 6 (Tel. 0599 234 931), has outdoor dining. There are two Chinese restaurants, both on Hoofdstraat.

Day 2: Borger to Dwingeloo (62.8 km)

Directional ANWB mushrooms will be useful route markers throughout the day.

From Borger to Orvelte, you will ride along a canal, on a forested bike path, and through farmland. In Orvelte (20.4 km), turn right into the parking area (P2). At the far end of the parking lot is an information booth with free maps of Orvelte.

Tiny Orvelte is a traditional 19th century Drenthe farming community, a "museum-village," where the villagers still dress and live as people did 200 years ago.

Drentse Fiets 4-Daagse

The Drentse Fiets 4-Daagse, a four-day cycling event held in Drenthe in mid-July, celebrates its 40th year in 2005. Around 25,000 cyclists gather each year for this, the country's biggest cycling event.

Not a race, the four days offer cycling programs with daily route choices and with various starting points in Drenthe. Routes are 30 km, 40 km, 60 km, 80 km, or 100 km long. These scenic routes are intended for leisurely cycling, and include routes for children. In 2004, the starting points were Assen, Hoogeveen, Meppel, Emmen, and Diever.

For information, phone 0521 594 130 (weekdays only), e-mail at info@fiets4daagse.nl, or go to the website at www.fiets4daagse.nl. From May through July, several of these four-day events are held throughout the country. The Dutch Bicycle Touring Union (www.ntfu.nl) has a calendar of these and numerous other events.

They are not putting on a show; this is how they really live. No cars are allowed in Orvelte. Walk the quaint streets and visit the dairy and the farmhouse; watch the potter, blacksmith, and clogmaker at work. The VVV is in the center (Tel. 0593 322 335, www.orvelte.net).

To continue on the route, go back to the parking area (20.4 km) and turn left to the Oranjekanaal. Turn left at 21.0 km, and notice the locks with the difference in water levels (21.7 km). Continue along the canal for 5 km, then turn off to Kamp Westerbork. (Note: The camp is about 10 km from the town of Westerbork). Cycle through open farmland and a birch and pine forest to the camp.

Kamp Westerbork was not a concentration camp. Originally, it was established to house Jewish refugees fleeing from Germany. When the Nazis invaded in 1940, it became a transit camp; every Tuesday, trainloads of people were transported east to concentration camps. It was from here that Anne Frank departed.

Today, only outlines of the buildings remain. As a memorial, a 20 m section of the otherwise demolished railway line remains. The museum, Herinneringscentrum Kamp Westerbork (www.westerbork.nl, open daily), is a moving commemorative, but there are other somber memorials as well. One is the former roll call area (32.3 km) on which are laid 102,000 bricks in the shape of the Netherlands, each brick symbolizing a person who was shipped from the camp. Another, just after mushroom #21668 (33.0 km), is five coffins representing the five concentration camps to where the Jews were sent.

From Westerbork, the route takes you through forests and farmland until you go through Beilen. At 46.4 km, do not turn left to the canal, but onto Gentiaan, the road angling off to the left. Cycle through Ter Horster Zand, open heath areas.

Cross the A28 into Dwingelderveld National Park. Quiet forested paths and small roads lead to Dwingeloo.

Cue Sheet

0.0	Start	VVV Borger go E on Oude Brink
90 m	R	Hoofdstraat
0.7	R	Westdorperstraat sign "Schoonloo"
0.9	L	Westdorperstraat
1.6	L	Westdorperstraat
2.2	R	bike path along canal, #22421
3.5	R	#22546
4.5	L	N374
6.5	L	cross N374, R forest bike path sign "Elp, Westerbork"
7.3	CS	#22368

8.3	L	#22463 N376
11.5	VR	#23159 bike path sign "Wezuperbrug"
13.3	VR	#23156 bike path, Ellertsveldroute sign
14.0	CS	#23334 sign "Wezuperbrug"
15.6	CS	cross canal (30 m), R Oranjekanaal (south side), T-Wezuperbrug
17.4	L	unmarked road – "*doorgaand verkeer*" (through traffic)
20.3	L	De Wiet

Map 9.2. Groningen & Drenthe Tour, Day 2.

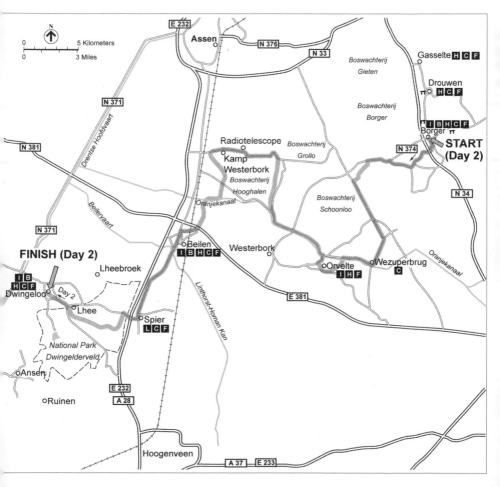

20.4	ST R	Orvelte at P2
20.4	L	(to Oranjekanaal)
21.0	CS	cross canal (30 m), L Oranjekanaal (north side)
21.7	CS	locks
26.0	R	#63441 sign "Kamp Westerbork," Zwiggelterweg
26.3	L	#24157 sign "Kamp Westerbork," Westerborken
29.5	R	#24158 sign "Kamp Westerbork" (into forest)
30.6	L	#24159 sign "Kamp Westerbork"
30.8	CS	#23166
31.2	VR	#24160
31.9	VL	#24161 sign "Kamp 300 m"
32.3	SSL	railway line and bricks
33.0	CS	#21668, coffins (on L)
35.0	L	to museum
35.3	-	Kamp Westerbork Museum
35.4	L	exit, west sign "Hooghalen"
36.4	L	#23392, Beilerdingspelroute sign
38.9	CS	#23393
40.3	R	#23394 Oranjekanaal
40.6	L	#24947 Klatering
43.0	R	#24944 sign "Beilen"
44.5	R	Breekamp (10 m), L Slootakker
44.9	RA L	Esweg sign "Centrum"
45.9	CS	T-Beilen
46.4	L !	Gentiaan (not canal)
46.5	CS	bike path, cross road
47.0	CS	Smalbroek sign "Dwingeloo"
47.9	L	Ter Horst sign "Dwingeloo"
48.7	R	#23862
49.2	R	#23861 sign "Dwingeloo"

49.6	SS	Ter Horster Zand
51.0	L	#23112 A28
53.8	R	sign "Dwingeloo," N855 (over A28)
54.7	R	sign "Dwingeloo," enter Dwingelderveld National Park
55.2	L	#21281 sign "Dwingeloo"
58.1	CS	#21272 sign "Dwingeloo"
59.0	L	Spiererweg to "Pesse"
59.2	VR	sign "Pesse," Information Center on L
59.3	R	bike path, #21270 sign "Dwingeloo"
59.3	R	(50 m) bike path (hard-packed dirt)
60.5	CS	#21267
60.6	R	unmarked road
60.7	L	unmarked road
60.8	CS	#24993, T-Lhee
61.0	R	#24992
62.7	L	Brink (VVV sign)
62.8	End	VVV Dwingeloo

Dwingeloo

Dwingeloo is different from most Dutch towns because it is centered on a *brink* (village green) instead of canals. Many of the houses around the brink have been converted into shops and cafés. The church, 14th-century St. Nicholaas, has an unusual onion dome on its steeple.

Most people come to Dwingeloo to enjoy walking and cycling in the nearby Dwingelderveld National Park, with its mix of forest and heath. On the edge of the park is the antithesis of nature, the Planetron (www.planetron.nl). This enormous blue sphere has movie theaters, a video game center, and an observatory. Just south of Dwingeloo is the giant radio-telescope (not open to the public).

Information:	VVV Dwingeloo at Brink 1 (Tel. 0521 591 331, www.vvvwesterveld.nl) has cycling and walking maps of the area for €4 or €5. Internet access is available at the library, Brink 4.
Bicycle Shops:	Both bike shops are on the Brink: Dolsma is at Brink 13 (Tel. 0521 591 428), and Reiber is at Brink 23 (Tel. 0521 591 326).

Where to Stay:	Right in the center, the stylish Hotel Wesseling, Brink 26 (Tel. 0521 591 544, www.hotelwesseling.nl), has singles for €62.50 and doubles for €95. Across the road, with the same owners and prices, is Hotel De Brink, Brink 30 (Tel. 0521 591 319). Hotel De Drift, Drift 4 (Tel. 0521 591 538, www.hoteldedrift.nl), charges €32 per person per night (€6.75 one-night surcharge).
	There are six B&Bs, including two on farms. Check with the VVV. Onder de Sterren, Esweg 18 (Tel. 0521 591 401), a pension/B&B, charges €29 per person per night.
	The closest campground is Camping Meisterhof, Lheebroek 33 (Tel. 0521 597 278, www.meisterhof.nl), 3 km north of Dwingeloo (open April through September).
Where to Eat:	Dwingeloo has many restaurants on the Brink. All three hotels (see "Where to Stay") have good restaurants. Onder de Eiken, Drift 20 (Tel. 0521 593 272, www.onderdeeiken.nl), serves Dutch food. For pancakes, go to Pannenkoekenboerderij In de Zaagkoele, Brink 36 (Tel. 0521 591 952, closed Mondays)

Day 3: Dwingeloo to Meppel via Giethoorn (45.0 km)

From Dwingeloo, cycle past the Planetron (1.0 km), then onto a hard-packed dirt bike path for 3 km until you exit the park. After Ansen, bump along the cobblestone road; the wooded area on your right is the Rheebruggen forest, a popular area for walking.

Cross the N371 (11.0 km) and follow Ruiterweg to the N353, where you turn right to the Havelteberg *hunebedden*. Cross the N353 (16.5 km) and cycle 150 m to the second largest *hunebed* in the Netherlands (on your left). Continue another 100 m to the southernmost *hunebed* (on your right). Return to the N353 and turn left. After 100 m (16.6 km), turn right onto the small road marked only by a mountain bike route sign. At 16.8 km, be sure not to continue south on Schierbosweg. Go a little further and turn onto the next road south, Dorlangenweg.

The forests disappear once you cross the A32, changing around De Wieden to a huge bog area. The lakes in this area are a result of past peat digging.

The side trip to the north, less touristy end of Giethoorn (30.8 km) is an absolute must. To get there, turn right on Kerkweg. In 1.1 km, turn right onto Molenweg. This is Noordeinde, the quieter, serene northern part of Giethorn.

You'll reach Giethoorn proper at 31.8 km. There are three museums, but the village itself is like a living museum. For 3 km, this storybook village, with its thatched roof houses and well-tended gardens, clings to both sides of the canal. You will cross no less than 40 wooden footbridges as you zigzag through the village. Giethoorn's only road is this canal-side path, just wide enough for one bicycle in each direction, but not for cars.

Giethoorn is a lovely overnight alternate to Meppel. VVV Giethoorn (outside the village) is on Beulakerweg 114A/N334 (Tel. 0900 567 4637, www.kopvanoverijssel.nl). There are several hotels in and around Giethoorn. Hotel Restaurant De Harmonie, Beulakerweg 55 (Tel. 0521 361 372, www.harmonie-giethoorn.nl), has singles for €70 and doubles for €85. De Waterlelie, Petersteeg 2 (Tel. 0521 361 317, www.dewaterlelie.nl), has rooms for €80. The VVV has a list of the available B&Bs; some are on the canal. Cafés, restaurants, and pancake houses can be found along Binnenpad and Beulakerweg.

Map 9.3. Groningen & Drenthe Tour, Day 3.

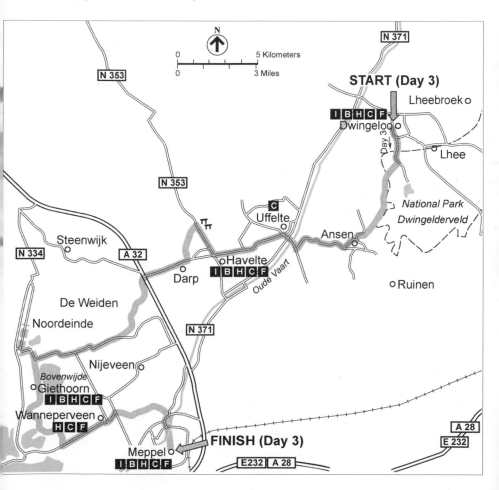

The VVV has a list of the many campgrounds in the area. Five campgrounds are right on Binnenpad (the route through the village), at Binnenpad 33, 49, 113, 137, and 141.

From Giethoorn, the route to Meppel travels through fields and farms alongside several small canals. Go through the linear town of Wanneperveen, follow the signs to the station, enter Meppel at the huge water tower, and go onto the busy ring road to the center.

Cue Sheet

0.0	Start	VVV Dwingeloo go S on Drift
0.2	CS	sign "Planetron," Drift
1.2	R	bike path (unpaved) sign "Uffelte," #21273
1.2	SS	Planetron
4.2	CS	#21505 end of park (paved bike path)
6.3	R	Voorlanden dir. "Uffelte," T-Ansen
6.4	L	Voorlanden
7.1	R	Hooidijk dir. "Uffelte"
10.2	R	Anserweg dir. "Uffelte"
11.1	CS	#20607 sign "Havelte," Ruiterweg
14.9	R	N353
16.5	ST R	RT = 500 m, two *hunebedden*, Havelteberg *hunebedden*
16.5	-	Turn S for 100 m
16.6	R	small (unmarked) road just after Theehuis 't Hunebed
16.8	L	Schierbosweg (30 m), R unmarked (not a continuation of Schierbosweg)
16.9	L	Dorlangenweg (becomes gravel)
18.0	R	small connecting road
18.2	R	Ruileterweg
18.7	CS	Darp
20.2	CS	bike tunnel under A32 sign "Meppel, Nijeveen"
21.0	L	A32 sign "Meppel, Nijeveen"
21.4	R	Spoorbaanweg

22.1	L	Bramenweg
23.0	L	Nijev. Kerkweg 3E
24.4	R	unmarked
26.0	CS	#25005, T-Kolderveense Bovenboer
30.8	L	Kerkweg/Binnenpad
30.8	ST R	RT = 5.0 km, sign "Noordeinde"
31.8	CS !	onto bike path
33.1	L	#24303 sign "Meppel"
33.2	R	sign "Wanneperveen"
34.1	L	#21359 sign "Meppel"
35.1	L	over high bridge, #21423 sign "Meppel"
36.6	CS	bike path
37.3	L	Weth. Vosstraat, T-Wanneperveen
39.7	R	Nieuwe Dijk
40.1	L	Mantenweg sign "Station"
42.2	R	sign "Station"
43.2	CS !	watch out for speed bumps

The quiet, well-kept bicycle paths of Drenthe through shady forests offer a delightful cycling experience.

43.5	RA CS	sign "Centrum," Steenwijkerstraatweg
44.2	R	Eendrachtstraat (police station on L)
44.8	L	Kerkplein
44.9	L	Kromme Elleboog
45.0	End	VVV/ANWB Meppel

Meppel

Meppel centers on the Kerkplein, with its 15th-century church replete with tall tower. Meppel has two lively markets, one on Thursday mornings and one on Saturday mornings. The Drukkerijmuseum (Printing Museum, www. drukkerijmuseum-meppel.nl, open Tuesdays through Saturdays, 1 p.m. to 5 p.m.) at Kleine Oever 11, explores the history of print, from paper making to book binding.

Information: VVV/ANWB Meppel is at Kromme Elleboog 2 (Tel. 0522 252 888, www.meppel.nl). Access the internet at unrealcafe.nl, Noteboomstraat 3 (Tel. 0522 247 419).

Bicycle Shops: The railway station bike shop at Stationsweg 72 (Tel. 0522 254 369) rents bicycles, as does bike shopb Hessels, Woldstraat 102 (Tel. 0522 241 880). Hoogeveen, Grote Kerkstraat (Tel. 0522 251 895), is in the center.

Where to Stay: There are two overpriced and ordinary hotels and no B&Bs in Meppel. (Giethoorn has better lodging options.)

Hotel De Poort van Drenthe, Parallelweg 25 (Tel. 0522 251 080, depoortvandrenthe@planet.nl), opposite the station, has singles for €50 and doubles for €70, and charges €1.25 for bike storage. Hotel De Reisiger, Dirk Jakobsstraat 6 (Tel. 0522 256 649, reisiger@home.nl) has €60 singles and €90 doubles.

For around €18 per person per night, Meppel's Inn, Leonard Springerlaan 14 (Tel. 0522 251 706, www.meppelsinn.nl), is a great hostel, in a big, airy house close to the station.

Camping De Kikkerije, Steenwijkerstraatweg 96 (Tel. 0522 254 639, www.kikkerije.info), 2 km from Meppel's center, is open mid-March through October.

Where to Eat: What Meppel lacks in hotels, it makes up for in eateries. There are several restaurants around the Kerkplein and Grote Kerkstraat, including Argentinian, Chinese, and traditional Dutch. At Woldstraat 30, Da Pasquale (Tel. 0522 460 021) serves excellent Italian food.

10.

Overijssel & Gelderland

THE THREE rides in this chapter, through the two provinces Overijssel and Gelderland, are all vastly different. The first, the Hanzeroute, follows the beautiful IJssel River from north to south, tracing the route through six historically rich Hanseatic towns (see boxed text "The Hanseatic League" on page 144). The second ride follows in part the Zevenheuvelenweg (Seven Hills Road), from which the ride takes it name. The third ride goes through two of the Netherlands' largest national parks, the Veluwezoom and Hoge Veluwe, with their hills, heaths, and forests.

Ride 1: Hanzeroute (Hanseatic Town Route)

Total Distance:	222.2 km
Duration:	4 days
Highlights:	Giethoorn, Blokzijl, IJssel River, Kampen, Zwolle, Hattem, Deventer, Zutphen, Bronkhorst, Doesburg, Nijmegen, Velorama Bicycle Museum.
Terrain:	Level
When to Go:	April through October, determined by the Jonen ferry, which is operational April through October only, and a portion of the LF3 through a nature reserve, open May through October. An alternate route outside the reserve is possible year-round.

Maps: Michelin 531 Noord-Nederland/Pays-Bas Nord, Michelin
                 532 Zuid-Nederland/Pays-Bas Sud, ANWB/VVV
                 Toeristenkaart Overijssel, ANWB/VVV Toeristenkaart Gelders
                 Rivierengebied, ANWB/VVV Toeristenkaart Achterhoek. The
                 LF3 Hanzeroute guidebook (Dutch only), in sections 3
                 through 6, provides maps and touring and lodging
                 information.

Start/Finish: Meppel/Nijmegen

Access: Railway stations: Meppel (start town), Kampen, Zwolle,
                 Deventer, Zutphen, and Nijmegen

Connecting routes: "Megaliths, Memorial, and Mini-Venice Ride" (Chapter 9),
                 "Veluwe & Het Loo Ride" (Ride 3 of this chapter), "Seven
                 Hills Ride" (Ride 2 of this chapter). By train from Nijmegen:
                 Den Bosch ("South of the Big Rivers Ride," Chapter 13),
                 Maastricht (both rides in Chapter 14), Utrecht (Day 2,
                 "Witches, Windmills, and West Coast," Chapter 11)

This ride follows part of the signed LF3a route, sectioned into the Rietlandroute, Hanzeroute, and Maasroute. From Meppel, you will ride to Blokzijl, the first Hanseatic town on the route. The bulk of the ride goes along the IJssel, a wide river with endless views, and wends its way through the once-prosperous Hanseatic towns.

From Doesburg, the southernmost Hanseatic town on the route, the ride continues to follow the IJssel to the confluence of the Rijn (Rhine River). Ferry across the Rijn to where it meets the Waal River, then ride along the Waal, through a small nature reserve, and into Nijmegen, home of the Velorama Bicycle Museum.

For information on Meppel, see Chapter 9, page 142.

The Hanseatic League

In the 14th century, several cities along major trading routes in northern Europe formed a powerful trading and economic alliance known as the Hanseatic League. At its height, the League included more than 200 cities, including cities such as London, Cologne, and Stockholm. For two centuries, merchants in the League traded items such as salt, fish, grain, beer, wine, timber, textiles, and fur.

Several Dutch cities, many along the IJssel River, which connects to the Rhine River, were *Hanzesteden* (Hanseatic towns, www.hanzesteden.info). The part of the LF3 route called the Hanzeroute passes through six of these well preserved, architecturally rich towns: Blokzijl, Kampen, Zwolle, Hattem, Deventer, Zutphen, and Doesburg.

Day 1: Meppel to Kampen (55.3 km)

From Meppel, cycle through rural terrain to Giethoorn, passing through the linear village Wanneperveen. This area is known for the lakes which formed after many years of digging out the peat (*veen*). At the end of town, note the church (9.0 km) with its unusual exterior bell.

The turn at 13.8 km is just before the best part of Giethoorn, which is well worth visiting (see Chapter 9, pages 138–139). (if you are overnighting in the area at the start of this ride, consider staying in Giethoorn rather than Meppel.) To explore Giethoorn, continue straight. To continue the route, go west from this point, following Bartus Warmersweg to the main road. On the other side of N334 (15.6 km), cross the bridge and curve right onto Jonenweg. Cycle 4 km, with the houseboat-lined canal on your right, to the Jonen ferry.

The tiny Jonen ferry operates by pulley. It runs from April 1 to November 1, 7 a.m. to 7 p.m., and costs 70 cents. When you arrive at the ferry, ring the bell to alert the ferry operator that you are there. She lives in the house adjacent to the ferry landing.

Ride through *polder* to Blokzijl, passing a few nicely located mini-campings on Duiningermeerweg. Join the LF3a route (24.0 km). It comes in from the north and is called the Rietlandroute until Kampen. Take the time to visit Blokzijl, a 14th-century Hanseatic town and prosperous Zuiderzee port, although now far from the IJsselmeer (the former Zuiderzee). The 17th-century Grote Kerk has an impressive interior. One of Blokzijl's finest buildings is the gabled Hotel Kaatje bij de Sluis, on Zuiderstraat 1. The picturesque harbor is lined with gabled 17th-century houses.

From mushroom #22809 (28.5 km), cycle from Leeuwte to St.-Jansklooster on a quiet road lined with thatched-roof houses. Continue on rural roads to the ferry (39.9 km), which operates daily until 11 p.m. and costs 55 cents.

In Genemuiden, the only thing of interest is Achterweg, perhaps the only street in the world where smoking is prohibited. Signs in this tiny backstreet indicate smoking is a risk to its historic wooden warehouses.

From Genemuiden, go south along the Kamperzeedijk for most of the way to IJsselmuiden. Around 50.0 km, cycle through farm areas dotted with greenhouses. Be sure to look for the thatched house (51.5 km) with its beautifully manicured vegetable patch. Go through IJsselmuiden and cross the IJssel into Kampen.

Cue Sheet

0.0	Start	Meppel Railway Station go W on Stationsweg
0.4	R	Zuideinde
0.8	CS	VVV Meppel 20 m on R at Kromme Elleboog 2
0.9	L	Kerkplein (at church)

1.0	R	Kleine Oever/Grote Oever
1.6	L	Steenwijkerstraatweg
2.3	RA L	follow signs for Kolderveenroute and Haveltebergroute
2.4	R	Nijeveenseweg
3.7	L	Matenweg
5.7	R	Nieuwe Dijk
6.1	L	Veneweg (at Wanneperveen info board), T-Wanneperveen
9.0	SS R	church with exterior bell
9.6	R	Bovenboersepad, sign "Giethoorn"
11.5	L	over high bridge, R bike path

Map 10.1. Overijssel & Gelderland, Hanzeroute Tour, Days 1 & 2.

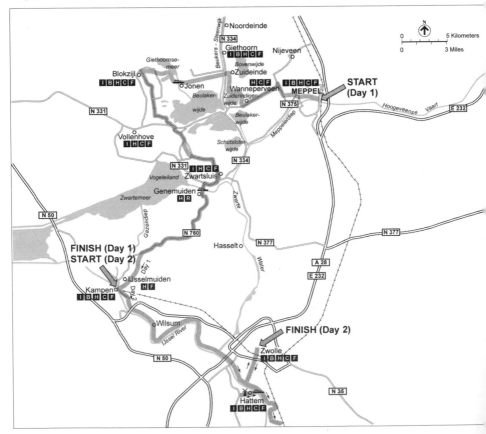

12.4	CS	#21359
13.4	L	Langesteeg (bike path)
13.5	VR	#24303, sign "Centrum Dorp"
13.8	L !	bike path
13.9	CS	Bartus Warmersweg
14.8	L	Bartus Warmersweg
14.9	R	Beulakerweg (N334), (VVV 1.2 km L)
15.2	L	over bridge to Dwarsgracht
15.3	VL	Kanaaldijk/Cornelisgracht
15.4	L	Jonenweg
15.6	CS	over bridge, curve R
17.0	CS	high bridge
17.9	CS	high bridge, Jonenpad
19.4	-	bike ferry, T-Jonen
19.4	CS	other side
20.3	R	#22752, sign "Blokzijl," Havenweg
21.3	R	#22751, sign "Blokzijl Duiningermeerweg"
24.0	CS	LF3a #22750, Duinweg sign "St.-Jansklooster"
24.0	ST R	RT = 1 km T-Blokzijl (follow LF3b signs to center)
28.5	L	LF3a #22809 sign "St. Jansklooster," Leeuwte
30.5	R	LF3a (under N331)
30.8	VR	LF3a Kloosterweg, T-St.-Jansklooster
32.1	L	LF3a sign "Zwartsluis," Barsbeek
34.1	L	LF3a #22575 Woldweg
36.0	R	LF3a #22574 Arembergerweg
37.9	R	LF3a Westeinde, T-Zwartsluis
38.2	R	LF3a bike path along N331
39.3	L	LF3a Veerweg
39.9	CS	ferry
40.0	CS	LF3a Veerweg, T-Genemuiden

40.2	R	LF3a Blokhuisweg
40.5	VL	LF3a Achterweg (SS see page 145)
41.3	R	LF3a dir. "Kampen," N760
42.2	L	LF3a sign "Zwolle"
42.4	R	LF3a Zwolsesteeg
43.4	R	LF3a Korenbeltweg
44.6	L	LF3a N760
48.3	L	(no LF3a sign) Zuiderzeeroute sign
49.4	L	LF3a Van Asseltweg
50.0	R	(no LF3a sign) Hartogsweg
51.1	L	LF3a
51.5	SS R	thatched house/vegetable garden
51.6	R	LF3a Koekoekseweg
52.7	R	LF3a Plasweg (10 m), L alongside church
52.8	L	LF3a Rondeweg
53.5	VL	LF3a Markerseplein, T-IJsselmuiden
53.6	R	LF3a Dorpsweg
53.7	L	LF3a Baan
54.2	L	LF3a Sportlaan
54.3	R	LF3a Burg. van Engelenweg
54.6	L	LF3a over IJssel River (Stadsbrug/bridge)
54.9	R	Oudestraat
55.3	End	VVV Kampen

Kampen

The Hanseatic town Kampen was an IJssel River trading port dating back to the Middle Ages. Its center is extremely well preserved. Kampen, famed for its beautiful skyline of spires, towers, and turrets, is best viewed from the bridge across the IJssel River. The Stadhuis is one of the most visited buildings: the Oude (old) Stadhuis was built in 1543, and the Nieuwe (new) built in the 18th century (closed weekends). The three *poorten* (city gates), Broederspoort, Cellebroederspoort, and Koornmarktspoort, are remnants from the old city fortifications. Two more sights are the 14th century St. Nicholaaskerk, or Bovenkerk, with its 70 m (230 ft) tower (open Mondays through Fridays, April through September) and the Nieuwe Toren (open Wednesdays and Saturdays, 2 p.m. to 5 p.m., May through September).

There are several boat trips on the IJssel and surrounding waterways that can be booked through the VVV.

Information:	Kampen's VVV (Tel. 0900 112 2375, www.vvvkampen.nl) and ANWB (Tel. 038 331 3500) share a location at Oudestraat 15. For internet access, the library is at Kennedylaan 4 (Tel. 038 331 2101).
Bicycle Shops:	At the station is Spruijt Rijwiel, Stationsplein 1 (Tel. 038 331 5079), and in the center, Potkamp, Oudestraat 152 (038 331 3495), does repairs and has rentals.
Where to Stay:	Book Kampen's two hotels in advance. Hotel van Dijk, on the river at IJsselkade 30 (Tel. 038 331 4925, www.hotelvandijk.nl), has singles for €49 and doubles for €72.50. Logement Het Buitenhof, Voorstraat 80 (Tel. 038 333 8998, hetbuitenhof@tiscali.nl), has rooms and apartments; single rooms are €30, doubles are €50, and breakfast is €7.50. Kampen has several B&Bs, which should be reserved but can be booked by the VVV when you arrive.
	There are three campgrounds in the vicinity: Camping Seveningen, Frieseweg 7 (Tel. 038 331 4891, seveningen@planet.nl, open April through October), Camping Roggebotsluis, Reeveweg (Tel. 038 331 7351, www.campingroggebotsluis.nl, open April through September), and Mini-camping De Kattewaard, Kattewaardweg 8 (Tel. 038 331 1866, www.kattewaard.nl, open April through October).

Kampen's famous skyline, viewed from across the IJssel River.

Where to Eat: Walk along Oudestraat and you'll find lots of dining, including Greek cuisine at Rhodos, Oudestraat 184 (Tel. 038 332 2777), and Chinese-Indonesian at Kota Radja, Oudestraat 119 (Tel. 038 332 4419). For fish and Dutch specialties, head to IJsselkade 45, D'Olde Vismark (Tel. 038 331 3490), or IJsselkade 59, Restaurant De IJssel (Tel. 038 332 1001).

Day 2: Kampen to Zwolle (22.4 km)

From the center, return to the east bank of the IJssel the way you came in. Here, the LF3a is now officially the Hanzeroute. You will be on top of the dike for part of the route, riding along pastures. Pass the small village of Wilsum, which boasts one of the oldest churches in the Netherlands, dating back to the 11th century. Although just a village today, it received its city charter in the 12th century.

Continue along the river. Around Zwolle is a mass of suburbs that have spread outward from the center to the river. After 't Engelse Werk gardens (18.8 km), the route turns left to the center, 4 km from the river.

Cue Sheet

0.0	Start	VVV Kampen
		go SE on Oudestraat
0.4	L	Vispoort (50m), CS Stadsbrug
0.7	R	LF3a Hanzeroute, Zwolseweg
1.6	VR	LF3a along IJssel (river on R)
6.1	CS	T-Wilsum
9.5	VR	LF3a along IJssel (river on R)
11.8	CS	LF3a
15.1	R	LF3a Turnhoutsweg (at bridge)
15.2	R	LF3a bike path
15.5	CS	LF3a unmarked (not Meenteweg)
15.6	R	LF3a Nilantsweg
16.4	R	LF3a over two small bridges
16.6	CS !	LF3a R, then L onto bike path
17.0	R	LF3a
17.1	CS	LF3a 't Engelse Werk

17.3	R	LF3a
18.2	CS	Schellerdijk
18.8	L !	LF16a Schellerenkweg/Schellerallee
20.6	L	LF16a Schellerweg
20.8	CS	under railway (50 m), VR Van Karnebeekpad
21.4	CS	Van Karnebeekstraat
21.8	L	Burg. van Roijensingel
21.9	R	Sassenpoort (SS see Zwolle, below)
22.1	CS	Sassenstraat
22.3	R	follow Sassenstraat
22.4	End	VVV Zwolle

Zwolle

The rich history of this Hanseatic stronghold is evidenced by a star shaped moat and remnants of ancient fortifications which separate the center from the suburbs. The magnificent Sassenpoort (21.9 km), with its four octagonal turrets, built in 1406, still guards the southeastern entrance to the city.

In the center, the Grote Kerkplein is framed by the 14th century Grote Kerk (St. Michaelskerk), with its 17th century, 4000-pipe Schnitger organ, and the old and new town halls. The Stedelijk Museum Zwolle, Melkmarkt 41 (www. museumzwolle.nl, closed Mondays), with its 17th century furnishings, ceramics, and silverware, has contemporary art exhibits in the new wing.

A specialty of Zwolle is *blauwvingers* (blue fingers), a shortbread finger with a chocolate tip. Excellent ones can be found at Van Orsouw bakery, on the corner facing the Grote Kerk.

Information:	VVV Zwolle is at Grote Kerkplein 15, but enter on Sassenstraat (Tel. 0900 112 2375, www.vvvzwolle.nl). The ANWB is at Dijkstraat 53 (Tel. 038 422 5940). Internet access is at the library, Diezerstraat 80 (Tel. 038 421 7278).
Bicycle Shops:	At the station is Rijwielshop Zwolle, Stationsplein 15 (Tel. 038 421 4598), and in the center is Scholten Tweewielers, Luttekestraat 13 (Tel. 038 421 7378). Both offer rentals.
Where to Stay:	For a city of Zwolle's size, hotels are scarce and expensive. An alternative is Hattem (see below), or one of the half dozen B&Bs in Zwolle. Centrally located and reasonably priced, City Hotel is at Rode Torenplein 10 (Tel. 038 421 8182, www.hotelzwolle.com); singles are €74.50 and

doubles are €82. Bilderberg Grand Hotel Wientjes, Stationsweg 7 (Tel. 038 425 4254, www.grandhotelwientjes. nl), is a grand hotel with grand prices; singles are €175 and doubles go for €210.

Camping Agnietenberg, Haerstereerweg 27 (Tel. 038 453 1530, www.campingagnietenberg.nl, open April through September), is on the Vecht River northeast of town. Mini-Camping De Bakspieker, Hessenweg 14 (Tel. 038 453 3999), is open April through October.

Where to Eat: City Hotel (see "Where to Stay") has a Balkan restaurant. For Italian food, Ristorante Michelangelo is at Sassenstraat 27 (Tel. 038 423 0943, closed Mondays), and at Sassenstraat 54, La Cucaracha (Tel. 038 421 8172, www.cucaracha.nl), specializes in Mexican meals. For Chinese-Indonesian fare, there is Kota Radja, Melkmarkt 50 (Tel. 038 421 3534). There are plenty of restaurants around the Grote Kerkplein.

Hattem

Across the IJssel and southwest of Zwolle is the small Hanzestad Hattem, a side trip or a lovely alternative to staying in Zwolle. There are four B&Bs, two campgrounds, several restaurants, and two bike shops.

It can be reached by using the small ferry 't Kleine Veer (see Day 3, 4.5 km), which operates mid-April to mid-October, 10 a.m. to 6 p.m., and costs €1 for an adult and bike. On the Hattem side of the river, follow the bike path about 1 km until you cross a bridge, where a sign will point you toward the center. If you are traveling outside ferry operating times, Hattem can be reached from Zwolle by using the bridge over the IJssel just north of 't Engelse Werk.

Hattem received its city charter in the 14th century. On the main square is the Dutch Reformed Church, parts of which date to the 12th century. The Stadhuis, built in 1619, is also on the main square, close to the VVV, Kerkhofstraat 2 (Tel. 038 444 3014, www.vvvhattem.nl). On the west side of town, part of the old castle walls remain, although the castle is gone. At the edge of town is an elegant windmill. Hattem has three small museums, including the Bakkerijmuseum (Bakery Museum, Kerkhofstraat 13, Tel. 038 444 1715, closed Mondays).

Return to Zwolle either by ferry or via the bridge about 1 km north of Hattem across the IJssel.

Day 3: Zwolle to Zutphen (59.1 km)

From the center of Zwolle, rejoin the LF3a alongside the IJssel (3.5 km). The side trip (4.5 km) indicates the turn to the ferry to Hattem (see "Hattem" above).

A blemish on the route is the large power plant (6.0 km). The LF3a route skirts the power plant; you will turn left onto Harculosepad about 50 m before the power plant.

Continue until you reach the tiny village of Windesheim, not much more than a cluster of houses. Just as you turn (11.7 km), note the impressive gateway on your left, the entrance to the 16th century Windesheim House. In 1944, bombs destroyed all but the smaller outbuildings, the grounds, and this gate.

At 16.1 km, the route goes through a *natuurgebied* (nature area), a breeding and nesting area for birds. This bike path is open from May 1 to November 1. (From November through April, LF3a signs offer an alternate route along the N337 and through Wijhe, rejoining the route at 19.4 km.)

From Wijhe, the route veers away from the IJssel to Olst. At 28.6 km, notice the 15th century castle, Kasteel Groot Hoenlo, guarded by two ferocious stone lions. From here, cycle along a canal, and then through a forest laced with walking paths. Trail maps are available at the information center (31.2 km). The forest continues to Diepenveen.

From Diepenveen, cycle through a farming area. At 36.2 km, don't be tempted to follow the road; turn onto the dirt path, Kozakkenweg, and follow that 300 m before making a quick turn onto the IJsseldijk, which leads back to the IJssel and to Deventer.

At 40.6 km, you reach the small ferry (it operates daily until 8 p.m., fare is 75 cents for an adult with bike). At this point, the LF3a crosses the IJssel. To visit Deventer, continue straight for 200 m, turn left, and go for 50 m on the tiny passage that leads to the Grote Kerkhof (past the massive Grote Kerk). Then turn left onto Lange Bisschopstraat. After 200 m, turn right onto Korte Bisschopstraat, and in 100 m, you arrive at the Brink, Deventer's center. On your left is Keizerstraat, on which, 200 m further, is Deventer's VVV.

Since Deventer is as suitable a place to break for the night as Zwolle or Zutphen, details about the city are provided below. To continue to Zutphen, see page 158.

Cue Sheet

0.0	Start	VVV Zwolle
		go SE on Sassenstraat to Sassenpoort
0.3	VR !	R side of Sassenpoort (20 m) R
0.4	L	Burg. van Roijensingel (60 m), R Van Karnebeekstraat
1.0	CS	under railway
1.4	L	Schellerweg
1.6	R	Schellerallee/Schellerenkweg
3.3	VL	Schellerdijk
3.5	CS	LF3a (Hanzeroute)

Map 10.2. Overijsssel & Gelderland, Hanzeroute Tour, Day 3.

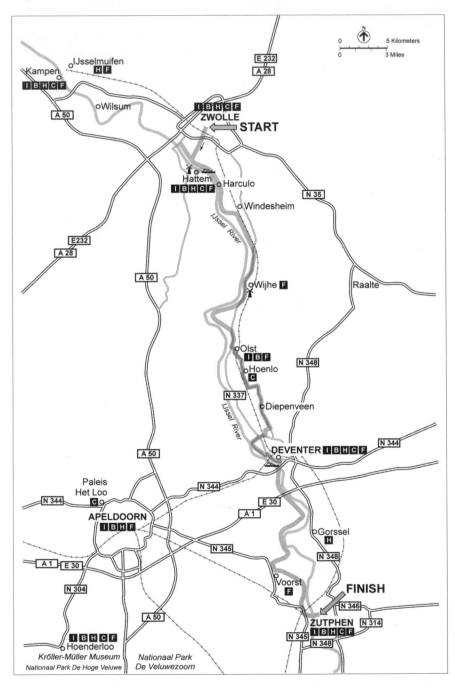

4.5	ST R	Hattem (Kleine Veerpad to ferry 500 m)
4.7	L	LF3a Kleine Veerweg
4.8	R	LF3a Oldeneelweg
5.2	R	LF3a Oldeneelweg
5.9	VR	bike path up to dike
7.0	L	LF3a Prof. Feldmannweg
7.3	R	LF3a unmarked
8.0	L	LF3a Harculosepad
8.3	L	LF3a Harculosepad
8.7	R	LF3a Jan van Arkelweg
8.9	L	LF3a Fabrieksweg
9.9	R	(no LF3a sign) Fabrieksweg
11.0	L	Windescheimerweg
11.7	R	Bulderingseweg (SS castle on L)
13.0	R	LF3a (to dike)
13.2	L	LF3a onto dike
16.1	R	LF3a Natuurgebied (Nature reserve)
18.5	L	LF3a Veerweg
19.0	L	(cross N337) Raalterweg
19.4	R	LF3a Enkweg, T-Wijhe
20.3	VR	LF3a Scherpenzeelseweg
21.6	R	(cross N337) bike path through forest (dirt bike path 1 km)
22.8	L	LF3a Fortmonderweg
23.2	L	LF3a Fortmonderweg
23.8	CS	onto dike
24.6	CS	(cross N337) Rijksstraatweg
26.0	L	LF3a De Meente
26.1	R	LF3a Kornet van Limburg/Stirumstraat
26.8	L	LF3a Aaldert Geertsstraat, T-Olst
27.3	R	LF3a Koekoeksweg

27.6	R	LF3a Diepenveenseweg
28.6	L	LF3a Hoenloseweg
28.6	SS L	Groot Hoenlo (castle)
29.3	R	LF3a Eikelhofweg
30.2	R	LF3a #20534 Molenweg
32.8	R	Randerstraat (10 m), L Molenweg #23924 sign "Deventer"
34.1	VR	#23922 Molenweg sign "Deventer"
34.4	L	LF3a Dorpsstraat, T-Diepenveen
34.7	VL	LF3a Oranjelaan
35.1	R	LF3a Wetermansweg
36.2	CS !	LF3a Kozakkenweg (dirt path)
36.5	L	LF3a IJsseldijk (10 m), R bike path (to IJssel)
37.9	R	LF3a Rembrandtkade/Onder de Linden
40.6	U R	LF3a to ferry
40.6	ST L	800 m to VVV Deventer T-Deventer
40.7	-	ferry (across IJssel)
40.7	L	LF3a (other side) Bolwerksweg
44.1	R !	#23694 (20 m), L Oyseweg
45.0	R	LF3a Oyseweg
46.0	R	LF3a Oyseweg
46.6	R	LF3a Marsstraat
47.2	L	LF3a #23815 Houtwalstraat
48.6	R	LF3a #23849 Nijenbeekseweg
49.5	L	LF3a De Halmen (1 km dirt bike path)
50.6	L	LF3a Rijksstraatsweg (unmarked)
51.3	L !	(no LF3a sign) Wilhelminaweg
51.7	L	LF3a Kerkstraat
52.2	L	LF3a Voorsterklei
55.8	L	LF3a IJsselstraat
57.6	L	LF3a Weg naar Voorst

58.0	L	over Oude IJsselbrug (bridge)
58.7	CS	Molengracht
59.0	L	Stationsstraat
59.1	End	VVV Zutphen (on R), railway station (ahead)

Deventer

This Hanzestad centers on the Brink, where the highlight is the Waag, the 15th century weigh house. Today a museum of local history, it also has an exhibit of antique bicycles. Also on the Brink is the Speelgoed en Blikmuseum (Toys and Tins Museum), with its collection of vintage toys and antique packaging tins. The website for both museums is www.deventermusea.nl; both are closed Mondays.

Head up Bergstraat to the Bergkwartier (Hill Quarter). View the town and Deventer's other famous church, the Romanesque St. Lebuinuskerk, from the 12th century St. Nicholaas Church, or Berg Church.

Information:	The VVV/ANWB is about halfway between the Brink and the railway station, at Keizerstraat 22 (Tel. 0570 691 410, www.vvvdeventer.nl). Internet access is at the library, Brink 70 (Tel. 0570 675 700).
Bicycle Shop:	Dicks Fietspoint is at Stationsplein 2 (Tel. 0570 613 832) and has rentals.
Where to Stay:	The charming Hotel De Leeuw, Nieuwstraat 25 (0570 610 290, www.hoteldeleeuw.nl), has rooms from €83. The Gilde Hotel, Nieuwstraat 41 (Tel. 0570 641 846, www.gildehotel.nl), once a convent, has singles from €85 and doubles from €100. There are six B&Bs in Deventer; check with the VVV.
	The nearest hostel, Stayokay Gorssel, Dortherweg 34 (Tel. 0573 431 615, www.stayokay.com/gorssel), is halfway between Deventer and Zutphen, on the other side of the river from the route, and is 5 km east of Gorssel.
	Camping De Worp, Worp 12 (Tel. 0570 613 60, www.idemax.nl), across the IJssel River and to the right of the ferry, is open April through September.
Where to Eat:	There are many restaurants on the Brink. Deventer's ethnic offerings include Balkan, Greek, Indian, Japanese, Thai, Dutch, and Indonesian food. The VVV has a free pamphlet, *Lekker Eten in Deventer*, listing about 40 restaurants.

To continue to Zutphen, take the ferry. LF3a signs direct you left (south) along the IJssel. From Deventer to Zutphen, the peaceful route takes you along the river and beside fields. Be careful to follow the LF3a at 44.1 km, mushroom #23694, as it's easy to continue along the river and miss the turn inland.

The route skirts Voorst and heads back toward the IJssel, which you cross by bridge to enter Zutphen.

Zutphen

Zutphen received its city charter in 1190, and was an important Hanseatic trading port at the confluence of the IJssel and Berkel Rivers. The city radiates from the Wijnhuis, an architecturally striking 17th century building, where Groenmarkt and Houtmarkt meet.

On the 's-Gravenhof square is the 15th century Stadhuis, as well as the13th century Romanesque St. Walburgskerk, with its frescoes and 15th century chandelier. The library (www.walburgskerk.nl, open May through September, closed Sundays), one of the oldest in Western Europe, is entirely original, including several books chained to the lecterns where they were read. Among the items on display are illuminated manuscripts and a 16th-century tomes. Near 's-Gravenhof, in the ramparts, is Drogenapstoren, an impressive turreted city gate dating to 1444.

Zutphen has three museums: the Stedelijk Museum at Rozengracht 3 exhibits silver, glassware, and clocks; the Grafisch Museum, Kerkhof 16, has a collection of printing presses; and the Museum Henriette Polak, Zaadmarkt 88, has contemporary art, as well as a secret chapel (dating from 1628), a refuge for Catholics. All museums are closed Mondays.

Information:	VVV/ANWB Zutphen are at Stationsplein 39 (VVV Tel. 0900 269 2888, www.vvvzutphen.nl, ANWB Tel. 0575 519 0355). Internet access is at the library, Broederenkerkplein 2 (Tel. 0575 512 926).
Bicycle Shop:	Rijwielshop Kranendijk is at Stationsplein 12 (Tel. 0575 519 327) and has rentals.
Where to Stay:	Die Schuyt, 's-Gravenhof 20 (Tel. 0575 543 501, www.overnachtenzutphen.nl), is in a 15th century house; singles are €39 and doubles are €54. The charming Berkhotel, Marspoortstraat 19 (Tel. 0575 511 135, www.berkhotel.nl), has singles from €40 and doubles from €55. The historic Hotel Volkshuis, Houtmarkt 62 (Tel. 0575 513 580, www.volkshuis.nl), has singles from €35, doubles from €55. There are about ten B&Bs in Zutphen listed on the VVV website.
	Both the campgrounds are about 3 km east in Warnsveld. The small Mini-camping 't Olthof (Tel. 0575 551 378) is at

Dennendijk 12. Camping Warnsveld, Warkenseweg 7 (Tel. 0575 431 338), is larger. Both are open April through October.

Where to Eat: Zutphen's most well-known restaurant, famed for vegetarian cuisine, is De Kloostertuin in the Berkhotel (see "Where to Stay," closed Mondays). In the Wijnhuis, Groenmarkt 40, Primo Piano (Tel. 0575 549 036) serves Italian food, and in the cellar, Tapasbar Loona-tic (Tel. 0575 549 962) serves tapas and Spanish fare. Tong Ah, Groenmarkt 27 (Tel. 0575 519 370), has Chinese-Indonesian food. At Turfstraat 5, De Gelaardse Kat (Tel. 0575 545 541) specializes in meals cooked on a lava grill (closed Tuesdays). Next door, at Turfstraat 7, Grand Café Chapeau (Tel. 0575 547 768) serves Dutch and French cuisine (closed Sundays).

Day 4: Zutphen to Nijmegen (85.4 km)

Continue along the IJssel, stopping in Bronkhorst and Doesburg. Although this is a long day, the cycling is easy along the river. Doesburg makes a pleasant overnight stop for if the ride is too long. Halfway through the day, the LF3a changes its name from the Hanzeroute to the Maasroute.

Today, you cross the IJssel twice. The first crossing (4.0 km) is over an enormous bridge on the N348 south of Zutphen. On the other side, cycle through fields to the second crossing (11.3 km), this time via the Veerpont Bronkhorst, a small cable-operated ferry (60 cents, June through September, weekdays until 8 p.m., weekends until 6 p.m.; October through May, weekends only).

Tiny Bronkhorst received its city charter in 1482. Today, with its 200 inhabitants, this "city" of thatched cottages and cobbled streets is the smallest chartered city in the Netherlands. Picturesque Bronkhorst is popular with Dutch tourists who frequent its galleries, antique shops, and restaurants. A surprise for Dickens fans is the Dickens Museum, Onderstraat 2 (Tel. 0575 451 623, www. dickensmuseum.nl), full of Charles Dickens memorabilia. Outside Bronkhorst is the Bronkhorster Molen (13.0 km), a grain mill (open Saturdays, 10 a.m. to 5 p.m.).

Continue through rural landscape, skirting the town of Rha, to Olburgen. You will see signs for the Canadian Pancakehouse (with Canadian-style pancakes) as you leave Olburgen. The beautiful bike path along the river from Olburgen is popular with both Dutch and German cyclists. It's no surprise that several campgrounds are located here. Be careful of the several cattle grates on this bike path.

Doesburg, a prosperous town in the Middle Ages, is also a Hanzestad. Two stunning buildings are the Waag and the Stadhuis. The gabled Waag, with tall, shuttered windows, dates from 1478 and is now a restaurant. Close by is the 15th century Gothic Martinikerk. The Mosterd en Azijnmuseum (Mustard and Vinegar Museum, Boekholtstraat 22, Tel. 0313 472 230, closed Sundays and Mondays) is a mustard factory founded in 1457 which still makes mustard traditionally in small wooden barrels.

VVV Doesburg is at Kerkstraat 6 (Tel. 0313 479 088, www.vvvdoesburg.nl). Doesburg has one hotel, about ten B&Bs, and several restaurants.

From Doesburg, the LF3a route hugs the IJssel, above the river on car-free dikes and bike paths or small dike-top roads. There are more cattle grates. Two with especially widely spaced grates are at 27.9 km and 29.9 km. The only blot, a huge water management plant (40.0 km), is just before you go under the freeway. After the A12, the LF3a sign pointing out the route on the IJsseldijk is missing (41.6 km).

At 47.9 km, the Hanzeroute becomes the Maasroute. You have left the IJssel and are cycling along the Pannerdens Kanaal to the Rijn (Rhine River). At 51.0 km, the route descends the dike. At the time of writing, the new Betuwe railway line was being constructed here, and no compensation had been made for the interrupted LF3a route. The directions from 51.0 km to 55.8 km take you alongside, then over the railway lines on a bridge, and back to the Pannerdens Kanaal. This portion may be different when the railway is completed.

Once back on the LF3a route along the canal, cycle to the Millingen ferry to cross the Rijn. It runs hourly from 8 a.m. to 6 p.m. from April through September, and every two hours until 5 p.m. the rest of the year. From April through September, there is one extra boat at 8 p.m. The cost is €1.10 for an adult and bike. In Millingen is one hotel and there are a few B&Bs.

The LF3a to Nijmegen begins on the dike high above the Waal River. It turns inland through farmlands and passes the village of Ooij. From here, the LF3a route traverses an area called Groenlanden, a "green" area of lakes, ponds, and shade trees, before heading to Nijmegen on the Ooijse Bandijk. Enter Nijmegen (83.0 km) along the Waal, and pass the Velorama Bicycle Museum (83.4 km) on Waalkade before continuing uphill to the station. The VVV is 300 m east of the station.

Cue Sheet

0.0	Start	Zutphen Railway Station/VVV go SE on Stationsstraat
0.1	R	Molengracht
0.4	L	LF3a IJsselkade
0.6	L	LF3a Marspoortstraat
0.9	R	LF3a Lange Hofstraat
1.2	L	LF3a Martinetsingel/Vispoortplein
1.3	R	LF3a Vispoortstraat
1.8	R	LF3a bike path
3.7	R	LF3a (90 m), CS LF3a (to bridge)

4.0	CS	LF3a bridge over IJssel
6.1	R	LF3a unmarked
7.4	CS	Cortenoeverseweg
9.6	L	LF3a Bronkhorsterweg
10.3	L	LF3a to ferry
11.3	-	LF3a ferry - Veerpont Bronkhorst

Map 10.3. Overijsssel & Gelderland, Hanzeroute Tour, Day 4.

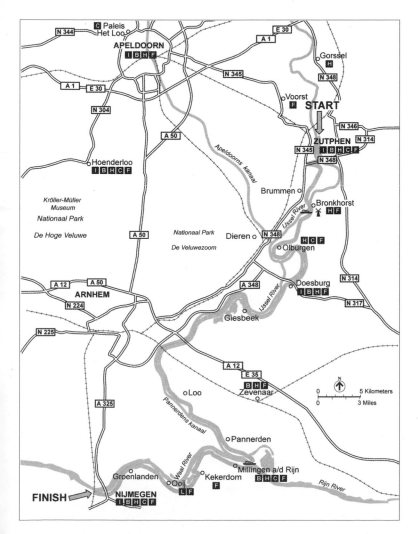

11.3	CS	(other side) Veerweg
11.9	VR	LF3a Bovenstraat, T-Bronkhorst
12.3	R	LF3a Molenstraat
13.0	R	LF3a #24008 Spaenweertweg
13.0	SS L	Bronkhorster Molen (grain mill)
13.2	L	LF3a Emmerweg
15.6	L	LF3a #23666 Rhabergseweg
15.7	R	LF3a Prinsenmatweg
16.8	L	LF3a Rhabergseweg (20 m), LF3a Olburgseweg
18.2	CS	Olburgseweg/Dierenseweg, T-Olburgen
18.7	L	LF3a bike path along IJssel
22.6	CS	LF3a bike path along IJssel
23.3	VR	LF3a bike path along IJssel
24.2	VR	LF3a bike path along IJssel
25.3	L	LF3a Verhuellweg
25.4	R	LF3a Panovenweg
25.9	CS	LF3a Koepoortdijk
26.3	L	LF3a Koepoortstraat, T-Doesburg
26.5	SS	Waag and Stadhuis
26.6	CS	Kerkstraat, VVV on R
27.7	R	LF3a Kosterstraat/Kloosterstraat
26.9	L	LF3a Veerpoortwal
27.2	R	LF3a Barend Ubbinkweg
27.7	SS	locks
27.9	R	LF3a bike path along the IJssel
29.9	R	LF3a/N338
31.2	VR	LF3a bike path along the IJssel
32.7	R	LF3a (not to Giesbeek)
32.9	VL	LF3a bike path along the IJssel
33.8	R	LF3a Kerkstraat

33.9	L	LF3a Strandpad
35.8	L	LF3a (10 m), R bike path along N338
37.2	CS	LF3a Bandijk
40.6	R	LF3a under A12
41.6	R !	(no LF3a sign) IJsseldijk
43.7	R	LF3a Veerdam
44.0	VL	LF3a Pleydijk
44.6	VR	LF3a bike path
47.1	R	LF3a
47.9	CS	Hanzeroute/Maasroute, Loodijk
50.4	VR	LF3a bike path along Pannerdens Kanaal
51.0	VL	LF3a bike path
51.3	R	LF3a sign "Pannerden," Den Oldenhoek (along railway line)
53.1	R	Schraleweidsestraat
53.6	R	Rijnstrangenweg
55.3	L	to Kanaal
55.8	L	bike path along Pannerdens Kanaal
58.8	CS	Rijndijk, T-Pannerden (on L)
60.9	R	LF3a sign "Millingen," Lobberdenseweg
62.4	L	LF3a Kijwaard voetveer (pedestrian/bicycle ferry)
63.0	R	ferry
63.7	R	LF3a to ferry
63.8	-	ferry
63.9	CS	up ramp (other side)
64.0	R	LF3a Maasroute Rijndijk (along Rijn)
65.8	CS	Millingse Bandijk/Duffeltdijk
67.0	CS	T-Kekerdom
70.3	CS	(no LF3a sign) Duffeltdijk
71.7	CS	LF3a Kapitteldijk
73.7	R	LF3a Kerkdijk

75.7	L	LF3a Kerkdijk, T-Ooij
75.8	R	LF3a Kerkdijk
76.9	R	LF3a Spruitenkamp
77.7	L	LF3a Ooijse Bandijk
78.3	L	LF3a Langstraat
78.7	SS	Groenlanden
79.9	L	LF3a Ooijse Bandijk
83.0	R	LF3a 't Meertje/Waalkade
83.4	SS L	Velorama Bicycle Museum
83.9	RA VR	LF3a sign "Station"
84.4	L	Veemarkt sign "Station"
84.6	L	LF3a Lange Hezelstraat
84.7	R	Kronenburgersingel
84.9	R	LF3a Kronenburgersingel
85.4	End	Nijmegen Railway Station

Nijmegen

Nijmegen is the oldest city in the Netherlands, and the only one built on several hills. From the remains of the Valkhof Palace, built on one of these hills, there are fabulous views over the Waal River. The belvedere, originally a 17th-century tower (part of the city walls), is now a restaurant.

Nijmegen was badly damaged in World War II. On the Grote Markt are the Waag, built in 1612, and the massive 13th-century Gothic St. Stevenskerk have

Housed in a historic building on the Waalkade in Nijmegen, Nationaal Fietsmuseum Velorama has one of Europe's finest bicycle history collections on display.

survived. Climb its tower for panoramic views (open June through August, closed Sundays and Mondays).

Every cyclist will want to visit the Nationaal Fietsmuseum Velorama (Bicycle Museum), Waalkade 107 (Tel. 024 322 5851, www.velorama.nl, open daily; see boxed text "Velorama" below). The Museum Het Valkhof, Kelfkensbos 59 (www. museumhetvalkhof, closed Mondays), has local history and art, plus Roman artifacts.

Annually, in mid-July, Nijmegen hosts the Wandelvierdaagse, a four-day, 200 km walking event in the area around Nijmegen that draws thousands of people.

Information:	VVV Nijmegen is at Keizer Karelplein 2 (Tel. 0900 112 2344, www. vvvnijmegen.nl). The ANWB is at Bisschop Hamerstraat 3 (phone 024 322 2378). Internet access is available at the library, Marienburg 29 (Tel. 024 327 4911).
Bicycle Shops:	You can rent bikes at Rijwielshop Nijmegen, Stationsplein 7 (Tel. 024 322 9618). In the center is Kersten Wielersport at Stikke Hezelstraat 19 (Tel. 024 322 6362, www.kerstenwielersport.nl).
Where to Stay:	The City Park Hotel, Hertogstraat 1 (Tel. 024 322 0498, www. cityparkhotel.nl), has singles for €48 and doubles from €75. About 1 km from the center is Catharina Hotel, St. Annastraat 64 (Tel. 024 323 1251, www.hotel-catharina.nl), where singles without private facilities cost €27 and doubles are €54; singles with private facilities are €33 and doubles are €65. Nijmegen has about six B&Bs; check with the VVV.
	Camping de Kwakkenberg, Luciaweg 10 (Tel. 024 323 2443), is 3 km south of town. Near Berg en Dal, Camping Maikenshof is at Oude Kleefsebaan 134A (Tel. 024 684 1651). Both are open April through October.
Where to Eat:	There are several restaurants around the Grote Markt. Waalkade is lined with restaurants and cafés. In the City Park Hotel (see "Where to Stay"), the Oporto Restaurant has excellent Mediterranean-style food. Humphreys, Vismarkt 7 (Tel. 024 360 2880, www.humphreys.nl), has interesting, reasonably priced three-course meals for €17.

Velorama: National Bicycle Museum

Housing the largest collection of historic bicycles in western Europe, this museum has over 250 bicycles dating from the early 19th century to the present, plus other bicycle-related items, including military bicycles and authentic cycling posters from the early days of advertising. A separate room is devoted to the Dutch bicycle industry. The museum has a café, appropriately named Café Velocitas.

Ride 2: Seven Hills Day Trip

Total Distance:	22.3 km
Duration:	Half day
Highlights:	Hills, views to Germany, Zevenheuvelenweg
Terrain:	Low hills
When to Go:	Year-round
Maps:	Michelin 532 Zuid-Nederland/Pays-Bas Sud, ANWB/VVV Toeristenkaart Gelders Rivierengebied
Start/Finish:	Nijmegen/Nijmegen
Access:	Nijmegen Railway Station
Connecting routes:	Link to "Hanzeroute" (page 143)

This ride dispels the theory that the Netherlands is flat. Leave your luggage at your lodging for a more enjoyable ride. Most of the hills aren't difficult, but there is one short, steep climb.

From Nijmegen, cycle along a small river, passing the village of Persingen, before turning right to Beek. Go through Beek, past the churches in the center (7.8 km). You will see the ascent as you round the corner (7.9 km); the next 700 m are the steepest climb of the day.

At the top, in Berg en Dal (8.9 km), turn left and then immediately right onto Zevenheuvelenweg (Seven Hills Road). Zevenheuvelenweg continues to Groesbeek.

A side trip en route (9.6 km) takes you to the Afrikamuseum. Turn right onto Meerwijkselaan and go 800 m; then turn left onto Postweg and ride 200 m. The museum (www. afrikamuseum.nl, open daily, closed Mondays November through March) has African masks, sculptures, plus reconstructions of dwellings.

Return to Zevenheuvelenweg. To the east is Germany (11.5 km). On the left (11.7 km) are solemn reminders of the ravages of war, the Canadian War Cemetery and the Groesbeek Memorial.

At 13.2 km, turning left and descending 1.0 km takes you into pleasant Groesbeek, with its shops, restaurants, and a windmill. En route, the Bevrijdingsmuseum (Liberation Museum, Tel. 024 397 4404, open daily), is located where the 82nd Airborne Division landed in 1944. The Dome of Honor, shaped like a stylized parachute and visible from Zevenheuvelenweg, honors the hundreds of Allied soldiers who died in Nijmegen. Turning right takes you along Nieuweweg and back to Nijmegen.

Once on Nijmeegsebaan (14.3 km), you glide down into the outskirts of Nijmegen on a forested road for 4 km. In Nijmegen, pass the university and rows of stately homes to reach the station.

Cue Sheet

0.0	Start	Nijmegen Railway Station go N on Stieltjesstraat (LF3b sign)
0.3	VL	LF3b Kronenburgersingel
0.5	L	Lange Hezelstraat (40 m), R Veemarkt
0.8	R	~~Waalkade~~
1.4	RA CS	LF3b Waalkade
1.3	SS R	Velorama Bicycle Museum
1.9	CS	Ubbergseweg (under Waalbrug)
2.2	L	LF3b Ooijsedijk
2.3	R	Dijkgraaf van Wijckweg
4.9	R	Persingensestraat
5.5	CS	T-Persingen
6.3	R	sign "Beek," St. Hubertusweg/Verbindingsweg
7.0	CS	cross N325

Map 10.4. Overijsssel & Gelderland, Seven Hills Day Trip.

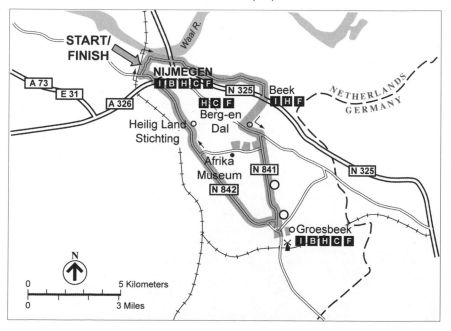

167

7.4	L	Waterstraat
7.7	R	Waterstraat, T-Beek
7.9	L !	Van der Veurweg/Bosweg (steep climb)
8.4	VR	Nieuwe Holleweg
8.6	VR	Nieuwe Holleweg (bike path on L)
8.9	L	Oude Kleefsebaan, T-Berg en Dal
9.0	R	Zevenheuvelenweg
9.3	VR !	Zevenheuvelenweg (N841)
9.6	L	Zevenheuvelenweg (N841)
9.6	ST R	RT = 2 km, Afrikamuseum
11.5	SS L	views of Germany
11.7	SS L	Canadian War Cemetery and Groesbeek Memorial
13.2	ST L	RT = 2 km, sign "Groesbeek, Bevrijdingsmuseum"
13.2	R	sign "Nijmegen," Nieuweweg
14.3	VR	sign "Nijmegen," Nijmeegsebaan (N842)
17.9	RA CS	Nijmeegsebaan (N842)
20.0	CS	Groesbeekseweg
20.8	SS L	university and houses
21.7	RA !	at Keizer Karelplein (VVV on R)
22.0	R	Van Schaeck Mathon Singel
22.3	End	Nijmegen Railway Station

Cycling the Dutch way—
wearing wooden shoes.

Ride 3: Veluwe & Het Loo

Total Distance:	102.1 km
Duration:	2 days cycling, plus 1 extra day (see note below)
Highlights:	Veluwezoom and Hoge Veluwe National Parks, Kröller-Müller Museum, Het Loo Palace
Terrain:	Low hills
When to Go:	Year-round
Maps:	Michelin 532 Zuid-Nederland/Pays-Bas Sud, ANWB/VVV Toeristenkaart Gelders Rivierengebied, ANWB/VVV Toeristenkaart Achterhoek
Start/Finish:	Zutphen/Zutphen or Deventer/Deventer
Access:	Deventer Railway Station or Zutphen Railway Station
Connecting routes:	Link to "Hanzeroute," where you can pick up the route on Day 3 of the ride in Deventer or Zutphen.

This is a circuit ride, and can begin in either Zutphen or Deventer. By starting in Deventer, you add the distance from Deventer to Zutphen (about 20 km) to Day 1, which makes it a 70 km day.

The ride takes two days, but an extra day should be allowed to fully appreciate the Hoge Veluwe National Park and the Kröller-Müller Museum (see boxed text, "A Day in the Park," page 171).

This ride, through two of the Netherlands' largest national parks, showcases the hilly heart of the country. The area known as the Veluwe encompasses two national parks: the larger Hoge Veluwe National Park and the Veluwezoom National Park. The route back to Deventer on Day 2 stops at Het Loo Palace and finishes on a serene stretch of the IJssel River.

For information on Zutphen and Deventer, see "Hanzeroute Ride" (pages 153, 157–158).

Day 1: Zutphen to Hoenderloo (49.6 km)

Cycle through the Veluwezoom National Park, going to the highest point in the Veluwe region, and end the day on the edge of the Hoge Veluwe National Park in the village of Hoenderloo.

Navigation note: Both parks are crisscrossed with largely unnamed bike paths which look the same. You will need to reference the map *ANWB/VVV Touristenkaart Gelders Rivierengebied* and pay close attention to the ANWB mushrooms.

Leave Zutphen to the south, through farmland, then forest, passing a small manor house (5.7 km) in the woods. Go through the village of Hall, and then to the

Apeldoorns Kanaal for 3 km of canal-side cycling. Soon after leaving the canal, you enter the Nationaal Park Veluwezoom (16.0 km). The 11,362-acre park is hilly, mainly pine and birch forest, with areas of heath.

At 17.2 km, you will notice an incline ahead. It's roller-coaster cycling on bike paths through forests and open heath throughout the park. The side trip to the Posbank takes you to an area of walking paths and up to 100 m (330 ft), the highest viewpoint in the park. On a clear day you can see Germany. The statue outside the restaurant near the top of the Posbank is of Queen Beatrix.

At mushroom #23444 (25.2 km), you may spot oxen grazing. At 26.5 km, the tower marks the highest point in the Veluwe, 110m (350ft). Watch for the turn at 28.3 km; mushroom #21063 was missing at the time of writing, but there is a Veluwezoomroute sign. Continue through the park; you may spot more buffalo or oxen around 30.0 km. Cycle through the Zilvense Heide, a heath area, and on to Loenen, where you exit the park.

From Loenen, the road takes you over the A50. For about 2 km before the freeway, there is no bike path; cycle on the road. After the A50 overpass, the bike path to Hoenderloo resumes.

Cue Sheet

0.0	Start	Zutphen Railway Station/VVV go SE on Stationsstraat
0.1	R	Molengracht
0.4	CS	Oude IJsselbrug
1.0	R	Kanaaldijk (over N345)
1.1	L	Oude Kanaaldijk/Zutphensestraat
3.3	R	Windheuvelstraat
5.7	SS R	manor house
8.5	L	#06934 Hallsedijk
9.3	R	#23182 Vosstraat/Dorpsstraat
10.0	CS	#21473 (at church), Hallseweg, T- Hall
11.4	L	#24032 Apeldoorns Kanaal, Rheinderenstraat
11.5	R	#23031 sign "Dieren," (tow path) along canal
12.6	CS	#24028 cross Eerbeekseweg
14.7	R	sign "Laag-Soeren," over canal
14.8	L	#20349/07735 Kanaalweg
14.9	L	Badhuislaan

15.1	CS	sign "Posbank"
15.8	VL	Badhuislaan
16.0	CS	enter Nationaal Park Veluwezoom, Schaapsallee
17.2	CS	#24245
20.4	L	#20358 sign "Posbank," Lange Juffer
20.9	R	Burg. Bloemersweg
23.9	ST L	RT = 2.2 km, sign "Posbank," #22800
23.9	R	LF4b
25.2	R	#23444 sign "Loenermark"
26.1	CS	#21064
26.5	SS L	tower/high point #21061
28.3	R !	#21063 (missing) Veluwezoomroute sign
30.4	CS	#20353
32.4	L	#24521
33.2	R	follow bike path Zilvense Heide (on L) Eerbeekse Veldpad

A Day in the Park

Hoge Veluwe National Park (www.hogeveluwe.nl), the largest nature reserve in the Netherlands, covers 13,585 acres. There are 42km of bike paths, and over 400 white bikes are offered free to visitors at the park entrances. You can buy a map of the park or simply follow the well-marked paths.

Within the park there are natural areas of heath, woodland, sand dunes and grassy fields where animals such as deer, wild boar, foxes and moufflons (wild sheep) roam. Originally the estate of Willem Kröller and his wife Hélène Müller, in the 1930s it was bequeathed to the nation.

The park truly reflects the harmony of art and nature. Located in the center is the park's highlight, the Kröller-Müller Museum (www.kmm.nl, closed Monday). Its focal point is a fabulous collection of 278 Van Goghs (they don't show all at once) plus works by Mondrian, Picasso, Toroop and other 19th and 20th-century artists, and ceramics. Surrounding the building is Europe's largest sculpture garden, covering 27 acres including pieces by Rodin, Moore and others.

North of the museum is Jachtslot St Hubertus, the Kröller-Müller's 1920s art deco hunting lodge (daily, tours only, closed January). Also in the park is Museonder (daily), an underground museum featuring displays of subterranean animals. The park has lots of picnic possibilities, plus refreshment areas. The park is best visited in good weather; avoid Monday when the museum is closed.

33.8	R	#24520 sign "Loenen"
34.0	L	#24508 (hard-packed dirt 3.5 km)
34.6	R	#24506
34.7	L	#24698
34.8	R	#24699
35.0	CS	#24507
35.7	R	no sign
36.6	VL	#24518
36.8	CS	#24532 (loose gravel)
37.1	R	#24519 sign "Loenen"
37.8	CS	unmarked road
38.4	L	Droefakkers
38.5	L	Eerbeekseweg
38.6	L	dir. "Hoenderloo," Groenendaalseweg
40.1	CS	#24516 (bike path on other side of road)
43.4	R	over A50/Oude Arnhemseweg
44.0	L	Woeste Hoefweg
47.7	CS	De Pampel camping
48.5	L	Krimweg sign "VVV"
49.6	VL/end	Krimweg (20 m), L Paarlbergweg, VVV Hoenderloo

Hoenderlo

Hoenderloo, at the northeast edge of the park, is a good base for exploring the park. It is also less than 4 km from the Kröller-Müller museum.

Another overnight option is Otterlo (www.vvvotterlo.nl), with one hotel, B&Bs, camping, and places to eat. It is only 8 km from Hoenderloo on the N304.

Information: The VVV is at Krimweg 6 (Tel. 055 576 3090, www.hoenderloo.nl).

Bicycle Shops: Essie Tweewielers, Paalbergweg 85 (Tel. 055 378 1034, www.fietsverhuur.com), rents bikes. Buitenhuis, de Fietsspecialist is at Krimweg 22 (Tel. 055 378 1318).

Where to Stay: Boerenkinkel, Middenweg 7 (Tel. 055 378 1256, www.boerenkinkel.nl), has rooms from €50. At

Apeldoornseweg 30, 1 km from the VVV, Buitenlust (Tel. 055 378 1362) is a stylish hotel with rooms for €75.

There are several campgrounds. Camping de Pampel, Woeste Hoefweg 35 (Tel. 055 378 1760, www.pampel.nl), is on the on the route (47.7 km). A small park campground is located at the Hoenderloo entrance to the park. Reservations aren't accepted, so check availability (Tel. 055 378 2232, open April through November).

Map 10.4. Veluwe & Het Loo Tour.

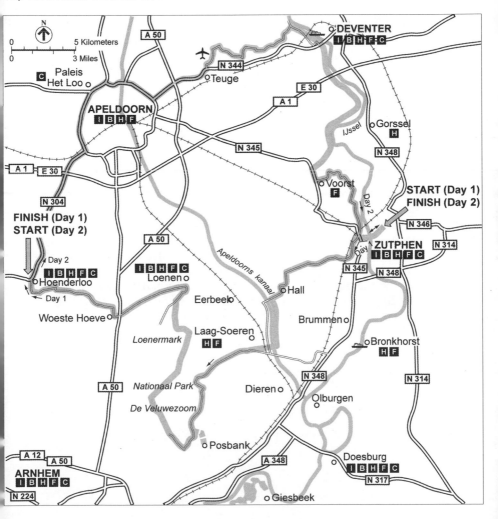

Where to Eat: Both the hotels (see "Where to Stay") have restaurants. Eetcafé De Lakai, Krimweg 28 (Tel. 055 378 1818), has traditional eetcafé fare. For pancakes, 't Pannekoekenhuis is at Krimweg 93 (055 378 1205, closed Mondays). Het Deelerhof, Krimweg 35 (055 378 1721, www.deelerhof.nl), serves Dutch, Asian, and vegetarian meals.

Day 2: Hoenderloo to Zutphen (52.5 km)

The road from Hoenderloo to Apeldoorn follows the N304, but the bike path tends to be away from traffic and is mainly through forest.

Just before you arrive at the ring road in Apeldoorn, cross Europaweg (9.2 km). This is not actually a right turn, but you cross the road to the right. At 10.8 km, you reach the ring road, which you follow through the suburbs to Column Willem III and Emma (15.2 km). At this point, there are two ways to enter the grounds of the Paleis Het Loo: go left and ride 400 m on Amersfortsweg or turn left just after the column and cycle 300 m to the entrance.

Apeldoorn itself has little appeal, but the Paleis Het Loo (www.hetloo.nl, closed Mondays) is spectacular. The magnificent 17th-century palace has been restored to exemplify the lifestyle of the House of Orange, with its art, furnishings, and tapestries. Allow time for a stroll through the well-tended formal gardens.

From the palace, continue another 4 km on the ring road. You can't turn at 17.4 km (a sign indicates "Deventer'), as this is a highway for cars only. Rather, continue to Deventerstraat/N344 (19.4 km), where there is a bike path.

Continue on the N344 until the west edge of Teuge (23.5 km). Turn onto De Zanden. This street makes three turns, but retains the same name. Pass the tiny airport (look for hang gliders if it's windy). At 29.2 km, pass a group of stylish manor houses. The route joins the IJssel River (32.1 km), along which you will cycle to Deventer. If you want to go into Deventer, take the ferry (34.1 km) across the IJssel. (See the "Hanzeroute Ride," Day 3, for directions and information.) Or continue on to Zutphen using directions from the "Hanzeroute Ride," Day 3, starting at the 40.7 km cue (Deventer to Zutphen, pages 153–157).

Cue Sheet

0.0	Start	VVV Hoenderloo go N on Paarlbergweg (20 m), L Krimweg
0.5	R	Apeldoornseweg
1.2	RA R	sign "Apeldoorn," N304 (separated bike path)
1.5	L	(30 m) R N304
7.2	L	#62865
7.3	L	#24398 (cross N304 to bike path on other side)

7.4	R	sign "Apeldoorn," N304
8.8	CS	under A1
8.9	R	sign "Apeldoorn," Van Heeckerensweg
9.2	R !	sign "Apeldoorn," cross road to Europaweg
10.8	L	(ring) Laan van Spitsbergen
12.5	CS	(ring) #20679 Laan van Spitsbergen
12.9	CS	(ring) Jachtlaan
15.2	SS L	column Willem III and Emma
15.2	ST L !	sign "Paleis Het Loo," Amersfoortsweg (N344)
15.3	CS	(ring) Zwolseweg
15.8	R	(ring) sign "Deventer," Hertenlaan (N344)
16.1	CS	(ring) Edisonlaan (N344)
17.4	CS !	(ring) Laan van Zevenhuizen (N344) dir. "Deventer"
19.5	L	sign "Deventer," Deventerstraat (N344)
23.5	L	De Zanden, T-Teuge
24.0	R	De Zanden
25.3	R	De Zanden
25.8	R	Oude Wezveldseweg
27.5	L	Quabbenburgerweg
28.3	R	Blikkenweg
29.5	L	Kruisvoorderweg
30.7	CS	unmarked, 200 m (gravel road)
30.9	L	Dijkhofstraat
31.4	R	Meemuidenseweg
32.1	R	Lage Steenweg (IJssel on L)
34.0	CS	Camping De Worp
34.1	L	ferry to Deventer
34.1	CS	to Zutphen (see "Hanzeroute," Day 3)
-	-	+ 18.4 km "Deventer," to "Zutphen"
52.5	End	VVV Zutphen (on R), station (ahead)

11.

Utrecht & South Holland

THIS RIDE goes through three provinces: North Holland, a small part of Utrecht, and South Holland. The four major cities, Amsterdam, The Hague, Rotterdam, and Utrecht, are all in the area known as the *Randstad* or Rim City, home to 40% of Dutch residents. Surprisingly, riding through this area will not feel crowded, and you will be surprised at the beauty and open space in this highly populated area. The area of lakes, rivers, and villages between the four major cities is known as *"Het Groene Hart"* (The Green Heart), or the "back garden of the Randstad." South Holland is filled with Dutch icons: tulip fields, windmills, the home of Gouda cheese.

Witches, Windmills, and the West Coast

Total Distance:	328.3 km
Duration:	7 days
Highlights:	Utrecht's Oudegracht, Kasteel de Haar, Oudewater's "witchery," Gouda, Kinderdijk windmills, Delft, Leiden's museums, tulip fields, Haarlem, Zaanse Schans, Het Twiske.
Terrain:	Level
When to Go:	Optimal months are April through October. If tulips are in your itinerary, plan from mid-April to early May. Each day starts and ends at a town with a railway station, which makes it suitable for winter day rides as well.

Maps:	Michelin 531 Noord-Nederland/Pays-Bas Nord, Michelin 532 Zuid-Nederland/Pays-Bas Sud, ANWB/VVV Toeristenkaart Utrecht, ANWB/VVV Toeristenkaart Zuid Holland
Start/Finish:	Amsterdam/Amsterdam
Access:	This ride can also start or conclude in Utrecht, Woerden, Gouda, Delft, Leiden, and Haarlem, all of which have railway stations.

Connecting routes: "Tour of North Holland" (page 67); all day trips from Amsterdam (see chapter 6)

This ride takes you through "*Het Groene Hart,*" the green heart of Holland, with its mostly level terrain. You will cycle through farmlands, forests, and sand dunes, see the highest concentration of windmills in the nation, pedal through the famous flower fields, and visit historic towns, as well as some of the main urban centers in the country.

Those who love museums of any type may have trouble getting through this route, as the selection of museums, art galleries, and cultural activities offered in the cities along the way is staggering. Haarlem, Leiden, and Utrecht are filled with world class exhibitions.

Day 1: Amsterdam to Utrecht (52.2 km)

The route takes you to Utrecht via three rivers: the Amstel, the tiny Angstel, and the gorgeous Vecht.

From the Amsterdam Centraal Station, head south on Damrak on the bike path that is often crowded with tourist pedestrians. Turn left at Muntplein onto Amstel—the name of both the river and the street. Cross the Amstel River on the Blaubrug, dating from 1883, a copy of the Alexandre III bridge in Paris, turning right onto Amstel (still the same street). On your left is the Waterlooplein. The circular building is the Stopera. The name is a combination of the words *stadhuis* (city hall) and opera, both of which are housed in this building.

The Amstel River is on your right. At 2.0 km, you'll see the Magere Brug (Skinny Bridge), a wooden drawbridge constructed in 1650. The Carré Theatre (2.1 km), with a white sculpted façade, was built in the late 19th century. The magnificent Amstel Hotel (2.3 km), overlooking the river, is one of the top hotels in the city. Look slightly right as you cross the Nieuwe Amstelbrug (2.7 km) and note the turreted buildings. You are now on the Amsteldijk; the river will be on your left until Ouderkerk a/d Amstel.

Zorgvlied Cemetery (5.7 km), built in the 18th Century, is the final resting place of many famous Amsterdammers. At 7.3 km are the Molen De Rieker, built in 1636 (closed to the public) and a statue of Rembrandt. The big wooden clog

(8.4 km) is the only indication of the Rembrandt Hoeve, a traditional cheese farm and clog maker since 1906 (Tel. 020 643 1323, closed Sundays). Look left across the Amstel (around 10.0 km); what you see is not a spaceship, but the new Ajax soccer stadium.

Ouderkerk a/d Amstel, its streets lined with lovely old row houses, dates to the 12th century. Here, you leave the Amstel, following Holendrecht on your right, winding through farmlands. At 14.9 km, go through the gate and continue on the bike path where, unlike the Damrak bike path, you will dodge sheep instead of tourists.

Cross the Angstel River in Abcoude, and continue to Baambrugge and Loenersloot. Loenersloot, the small moated castle, will be on your right (26.6 km).

It's tricky getting onto the N201 and crossing the Amsterdam-Rijnkanaal (26.9 km). Carefully follow the signs. Ultimately, you'll go east on the N201 to Vreeland, a picturesque village on the Vecht River. Just before the turn at 30.0 km, indulge yourself at Pancake House Noord Brabant (see "Lakes and Rivers Ride," page 62).

Cycle along the Vecht past stately homes and through the villages of Loenen, Nieuwersluis, and Breukelen (after which Brooklyn, New York was named). If you want to visit these villages, cross the bridges (right), then return to the route, keeping the Vecht on your right. In Breukelen, you can cross the original Breukelen Bridge, a mere 7 m (20ft) long, and wide enough for one car—hardly comparable to its New York namesake.

Before Maarssen (41.5 km), the route veers away from the Vecht, rejoining it just north of Utrecht. Go through Maarssen, and at the roundabout (43.6 km), look for the small street with a canal, the LF7a sign, and the bike sign to Maarssenveen.

After the two windmills (45.7 km), the bike path goes through 2 km of forest to the outskirts of Utrecht and rejoins the Vecht, which will be on your right (48.0 km). Starting at 49.4 km, pass a 600 m stretch of Vecht houseboats, a Red Light district. Continue through Utrecht's suburbs to the VVV.

Cue Sheet

0.0	Start	Amsterdam Central Station go S on Damrak/Rokin
1.0	L	Amstel (at Muntplein)
1.5	L	Blauwbrug (over Amstel River)
1.6	R	Amstel
1.6	SS L	Waterlooplein and Stopera
2.0	SS L	Magere Brug
2.1	SS R	Carré Theater

2.3	L	Sarphatistraat (10 m), R Prof. Tulpplein/Weesperzijde sign "Utrecht"
2.3	SS L	Amstel Hotel
2.7	R	Nieuwe Amstelbrug (at Ruyschstraat)
2.9	L	Amsteldijk

Map 11.1. Utrecht & South Holland Tour, Days 1 & 2.

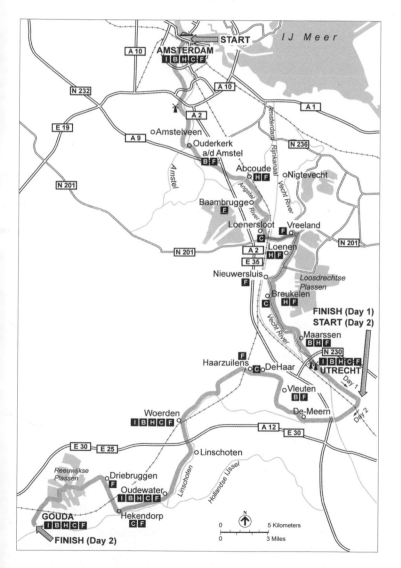

4.4	L	President Kennedylaan
4.5	R	Amsteldijk
5.7	SS R	Zorgvlied Cemetery
7.3	SS R	Molen De Rieker and Rembrandt Statue
8.4	SS R	cheese farm and clog maker
10.0	SS L	Ajax Stadium
11.3	L	over bridge, T-Ouderkerk a/d Amstel
11.4	R	Hoge Einde-Zuid/Dorpsstraat/Koningin Julianalaan/ Holendrechterweg
14.9	U L	sign "Abcoude," through gate
15.8	CS	through gate
17.3	R	sign "Abcoude," Holendrechterweg
18.2	R	sign "Abcoude and Utrecht," Abcouderstraatweg
19.1	R	sign "Utrecht," Broekzijdselaan
19.2	L	Amsterdammerstraatweg
19.5	R	Brugstraat (50 m), L Voordijk (cross Angstel River)
19.9	R	LF7a Raadhuisplein T-Abcoude
20.0	L	LF7a Koppeldijk
20.8	L	sign "Baambrugge"
23.5	L	Krugstraat, T-Baambrugge
23.6	R	(cross Angstel River) Rijkstraatweg
26.6	SS R	Loenersloot, T-Loenersloot
26.9	VR !	under N201 sign "Loenen and Utrecht"
27.0	L	sign "Loenen and Utrecht"
27.2	L U !	onto ramp
27.3	L U !	N201 (cross Amsterdam-Rijnkanaal)
28.1	CS	sign "Vreeland," N201
29.2	L	sign "Vreeland" (cross N201)
29.4	R	Spoorlaan
29.9	L	Duinkerken (30 m), R (over Vecht) Breedstraat

30.0	R	LF7a Lindengracht
30.2	R	sign "Loenen and Breukelen," Boslaan
32.9	CS	T-Loenen (on R)
34.9	CS	T-Nieuwersluis (on R)
37.7	CS	T-Breukelen (on R)
38.7	SS R	Nijenrode (view castle across Vecht)
41.5	CS !	follow Diependaalsedijk (road)
41.7	R	LF7a Diependaalsedijk/Nassaustraat
42.7	R	Kaatsbaan, T-Maarssen
42.8	L	LF7a Langegracht (along canal)
43.1	R	LF7a Schoutenstraat
43.2	L	LF7a Huis ten Boschstraat
43.6	RA L !	LF7a sign "Maarssenveen," Maarssenveense Vaart
43.9	R	LF7a sign "Maarssenveen" (80 m), cross road to Tuinbouwweg
44.8	CS	sign "Maarssenveen," Tuinbouwweg
45.3	L	LF7a (under A2) sign "Oud-Zuilen and Utrecht"
45.7	SS	Westbroekse Molens
45.7	L	LF7a footbrdge/Groenweg/Polderweg 2E
47.9	R	LF7a Franciscusdreef
48.0	L	LF7a Vechtdijk (along Vecht)
48.4	VR	LF7a Vechtdijk/Zandpad/Jagerskade (along Vecht)
49.4	SS R	houseboats
50.3	L	LF7a Loevenhoutsedijk
50.4	R	LF7a Anthoniedijk/Lauwerecht
51.4	CS	cross Adalarstraat, Bemuurde Weerd OZ
51.7	CS	cross bridge onto Oude Gracht
52.1	L	Drakenburgstraat
52.2	R/end	Vinkenburgstraat, VVV Utrecht

Utrecht

Utrecht, like Groningen, is both a city and a province (the smallest of the 12). This bustling city is home to a large university, several excellent museums, and impressive churches. Stroll along the Oude Gracht (canal) lined with warehouses dating to the 13th century. Much of Utrecht's activity and attractions are centered on the Domplein.

The Domtoren (www.domtoren.nl), located on the Domplein, is the tallest tower (112 m/367 ft) in the Netherlands. Climb the 465 steps for a magnificent view; if it's a clear day, you can see as far as Amsterdam. Adjacent to the Domtoren, is the Domkerk (www.domkerk.nl), begun in 1254 and completed 250 years later. In the same vicinity is Pieterskerk, the oldest Romanesque church in the Netherlands, built in 1048.

Off the Oude Gracht is the Nationaal Museum van Speelklok tot Pierement (Mechanical Musical Museum), located in the Buurkerk (Buurkerkhof 10, www. museumspeelklok.nl, closed Mondays). Musical instruments from the 18th to 20th centuries, everything from music boxes to street organs to musical clocks, are exhibited. A few blocks south, at Nieuwe Gracht 63, is the Rijksmuseum Het Catharijneconvent (www.catharijneconvent.nl, closed Mondays). The former convent is now a museum documenting the story of Christianity in the Netherlands, with the largest collection of medieval art in the country.

Utrecht has many more museums: the Centraal Museum (www. centraalmuseum.nl) exhibits paintings; the Nederlands Spoorwegmuseum (Railway Museum, www.spoorwegmuseum.nl); the Universiteitsmuseum (www. uu.nl), with interesting old instruments formerly used by members of the university; and the Museum voor het Kruideniersbedrijf (Grocery Museum), an old-fashioned grocery store. Other buildings to visit are the Stadhuis, some of the cloisters, and the buildings along both the Oude Gracht and the Nieuwe Gracht.

Information:	VVV Utrecht is at Vinkenburgstraat 19 (Tel. 0900 128 8752, www.utrechtstad.com). The ANWB is in the huge Hoog Catharijne Mall above the railway station (Tel. 030 232 1421). At Oudegracht 112A, Time2Surf has about 100 computers for internet access.
Bicycle Shops:	For bike rentals and repairs, head to Laag Catharijne, Catharijnesingel 34, adjacent to the railway station (Tel. 030 231 6780). A bike shop in the center is Wim Kok, Nachtegaalstraat 51 (Tel. 030 231 5780, fietsen@wimkok.nl).
Where to Stay:	Hotels don't come cheap in Utrecht. Across from the station is Best Western's modern Amrath Hotel (030 233 1232, www.amrathutrecht.nl), with singles for €80 and doubles for €90 on weekends (add €50 for week nights) and €14 for breakfast. Housed in two 1883 mansions is the lovely Hotel

Malie, Maliestraat 2 (Tel. 030 231 6424, www. maliehotel.nl). Singles start at €99 and doubles at €120. Overlooking a canal, the cozy Hotel Ouwi, F.C. Dondersstraat 12 (Tel. 030 271 6303, www.hotel-ouwi.nl) has singles for €75 and doubles for €85.

In the center, the Strowis Hostel, Boothstraat 8 (Tel. 030 238 0280, www.strowis.nl), offers dorm rooms from €13 and doubles for €50, with kitchen facilities and e-mail service. The hostel B&B, Lucas Bolwerk 4 (Tel. 06 5043 4884, www.hostelutrecht.nl), has dorms from €16, singles from €55, and doubles from €65, and includes breakfast, lunch, and free internet access. Stayokay Hostel Bunnick, Rhijnauwenselaan 14 (Tel. 030 656 1277, www.stayokay.nl/bunnick), is 6 km southeast of Utrecht.

Camping de Berekuil, Arienslaan 5 (Tel. 030 271 3870), is 2 km east in a park.

Where to Eat: Utrecht is a cosmopolitan city with lots of variety. Restaurants line the Oude Gracht, with ethnic options including Indian, Thai, French, Italian, Greek, plus eetcafés and tapas bars. Near the VVV, Café Le Journal, Neude 32-34 (Tel. 030 236 4839), has reasonably priced meals in a warm, old-world atmosphere. For Indonesian fare, Selamat Makan, Voorstraat 100 (Tel. 030 236 8917, www.selamat-makan.nl) serves both regular and vegetarian *rijsttafel* (closed Tuesdays and Wednesdays).

Day 2: Utrecht to Gouda (53.1 km)

Visit the magnificent Kasteel de Haar, and cycle through farmland to Woerden, where a stop at the Fietsvakantie Winkel is a must. Superb canalside paths lead to historic Oudewater. The day's *pièce de résistance* is the stunning cycling through the Reeuwijkse Plassen to gorgeous Gouda.

Leave Utrecht passing the railway station. At 0.7 km, don't take the first bike tunnel, but the second car/bike tunnel under the railway tracks. On Leidseweg and Kennedylaan, pass a windmill and several houseboats on the Leidsche Rijn. Follow LF4b signs over the Amsterdam-Rijnkanaal, through De Meern, and to Vleuten.

From Vleuten, cycle on farm roads and take a short side trip to Haarzuilens (13.6 km). Go right on Brinkstraat, under the welcome arch to the village with quaint 19th-century houses with colorful shutters, clustered around a *brink*, a grassy square. Back on the route, continue through a small forest to the Kasteel de Haar, Kasteellaan 1, Haarzuilens (Tel. 030 677 8515, www. kasteeldehaar.nl, open daily, tours). Built by P.J.H. Cuypers (architect of Amsterdam's Rijksmuseum) in 1892, this castle has moats, "pepperpot" towers, and landscaped gardens.

Cycle on to Woerden. A 300 m side trip (24.8 km) takes you to Woerden's well-preserved 15th-century moated castle across from the 1892 neo-Gothic church, Bonaventurakerk. Go a further 100 m to the center. The 16th-century Stadhuis houses a municipal museum (open weekdays).

A visit to Woerden wouldn't be complete without stopping at the Fietsvakantie Winkel, Spoorlaan 19 (Tel. 0348 421 844, www.fietsvakantiewinkel.nl, closed Sundays, closed Sundays and Mondays in winter months). This shop is a cyclist's dream, with a huge range of books (touring and literature) and maps, both in Dutch and English, plus an extensive range of worldwide cycling tours.

From the right of the station, take the bike path underpass to Linschoten. On the way out of Woerden, you will go under two underpasses, then under the A12, and soon turn onto Haardijk, 3 km of beautiful narrow road, easily mistaken for a bike path, along a tree-lined canal. At 29.9 km, ride for 4 km on the Noord Linschoterdijk, a tiny road beside the Lange Linschoten River to Oudewater. In Oudewater (34.4 km), do not follow the VVV sign at the second bridge; instead, continue on Donkere Gaard to the Markt, Oudewater's center.

Oudewater is full of 16th-century houses, cobblestone streets, and picturesque canals. Oudewater's Waag is a little different from that of other Dutch towns. Here, it is called the Heksenwaag (Witch's Weigh House). In the 16th-century, women suspected of being witches were brought here to be weighed, because, in order to fly, a witch must weigh considerably less than a normal human being. The Heksenwaag (Leeuweringstraat 1, www.heksenwaag.nl, April through October, closed Mondays) is now a museum. There is a great traditional market on Wednesdays. The VVV is at Kapellestraat 2 (Tel. 0348 564 636, www.vvvoudewater.nl), and the Stadhuis is around the corner. Oudewater has one hotel, a few B&Bs, camping, and several eateries.

Follow the Hollandse IJssel River out of Oudewater, and follow the quiet farm road to Hekendorp. In Hekendorp, the road turns north to Driebruggen. Just before the town (43.0 km), there is a tiny (not well-signed) bike path to the Reeuwijkse Plassen, the stunning lake area north of Gouda. For 5 km, narrow roads, several closed to car traffic, wind past the lakes and quaint houses with neatly tended gardens. At 48.2 km, the wooded path ahead is for pedestrians only. (Note: The route covers only a small section of the lake area.)

From the lakes, Aschpotpad takes you into Gouda's suburbs, where two canals, Burgvlietkade and Karnemelksloot, lead you to the Markt, Gouda's striking centerpiece.

Cue Sheet

0.0	Start	VVV Utrecht
		go SW on Vinkenburgstraat
60 m	R	Oude Gracht

0.2	L	Lange Viestraat/Vredenburg
0.7	R	LF4b sign "Woerden"
0.8	L	car/bike tunnel (under railway tracks)
1.2	L	Kanonstraat sign "Woerden"
1.4	R	LF4b Leidsekade/Leidseweg/Kennedylaan
3.3	VL	bike path
3.4	R	LF4b bike path (over Amsterdam-Rijnkanaal)
4.2	L	LF4b sign "De Meern"
4.9	R	LF4b Park Voorn sign "Woerden"
5.0	L	Zandweg (along canal)
5.7	R	LF4b Klifrakplantsoen, T-De Meern
6.2	L	LF4b Groenedijk
7.3	R	LF4b 't Zand
7.6 !	RA L	LF4b Alendorperweg (follow LF4b signs around RA, then R)
9.5	L	LF4b Utrechtseweg sign "Vleuten"
10.0	CS	cross railway tracks
10.3	RA VL	LF4b Hindersteinlaan
10.5	L	LF4b Pastoor Ohllaan
10.8	VR	LF4b Pastoor Ohllaan (at church)
11.1	L	LF4b Dorpsstraat, T-Vleuten
11.2	R	LF4b Schoolstraat
12.2	L	Thermaterweg, dir. "Haarzuilens," to Kasteel de Haar
13.6	L ST R	Elkslaan RT = 400 m T-Haarzuilens
13.7	R	Bochtdijk
14.6	SS R	Kasteel de Haar
14.8	L	LF4b Rijndijk (20 m), R Lagehaarsedijk
15.4	R	LF4b Kortjaksepad (bike path)
16.3	L	Gerverscop (not LF4b)
19.9	R	N198 (400 m busy road)

20.4	R	Houtdijk
20.6	L	Houtdijk
21.3	L	LF4b Houtdijksepad
21.6	L	LF4b N198 sign "Woerden"
21.9	L	bridge (20 m), R bike path
23.1	VL	sign "Centrum," Utrechtsestraatweg
24.8	L	sign "Linschoten," Stationsweg
24.8	ST CS	sign "Centrum" (T-Woerden) RT = 600–800 m
25.0	SS L	Fietsvakantie Winkel, Spoorlaan (opposite Woerden Station)
25.0	R	bike tunnel sign "Linschoten"
25.2	L	sign "Linschoten," Linschoterweg
25.3	R	Van der Valk Bouwmanlaan
26.3	R	Polanerzandweg (100 m after 2nd underpaass)
26.7	R	over bridge (10 m), L Korte Linschoterweg
27.0	VL	Lopikerwaardroute sign (100 m after A12 underpass, river on left)
27.1	R	Haardijk
29.9	R	Noord Linschoterdijk
34.4	CS	do not follow VVV sign
34.5	VL	Donkere Gaard/Markt/Peperstraat, T-Oudewater
34.8	VR	Wijdst
34.9	R	Noord IJsselkade (at church)
35.1	CS	bike path/road, Hekendorpse Buurt
35.3	L	Oude Hekensdorperweg (unsigned)
39.5	VR	sign "Reeuwijk," dir. "Driebruggen" (lower street)
39.7	R	Opweg T-Hekendorp
41.0	CS	Hoogeind (under railway), T-Hogebrug
43.0	L !	sign "Gouda and Reeuwijkse Plassen," bike path, T-Driebruggen
44.9	L	sign "Gouda and Reeuwijk," Oukoopsedijk
45.3	R	sign "Gouda," Nieuwebroeksedijk

46.5	L	Ree
48.2	L	Korsendijk
49.3	R	Platteweg (restaurant on corner)
50.6	L	cross road, then R
50.7	L	(10 m) L Aschpotpad bike path
50.9	VR	Aschpotpad bike path
51.4	R	Dijksgraafslag
51.5	R	Achterwillemsweg
51.7	R	(after canal) Burgsvlietkade
51.9	L	under railway tracks
52.0	L	Zuidelijke Burgsvlietkade
52.2	L	over bridge (10 m), R Karnemelksloot
52.7	CS	Lange Tiendeweg
53.0	R	Korte Tiendeweg
53.1	End	Markt, VVV Gouda

Gouda

Most people identify the lively town of Gouda with cheese. Every Thursday morning in the summer months, you can sample Gouda cheese at the market in the town's center. Farmers weigh their cheese at the Waag, now also a cheese museum (Markt 36, April through October, closed Mondays).

You can't help but be impressed by the Stadhuis in the center of the Markt, built in 1450 (open daily), and the Grote St. Janskerk at Achter de Kerk 16 (open daily, €2). St. Janskerk, the longest church in the Netherlands, has 70 of the most impressive stained glass windows you'll ever come across.

Museums in Gouda include the Stedelijk Museum Het Catharina Gasthuis (Achter de Kerk 14, open daily), once the hospital and the governor's mansion, but

Gouda: Cheese Town

Gouda (pronounced HOW-da with a gutteral "h") is both the name of the town itself, and the cheese that made the town famous. *Goudse kaas*, Gouda cheese, comes in various levels of maturity. Begin with the *jonge* (young), which is creamy and mild, and the work your way through the aging process to *belegen*, then *extra belegen*, and finally *oude* (old). *Oude kaas*, aged for at least 2 years, is the firmest Gouda, and has the strongest taste.

now housing everything from 16th and 17th-century paintings to 17th-century medical equipment in the old surgeon's room. It also has a period kitchen and antique toys. Museum De Moriaan at Westhaven 29 is an 18th-century tobacconist's shop and pipe museum (open daily). Gouda is also home to the Zuidhollands Verzetsmuseum, Turfmarkt 30, a remembrance and documentation of World War II (closed Mondays).

Information:	VVV Gouda is at Markt 27 (Tel. 0900 4683 2888, www.vvvgouda.nl). The ANWB is opposite the station at Stationsplein 1B (Tel. 0182 524 444). Log on at Tele-Inter, Vredebest 10 (Tel. 0182 686 125).
Bicycle Shops:	Rijwielshop Gouda, Stationsplein 10 (Tel. 0182 519 751), offers rentals and repairs. Leeuwen Tweewielers, Burg. Martenssingel 100 (Tel. 0182 513 520), is a full service bike shop.
Where to Stay:	In a renovated older building, the bike-friendly Hotel Utrechtse Dom, Guezenstraat 6 (Tel. 0182 528 833, www.hotelgouda.nl), has rooms with shared bath for €55, and with private bath for €72. Hotel Keizerskroon, Keizerstraat 11 (Tel. 0182 528 096), has single rooms with shared bath for €35, and doubles with shared bath for €48. Singles with bath are €55 and doubles are €70. The VVV has a list of B&Bs.
	Camping Elzenhof, Broekweg 6 (Tel. 0182 524 456), is west of Gouda, near the Julianasluis (see Day 4).
	Mini-Camping De Breevaart, Bodegraafsestraatweg 52 (Tel. 0182 588 426) is open April through October.
Where to Eat:	Café Centraal, Markt 23 (Tel. 0182 512 576), serves huge portions of traditional food and seasonal specialties. Behind the pub De Zalm at Markt 34 is De Goudsche Stal at Achter de Waag 20 (Tel. 0182 686 689, www.goudschestal.nl, closed Mondays), which offers three courses for €17.50. Sleek and modern, Mestizo, Wijdstraat 13 (Tel. 0182 687 088), has an inventive Mediterranean menu. Other choices in Gouda include Chinese, Middle Eastern, Greek, and Balkan cuisine.
	Visit 't Kaaswinkeltje, Lange Tiendeweg 30, a tiny cheese shop crammed with huge wheels of Gouda of all "ages" (closed Sundays).

Day 3: Kinderdijk Windmill Day Trip (61.6 km)

The Kinderdijk windmills (and the other windmills en route) are undoubtedly the highlights of the day. This windmill route follows some of the most idyllic paths along rivers and canals in South Holland. Allow time for the historic town of Schoonhoven.

From Gouda to the village of Haastrecht, follow the dike along the Hollandse IJssel. Cycle along the pretty Vlist River from Haastrecht to Schoonhoven. Make sure to veer right over the bridge (11.1 km) just after the village Vlist, and keep the river to your right. Just before Schoonhoven, pass a stately, dark green windmill.

Schoonhoven is at the confluence of the Vlist and Lek Rivers. The town itself is charming, but one of the reasons people come here is for the silver products produced over the centuries in many of the town's workshops. The Nederlands Goud, Zilver, en Klokkenmuseum (Gold, Silver, and Clock Museum, Kazernplein 4, closed Mondays) has a fine collection of gold and silver artifacts as well as antique clocks, many still chiming and cuckooing at regular intervals.

Other buildings of note along the Haven, the main waterway through town, are the 15th-century Stadhuis (15.1 km), with its 50-bell carillon in the steeple (also the home of the VVV), and the Waag from 1617, now a restaurant. The Veerpoort (15.4 km), built in 1601 and the only remaining town gate, is at the far end of town where you take the ferry across the Lek River (50 cents per adult and bike, daily, 5 a.m. to midnight). On the other side, cycle on the dike past a small industrial area to Groot Ammers.

Coming down off the dike in Groot Ammers, you see a line of four eye-catching windmills. The narrow canal-side bike path (19.7 km) gives you close-up views of these four windmills from the 18th century. Continue on quiet roads until after De Donk, where the route enters the Donke Laagten, a nature area (28.4 km). Watch for birds on this double-track foot/bike path next to a small canal. (At 27.7 km, cross two footbridges, but not the third).

At 31.2 km, cycle past two more windmills. At about 35.0 km, the first windmills of the Kinderdijk come into view. Here are the quintessential, picture-postcard Dutch windmills. Windmill after windmill appears for 2 km, 19 beautiful behemoths. These windmills were built in the 18th century to keep the polders drained of water, and were used until 1950. One mill (39.5 km) is open daily for vis-

National Windmill Day

If you are in the Netherlands on the second Saturday in May, you are in for a treat. Nationale Molendag (National Mill Day) is the day in which all the country's windmills operate, and many are open to the public. Kinderdijk is nothing short of magnificent, with many of the mills sporting colorful sails and spinning in unison. This is a good day to cycle the "Kinderdijk Windmill Day Trip." The Schermer area (see pages 72–73) and Zaanse Schans (see page 207) also have lots of windmills.

its April 1 to September 30. In 1997, the Kinderdijk was placed on the UNESCO World Heritage list of cultural historic objects.

Continue on the bike path past the mills to the north. Take the ferry across the Lek (55 cents per adult and bike, daily, 6 a.m. to midnight). Skirt Krimpen a/d Lek and make your way across the N210. From ANWB mushroom #21386 all the way back to Gouda, this open polder area is riddled with small canals.

Cue Sheet

0.0	Start	VV Gouda go S (20 m), then W on the Markt (past the Stadhuis)
0.1	L	Wijdstraat
0.2	CS	Westhaven
0.6	L	Nieuwe Veerstal
1.2	VR	Goejanverwelldijk sign "Hekendorp"
3.1	CS	stay on dike

Map 11.2. Utrecht & South Holland Tour, Days 3 & 4.

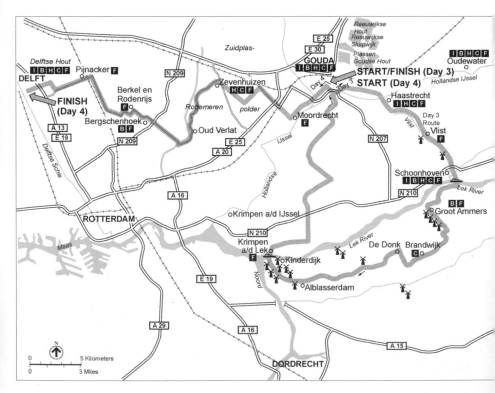

190

3.6	CS	#21509 sign "Haastrecht"
3.7	R	(10 m) L bike path
5.3	R	bridge sign "Schoonhoven," Veerstraat
5.4	R	(5 m) L Marktveld sign "Schoonhoven," T-Haastrecht
5.5	L	Kraanstraat sign "Schoonhoven"
5.6	R	sign "Schoonhoven and Vlist," Grote Haven/ Jan de Waardsingel
6.4	R	onto road
8.1	L	over bridge (20 m), R sign "Schoonhoven and Vlist"
11.1	VR !	over bridge (50 m), L sign "Schoonhoven," T-Vlist
13.7	L	sign "Centrum"
13.8	R	sign "Centrum," Vlisterweg
14.4	RA CS	cross N210
14.6	VL	Koestraat to "museum"
14.8	L	Uitdragersstraat (50 m), R Oude Haven/Dam/Haven
15.1	CS SS	VVV Schoonhoven/Stadhuis on L, T-Schoonhoven
15.3	L	Tol (20 m), R Veerstraat sign "Gorinchem and boat"
15.4	L	old city gate
15.6	R	ferry across the Lek
15.7	R	at top of ferry ramp dir. "Groot Ammers" Schoonhovenseveer
19.2	L	Kerkstraat (just before church), T-Groot Ammers
19.7	VR SS	bike path sign "Vier Molens" (four windmills)
21.8	R	over bridge after last windmill
22.0	L	Molenroute sign
23.2	CS	sign "Brandwijk"
26.4	R	sign "De Donk," Donkseweg
27.7	L	bike path along Grote Achterwaterschap (canal)
28.4	R	over bridge (edge. Donkse Laagten)
28.7	L !	over two bridges, then CS sign "Kinderdijk"
28.7	SS	enter Donkse Laagten

31.2	SS	windmills on route and north
31.5	L	#24220 sign "Kinderdijk"
31.7	R	sign "Kinderdijk"
36.7	CS	#20712 sign "Kinderdijk"
36.8	CS	cross bridge
37.9	SS L	"Welkom in Kinderdijk"
39.5	SS L	working windmill
40.2	L	Molenstraat sign "Krimpen a/d Lek"
40.7	R	sign "Gouda"
41.1	CS	ferry across the Lek
41.2	CS	dir. "Gouda," Kerkestoep, T-Krimpen a/d Lek
42.1	R	sign ""Gouda," Tiendweg
42.6	L	sign "Gouda," Breekade/N477
43.0	CS	do not follow "Gouda" sign
44.4	CS	across N210, over wooden bridge
44.5	CS	#21386 sign "Ouderkerk a/d IJssel"
45.7	R	LF2b over small, white, metal bridge
49.4	L	LF2b unmarked farm road
51.4	R	LF2b #22432 sign "Gouderak"
57.9	R	Gouderakse Tiendweg
59.6	L	LF2b N207/Goudseweg
60.2	R	Gouderaksedijk
60.3	RA L	LF2b N207 sign "Gouda"
60.5	L	LF2b sign "Centrum," Goejanverwelldijk
61.0	R	LF2b Oosthaven/Wijdstraat
61.5	R	Markt
61.6	VL/end	(30 m) VVV Gouda

Day 4: Gouda to Delft (40.2 km)

From Gouda, leave on Nieuwe Veerstal (0.6 km), where you cross to the other side of the road. After crossing the locks, the Julianasluis (2.1 km), go alongside the N207. At 2.7 km, make a U-turn onto the ramp, then another turn, which will take you under the N207 and along a quiet canal to Moordrecht (5.4 km). Middelweg takes you to the Zuidplas Polder, easy cycling through flat, open polder and green-houses.

In the town of Zevenhuizen, watch for the right turn onto Dorpsstraat (14.0 km). Go through the center, and turn left (14.7 km) to the lakes, the Rottemeren, and past the small village of Oude Verlat, and along the water to a footbridge (16.3 km), which crosses into Bergse Bos (forest). The huge expanse of buildings in the distance is Rotterdam. If you are interested in visiting the city, there is access at 22.3 km, where the route turns right. If you continue straight, you will reach Rotterdam. (A good map of Rotterdam is a necessity for finding your way around.)

The area around Rotterdam is densely populated, and from here, the route to Delft and to The Hague (Day 5) passes through many towns. Go through Bergschenhoek, then skirt the edge of Berkel en Rodenrijs to the N472, an unin-spiring road to Pijnacker. Shortly after Pijnacker, turn right at Noordeindseweg (36.0 km), where a forested area, the Delftse Hout, provides a "green reprieve" all the way to Delft.

Cross Koepoortbrug (39.4 km) and continue through Delft, passing the Markt (on your right at 39.8 km) to the tourist office (not a VVV).

Cue Sheet

0.0	Start	VVV Gouda go S (20 m), then W on the Markt (past the Stadhuis)
0.1	L	Wijdstraat
0.2	CS	Westhaven
0.6	R !	Nieuwe Veerstal/N207
1.1	R	Constantijn Huygensstraat
1.2	L	Van Baerlestraat
1.9	L	(10 m) R to "Moordrecht," N207
2.1	L	sign "Moordrecht," over Julianasluis (locks)
2.2	R	sign "Waddinxveen"
2.3	L	N207 (cross to other side)
2.7	U R !	under N207, Oosteringdijk (along canal)
5.4	R	Middelweg, T-Moordrecht (to L)

6.4	R	bike path
6.5	R	Middelweg
7.3	CS	Middelweg/N456 (under A20)
9.0	L	Zuidelijke Dwarsweg
10.7	R	Derde Tochtweg/Knibbelweg
13.1	L	Noordelijke Dwarsweg
14.0	R !	Dorpsstraat (tiny street) sign "Rottemeren"
14.7	L	Tweemanspolder sign "Rottemeren"
16.3	L	LF2a over footbridge #21390 sign "Oude Verlat"
16.4	R	40 m after footbridge
18.7	CS	to Oude Verlat along the Rottemeren (water on R)
19.5	CS	T-Oude Verlat
21.3	R	over footbridge, Bergse Bos sign "Bergschenhoek"
21.4	L	Rottekade (other side)
22.1	R	Van Schaikdreef
22.2	L	dir. "Bergschenhoek and Berkel en Rodenrijs"
22.3	R !	Hoeksekade/Julianalaan
24.8	CS	under N209
25.4	VR	Rondom, T-Bergschenhoek
25.5	R	Kerkstraat/Berkelseweg
26.8	RA L	onto road (no bike path)
27.3	R	D.S. van Koetsveldstraat, T-Berkel en Rodenrijs
27.3	L	(20 m) bike path (through residential area)
27.8	R	sign "Pijnacker and Delft," N472
32.9	RA L !	sign "Delft," Westlaan/Delftsestraatweg
33.0	CS	T-Pijnacker
36.0	R	sign "Delft," Noordeindseweg
37.1	CS	B&B/Camping de Uylenburg on R
37.4	L	Korftlaan sign "Delft and Delftse Hout"
38.2	CS	Camping Delftse Hout

38.8	CS	under A13 Korftlaan/Bieslandsekade
39.2	R	sign "Markt and Information," Oostsingel
39.4	L	Koepoortbrug/Nieuwe Langendijk/Oude Langendijk
40.0	R	Wijnhaven
40.1	R	cross bridge/Hippolytusbuurt
40.2	End	Toeristen Informatie Point Delft

Delft

Delft's claim to fame is Deltfware, the white porcelain painted with blue, developed in the 16th century to compete with chinaware from China. Delft spreads out from the Markt. Towering over the Markt is the Gothic Nieuwe Kerk, built in 1381, where the mausoleum of William the Silent is found. Climb the tower for a view of Delft, and to see the 48-bell carillon. Also at the Markt are the Waag, now a theater, the Vleeshal (Meat Hall), with its two ox heads on the gable, and the Vismarkt (Fish Market).

At Sint Agathaplein, Het Prinsenhof Museum (www.gemeentemusea-delft.nl, closed Mondays), originally a nunnery and then William's domicile, now houses tapestries, Delftware, and paintings. To see Delftware processed and painted, go to Koninklijke Porcelyne Fles, Rotterdamseweg 196 (www.royaldelft.com, open daily; closed Sundays November to March), founded in 1653. Another Delftware factory is De Delftse Pauw at Delftweg 133. They also offer demonstrations.

Delft comes alive on Thursdays between 9 a.m. and 5 p.m., when a huge, colorful market transforms the Markt. On Saturday, there is a market at the Brabantse Turfmarkt.

Information:	Delft has no VVV. Instead there is a privately owned tourist office at Hippolytusbuurt 4 (Tel. 015 215 4051, www.delft.com). The tourist office offers free internet access.
Bicycle Shops:	At the station, Rijwielshop Delft, Van Leeuwenhoeksingel 40A (Tel. 015 214 3033), has rentals. In the center, Piet Vonk is at Voldersgracht 20 (Tel. 015 212 3252, www.pietvonk.nl), and Halfords is at Wijnhaven 17 (Tel. 015 213 8558).
Where to Stay:	The most congenial and fun hotel in Delft is Herberg De Emauspoort, Vrouwenregt 9 (Tel. 015 219 0219, www.emauspoort.nl). Centrally located and with its own bakery, its single rooms are €77.50 and doubles are €87.50. Or stay in a gypsy caravan in their courtyard; singles are €72.50 and doubles are €82.50. On a quiet canal, Hotel Leeuwenbrug, Koornmarkt 16 (Tel. 015 214 7741,

www.leeuwenbrug.nl), has singles from €75 and doubles from €90. Near Koninklijke Porcelyne Fles, in a residential area, Hotel Juliana, Maerten Trompstraat 33 (Tel. 015 216 7612, www.hoteljuliana.nl), has singles from €78 and doubles from €96. Hotels in Delft fill up quickly, so reserve ahead.

There are two B&Bs in Delft: B&B Oosteinde 156 (Tel. 015 213 4238), and B&B Soul Inn, Willemstraat 55 (Tel. 015 215 7246, www.soul-inn.nl).

On the route and before Delft (38.2 km), the large Camping De Delftse Hout, Korftlaan 5 (Tel. 015 213 0040, www.delftsehout.nl), is a 5-minute bike ride from the center. Also on the route (37.1 km), a smaller campground, De Uylenburg, Noordeindseweg 70 (Tel. 015 214 3732, www.uylenburg.nl), also has B&B rooms.

Where to Eat:	The tourist office has a free list of restaurants and cafés. Several restaurants, with French, Spanish, Greek, Thai, and Chinese food, are on the Grote Markt and the streets radiating off it. There are about 100 types of pancakes at Stads Pannekoeckhuys, Oude Delft 113 (Tel. 015 213 0193). Next door, Restaurant L'Orage, Oude Delft 111 (Tel. 015 212 3629), serves French meals. For Greek food, try Rhodos, Wijnhaven 11 (Tel. 015 214 2609).

Day 5: Delft to Leiden (34.6 km)

This short riding day allows time for a stop in The Hague and the beach town of Scheveningen. From there, you will go through sand dunes and catch your first glimpse of tulip fields before entering Leiden, famed for its many and varied museums.

Leave Delft along the Vliet Kanaal, on bike paths and canal-side roads. At 1.9 km, notice the tiny ferry (which only operates weekdays). At 4.8 km, the route veers away from the canal and you travel on surface streets through Rijswijk and Voorburg on the outskirts of The Hague. For a short time, LF11b signs guide you through the streets and along canals. Pass the giant, blue coffeepot at 7.2 km.

Turn onto busy Rijswijkseweg (7.4 km); as you cross the canal, look right to see the windmill. At 8.2 km, go left into the traffic of Den Haag. Be careful crossing the several tram tracks.

At 9.1 km, you're in the center. Turn right on Lange Potten to go to VVV Den Haag, Koningin Julianaplein 30 (Tel. 0900 340 3505, www.denhaag.com), about 800 m further and located next to the Centraal Station.

Den Haag (the official name is 's-Gravenhage) is referred to in English as The Hague. Amsterdam is the country's constitutional capital, but Den Haag, a city of diplomats and officials, is the center of the Dutch government. Here, you will find the International Court of Justice (World Court) housed within the Vredespaleis (Peace Palace), and the royal residence.

For a good sightseeing start, head to the Hofvijver (9.3 km), a lake in the center of town, passing the Binnenhof (Inner Courtyard), the center of Dutch government for centuries (9.2 km). Weekday tours to the Ridderzaal (Hall of Knights), the Chambers, and more, leave from Binnenhof 8A.

The Hague has several museums. The Haags Historisch Museum, Korte Vijverburg 7 (www.haagshistorischmuseum.nl, closed Mondays), has paintings, furniture, and other relics tracing three centuries of Hague history. Mauritshuis, Korte Vijverburg 8 (www.mauritshuis.nl, closed Mondays), has a collection of 17th-century paintings, including Rembrandt's Anatomy Lesson of Professor Tulp and works by other Dutch masters. Rijksmuseum Gevangenpoort, Buitenhof 33 (closed Mondays), was a prison for centuries. Today you can tour the cells and view torture instruments. The Haags Gemeentemuseum (municipal art museum, Stadshouderslaan 41, www.gemeentemuseum.nl, closed Mondays), has Delftware, rare musical instruments, and impressionist and modern art, including Mondrians and Eschers.

There are three royal palaces: Noordeinde Palace at Noordeinde 68, Lange Voorhout Palace at Lange Voorhout 74, and Huis ten Bosch in the Haagse Bos. None of these are open to the public, but you can create your own "Royal Bicycle Tour" and cycle from one to the other.

The Hague has no shortage of hotels, but they are expensive due to the international and diplomatic nature of the city. There is a Stayokay Hostel. Accommodations in Scheveningen are a little cheaper. For meals, you'll find everything from *shoarma* to *rijsttafel* to fine dining for dignitaries.

Both of The Hague's railway stations, Centraal (Tel. 070 385 3235) and Hollandse Spoor (Tel. 070 389 0830), have bike shops. Du Nord Rijwielen, Keizerstraat 27-29 (Tel. 070 355 4060), is another option. Both railway stations have a *fietsenstalling*, and there is a guarded *fietsenstalling* near the Binnenhof.

A note about The Hague: The North Sea Jazz Festival, with acts from all over the globe, takes place every July and attracts 60,000 people. Plan around this.

Back on the route, pass the Vredespaleis (Peace Palace, www.vredespaleis.nl, tours weekdays only) and the International Court of Justice (10.8 km). About 100 m further, enter the forested area, the Scheveningense Bos.

Pass Madurodam (www.madurodam.nl, open daily), the Netherlands in miniature (12.2 km), and go under the viaduct, being careful at the turn (12.4 km), as the road is busy.

Scheveningen, once a seaside getaway for The Hague locals, is now an overdeveloped resort area. Modern structures have encroached upon the once beautiful centerpiece, the Kurhaus, and fast food places abound. The name Scheveningen is so difficult for anyone but a native Dutch person to pronounce, that it was used as a test in World War II to detect German infiltrators.

Scheveningen is also the gateway for the dune area to the north. From 16.3 km to 22.4 km, roll up and down through the dunes on a paved bike path, probably the only bike path in the Netherlands with speed bumps. Continue for 2 km through forest before coming to the farms and tulip fields west of Leiden, where, in the spring, you will get your first glimpse of tulips (27.2 km, 100 m on L). Be aware that Oostdorperweg curves right (27.2 km) but retains the same name.

For 3 km, cycle through farmland. The final 3 km will take you past modern buildings on a maze of intersecting bike paths. Watch carefully for signs to the Centrum and the station.

Cue Sheet

0.0	Start	Toeristen Informatie Point Delft go NW on Hippolytusbuurt/Voorstraat/Annastraat
0.6	VR	Annageer
0.7	CS	Nieuwe Plantage (cross Vrijenbaanselaan), water tower on L
0.8	CS	cross bridge, Weteringseweg (along canal)

Map 11.3. Utrecht & South Holland Tour, Day 5.

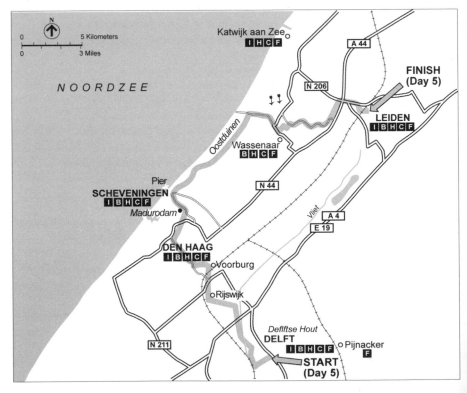

1.2	R	footbridge (20 m), R along canal
1.4	VR	Jaagpad
4.0	R	over bridge, sign "Voorburg"
4.8	CS	follow road under A13
4.9	R	Nassaukade sign "Voorburg"
5.8	CS !	cross Geesterweg (busy), T-Voorburg
6.2	L	LF11b Broekslootkade
6.5	R	LF11b Noordpolderkade
7.3	L	LF11b Laakkade
7.4	R	Rijswijkseweg sign "Centrum"
7.4	SS R	view windmill R
8.2	L	Pletterijkade/Spui/Hofweg sign "Centrum"
9.1	CS	Lange Potten (on R sign "VVV and Station" 800 m)
9.2	SS R	Binnenhof T-Den Haag
9.5	R	Lange Voorhout (50 m), R (at church) Parkstraat/ Alexanderstraat/Plein 1813
10.3	L	Javastraat sign "Scheveningen"
10.6	R	Scheveningenseweg
10.8	SS L	Vredespaleis (Peace Palace)
11.2	R	Prof. Teldersweg sign "Madurodam"
12.2	SS	Madurodam
12.2	L	(under viaduct) DR Aletta Jacobsweg/Plesmansweg
12.4	L	Nieuwe Parklaan sign "Scheveningen"
14.3	L	Kurhausweg
14.4	R	Gevers Deynootweg (Kurhaus ahead)
14.6	-	VVV Scheveningen on L
14.6	R	Zwolsestraat sign "Katwijk"
15.3	L	sign "Katwijk"
16.3	L	#22726 Meijendal (enter dune area)
23.2	R	#21733 sign "Wassenaar"

25.8	L	Dr. Mansveltkade
26.3	R	Zonneveldweg
26.6	L	Oostdorperweg
27.1	VL !	Oostdorperweg
27.2	R	Oostdorperweg (tulips 100 m L)
28.2	R	Hogeboomseweg
29.1	L	Maaldrift
30.1	L	bike path (after campground)
31.7	L	sign "Centrum" (at Hotel De Haagsche Schouw)
32.6	R	sign "Centrum" (soon after Holiday Inn)
32.7	CS	Van Ravelingenstraat
38.9	L	sign "Centrum"
33.0	R	sign "Centrum"
33.7	R	sign "Centrum"
33.8	L	sign "Centrum"
34.1	L	sign "Station"
34.3	R	sign "Centrum and Station"
34.4	L	sign "Centrum and Station"
34.5	R	Stationsweg
34.6	End	VVV/ANWB Leiden

Leiden

Leiden, home to the Netherlands' oldest university, is a city crisscrossed by canals. There are as many as 11 excellent museums. The Rijksmuseum van Oudheden at Rapenburg 28 (www.rmo.nl, closed Mondays), has the impressive mini-Egyptian Temple of Taffeh in the foyer, plus exhibits of Classical, Near Eastern, Egyptian, and Dutch archaeology. The mummies on the 2nd floor are well preserved and worth a peek. The Molenmuseum De Valk (Windmill Museum, www. home. wanadoo.nl/molenmuseum, closed Mondays) has been a working windmill for ten generations, from 1747 until 1964, and sheds light on the miller's lifestyle. The Museum de Lakenhal, Oude Singel 28 (www.lakenhal.nl, closed Mondays), the old cloth hall, now houses decorative arts, paintings, clothmakers rooms, and antiques.

Note the arched bridges crossing the Rapenburg Kanaal, as well as the grand houses of the aristocracy that line it. Close to Rapenburg is the 14th-century Gothic St. Pieterskerk, and at Rapenburg 73 is Hortus Botanicus (open daily), one of the world's oldest botanical gardens, with the first seeds planted in 1590.

Information:	VVV/ANWB Leiden is at Stationsweg 2D (Tel. 0900 222 2333, www.leidenpromotie.nl). For internet access, the library is on Nieuwestraat (Tel. 071 514 9943).
Bicycle Shops:	Leiden Rijwielshop (Tel. 071 512 0068) is on the station's west side and has rentals. Halfords is at Haarlemmerstraat 245 (Tel. 071 512 2890).
Where to Stay:	In a quiet setting south of the center, Pension Witte Singel, Witte Singel 80 (Tel. 071 514 2890, www.pension-ws.demon.nl), has singles from €36 and doubles from €55. In the center, Nieuw Minerva, Boommarkt 23 (Tel. 071 512 6358, www.nieuwminerva.nl) has singles from €75 and doubles from €100. Hotel de Doelen, Rapenburg 2 (Tel. 071 512 0527, www.dedoelen.com), has singles from €70 and doubles from €90, plus €8 for breakfast.
	Stayokay Hostel Noordwijk, Langevelderlaan 45 (Tel. 0252 372 920, www.stayokay.com/noordwijk), is the closest hostel to Leiden, 15 km northwest in Noordwijk.
	There is no campground close to Leiden, but there are plenty in the seaside area of Katwijk. On the way to Haarlem, just after Warmond (6.0 km), are about six campgrounds, many along Oosteinde.
Where to Eat:	Being a university town, Leiden has no shortage of reasonably priced restaurants and cafés. There are several overlooking the water at the Beestenmarkt, and many around the Pieterskerk and along Noordeinde. Near Pieterskerk, Bistro La Cloche, Kloksteeg 3 (Tel. 071 512 3053, closed Mondays), serves French food. Surakarta, Noordeinde 51-53 (Tel. 071 512 3524, www.surakarta.nl), has a traditional Indonesian menu. Oudt Leyden, Steenstraat 49 (Tel. 071 513 3144, www.oudtleyden.nl), serves pancakes and other food.

Day 6: Leiden to Haarlem (38.9 km)

After a quick ride out of Leiden, arrive in Sassenheim. In late April or early May, the bulb fields here are ablaze in color. Pass Lisse, the center of the bulb area, and on to the Keukenhof Gardens, a spectacular array of blooms that is open for only a few weeks per year. Continue through bulb fields and forests to Cruquius Museum, a former pumping station, and then to Haarlem.

If you wish to stay overnight in the bulb area, Sassenheim, Lisse, and Hillegom all have hotels and a few B&Bs. There is camping near Warmond and camping and a hostel on the coast in Noordwijk.

Soon after leaving Leiden, go under the railway bridge (1.0 km) and pass two windmills on a canal lined with houseboats. A small forest (2.1 km) brings you to the outskirts of Warmond. Go through Warmond; notice the stately homes lining Herenweg. After Warmond, pass several campgrounds (6.0 km). Go over the A44 and into Sassenheim (9.2 km), where a lively market is held on Friday mornings.

If you are cycling in bulb season, the color spectacle begins when you leave Sassenheim. You will see fields of tulips, daffodils, and hyacinths in every color imaginable. The route takes you north through the fields, but there are plenty of other roads for you to explore the fields on your own.

If you want to visit Lisse, turn right instead of left at 15.3 km. There's not much of interest in the town except one museum, Museum De Zwarte Tulp, Grachtweg 2A (open afternoons only, closed Mondays), devoted to the history and growing of bulbs.

At 15.3 km are the Keukenhof Gardens (open daily, 9.a.m. to 5 p.m., early April to mid-May only). The entrance for cyclists is 400 m R. The Keukenhof is a huge, 41,230-acre park of manicured gardens planted with over 6 million bulbs of every imaginable type and color. The gardens are crowded, but are well worth a visit. Avoid weekends and arrive early.

After the Keukenhof, cycle through more bulb fields. As a side trip, at 22.4 km continue straight (for up to 2 km) on the road to De Zilk, instead of turning right. This road has some stunning bulb fields contrasting with the deep green trees of the forest in the background. Return the same way.

Back on the route, the tiny Tweede Doodweg takes you through the last of the bulb fields before going through a forest and then through farms to Bennebroek. Cycle along the forested N208 from Bennebroek. Go through the gates into Groenendaal, a small wooded area.

Cruquius lies on the edge of the Haarlemmermeer, once a lake. Today, this reclaimed land, the Haarlemmermeerpolder (4.5 m or 14ft below sea level), is the location of Schiphol Airport. Cruquius (open daily, April through November), now a museum, was one of the original steam-driven pumping stations used to drain the Haarlemmermeer between 1849-1852. The steam pump itself and information about the history of land reclamation are the focus of this museum.

Cross the canal opposite Cruquius on the newly constructed bicycle bridge, Fietsbrug Cruquius. Cycle through farmland to the Spaarne River and along the Spaarne into Haarlem.

Cue Sheet

0.0	Start	Leiden Railway Station go NE under arch (SVB bank building)
0.1	CS	(cross Schuttersveld) Schipholweg sign "Warmond"
0.6	L	sign "Warmond" (80 m), L up railway ramp sign "Warmond"
0.9	U R	along railway tracks sign "Warmond"
1.0	R	under railway bridge Halemmerweg
2.1	L	sign "Warmond"
2.4	R	sign "Warmond," Abtspoelweg

Map 11.4. Utrecht & South Holland Tour, Day 6.

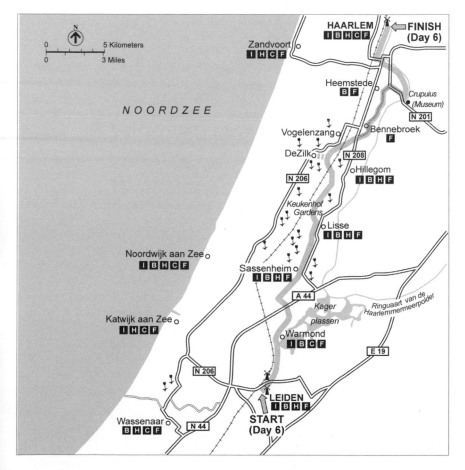

3.2	CS	cross Poelmeer (lake), Oranje-Nassaulaan
3.9	L	sign "winkelstraat" (shopping street) (10 m), R Padoxlaan/ Herenweg
6.0	CS	several campgrounds
6.6	-	over freeway
7.1	R	sign "Sassenheim, Lisse, and Haarlem," Hoofstraat
8.7	CS !	(at Parklaan/church) Hoofstraat
9.2	CS	T-Sassenheim (pedestrian area)
9.3	L	Teylingerlaan
10.0	L	sign "Voorhout and Noordwijk," N443
10.2	R	Oude Herenweg
11.3	R	Akervoorderlaan
11.4	L	Achterweg-Zuid
13.6	L	Spekkelaan
14.1	R	Van Lyndenweg (to Keukenhof)
15.3	L !	Stationsweg, Keukenhof Gardens (entrance 400 m R)
15.3	ST R	RT = 1 km to T-Lisse R
15.8	R	Loosterweg-Noord/Veenenburgerlaan
18.5	L	#4077 3E Loosterweg dir. "Vogelenzang"
19.5	VR	Wilhelminalaan
19.7	L	2E Loosterweg
20.9	L	1E Loosterweg (cross railway tracks)
21.7	L	Margrietenlaan
22.0	L	N206
22.4	R	Tweede Doodweg
22.4	SS CS	road to De Zilk, bulb fields, ST=approx. 4 km
23.1	CS	forest and farms
24.0	R	Bekslaan
24.4	CS	cross N206
25.0	CS	cross railway tracks (10 m), CS cross footbridge/ Hyacinthenlaan

25.3	L	Hyacinthenlaan
25.5	R	Zwarteweg
25.6	L	N208, T-Bennebroek
27.5	R	Sparrenlaan (through gateway)
27.7	CS	through wooden gate, Groenendaal
28.0	CS	through wooden gate
28.2	R	Bosbeeklaan
28.4	L	Glipperdreef
29.4	R	(at church) Heemstedsedreef
29.7	R	Cruquiusweg/N201
31.0	L	(cross N201) Cruquiusdijk
31.1	SS R	Cruquius Museum
31.8	L	cross Fietsbrug Cruquius
31.9	L	bike path (200 m hard-packed dirt)
32.1	R	Hommeldijk
33.5	VL	Zuid Schalkwijkerweg
35.0	CS	Noord Schalkwijkerweg (along Spaarne)
36.0	CS	along Spaarne
36.7	L	over Langebrug (bridge)
37.5	CS	on Spaarne (road; no bike path 400 m)
38.1	SS R	Molen De Adriaan (windmill)
38.2	L	Nieuwe Gracht
38.4	R	Jansweg
38.7	L	Stationsplein
38.8	CS	Haarlem Railway Station
38.9	End	VVV Haarlem

Haarlem

Haarlem, only 15 minutes by train from Amsterdam, doesn't have the big-city feel, and is a good place from which to take day trips to Amsterdam. It is also close to the tulip fields to the south and the sand dunes along the coast to the west. The focal point of Haarlem is the Grote Markt, dominated by the Grote St. Bavokerk, with its beautifully decorated 1738 Müller organ on which Mozart played. (Organ concerts are given in the summer months.) On the Grote Markt are also the medieval Stadhuis, the Vleeshal (Meat Hall), and the Vismarkt (Fish Market). On Saturdays, the Grote Markt hosts a colorful flower and fruit market. Haarlem is also sprinkled with *hofjes* (courtyards surrounded by small houses), originally almshouses for elderly women. Ask at the VVV for locations.

The painter Frans Hals was Haarlem's native son, and the city proudly houses many of his works, among others, in the Frans Hals Museum, Groot Heiligland 62 (www.franshalsmuseum.nl, closed Mondays), in a 17th-century almshouse. The Teylers Museum, Spaarne 16 (www.teylersmuseum.nl, closed Mondays), the Netherlands' oldest museum, dating to 1778, originally promoted arts and sciences, but today exhibits paintings and drawings (including a Michelangelo and a Rembrandt), fossils, coins, and scientific instruments. The Corrie ten Boomhuis, Barteljorisstraat 19 (www.corrietenboom.com, tours Tuesdays through Saturdays), is the house where Corrie ten Boom and her family hid Jews in World War II. The family ended up in a concentration camp, and only Corrie survived.

Information:	VVV Haarlem, Stationsplein 1 (Tel. 0900 616 1600, www.vvvzk.nl), is at the station. The ANWB is at Gedempte Oudegracht 39 (Tel. 023 531 9163). The most convenient internet access is Hotel Amadeus (see "Where to Stay").
Bicycle Shops:	Rijwielshop Station (Tel. 023 531 7066) is Haarlem's only place for rentals. Near the station is De Rijwielhal, Rozenstraat 24-26 (Tel. 023 532 5602), and in the center is Wolkenfietser, at Koningstraat 36 (Tel. 023 532 5577, jos@wolkenfietser.nl).
Where to Stay:	The friendly, centrally-located Joops Hotel, Oude Groenmarkt 20 (Tel. 023 532 2008, www.joopshotel.com), has rooms between €65 and €120 and apartments from €100; breakfast is €5 to €10 extra. Hotel Amadeus, Grote Markt 10 (Tel. 023 532 4530, www.amadeus-hotel.com), is a small hotel built in 1588; singles are €57.50 and doubles are €80. It has no place for bikes, but the secure *fietsenstalling* at Botermarkt 6 is only a two-minute walk away. Near the station, Golden Tulip Hotel Lion d'Or, Kruisweg 34 (Tel. 023 532 1750, www.goldentulip.com/goldentulipliondor), has singles from €145 and doubles from €170. VVV Haarlem can make local B&B reservations.
	Haarlem Stayokay Hostel, Jan Gijzenpad 3 (Tel. 023 537 3793, www.stayokay.com/haarlem), is 3 km north of the city.

Camping De Liede, Lie Oever 68 (Tel. 023 535 8666), is located 2.5 km east of Haarlem and open all year. In the summer, there is also camping on the coast around Zandvoort.

Where to Eat: Several restaurants with a variety of cuisines are located on the Grote Markt and on nearby Lange Veerstraat. Close to the Grote Markt, on Paarlaarsteeg 10, the cozy Rembrandt (Tel. 023 531 1699) serves French cuisine (dinner only, closed Mondays). Café 1900, Barteljorisstraat 10, is a charming eatery which serves snacks and light meals.

Day 7: Haarlem to Amsterdam

Follow the Spaarne River north from Haarlem to Spaarndam, a picturesque village surrounded by water regulated by locks. On one of the locks (5.5 km) is a statue of Hans Brinker, the little boy who prevented a flood by sticking his finger into a hole in the dike, according to American writer Mary Mapes Dodge, who wrote the mythical tale *Hans Brinker or the Silver Skates* in 1873.

Ride 4 km along the canal to the huge Noordzeekanaal, with its free ferry which runs 24 hours a day, every day of the year. On the other side, ride atop the dike to the tiny village of Nauerna. The houses appear to be one story tall, but look below.

Continue on the dike to 14.2 km, where you turn north to Westzaan. This village stretches along the road for 4 km, with many houses dating to the 17th and 18th centuries. The houses are painted in the traditional "Zaan" green with white trim. At the north end of the village, the old Stadhuis (17.9 km) is truly a centerpiece.

The Zaan region once had around 600 windmills, but only a few dozen remain. Soon after leaving Westzaan, you will see three windmills, with more to come.

Approaching Zaandijk, you will certainly smell chocolate in the air. The aroma of cocoa comes from the ADM plant (21.0 km). Wind through Zaandijk, following the signs to Zaanse Schans. Stop on the Julianabrug (21.6 km). From the bridge is a great view of Zaandijk and Zaanse Schans, with its characteristic windmills.

Zaanse Schans (www.zaanseschans.nl, open daily), an open-air museum, is a recreation of a typical 18th-century Zaan village. Houses were brought in from all over the area and assembled alongside the Zaan River. Visit the cheese farm, the clogmaker, the old-fashioned grocery store, and the four mills, including a mustard grinding mill.

From here, wind your way along canals and past the A7 freeway to Het Twiske, a man-made nature area, part of the Twiskepolder. Open grass areas, forests, and lakes make this a lovely spot for Amsterdammers escaping the city. LF7a route signs and ANWB mushrooms guide you 4 km through the area to the town of

Landsmeer. From Landsmeer, head to the Noordhollandskanaal for 7 km of canal-side cycling to the IJ ferry (free) which crosses the IJ River every 5 or 10 minutes to the Amsterdam Centraal Station.

Cue Sheet

0.0	Start	VVV Haarlem go W on Stationsplein
20 m	L	Kruisweg
0.2	L	Parklaan
0.7	L	Friese Varkensmarkt (along Spaarne)
3.3	R	Spaarndamseweg sign "Spaarndam"
4.6	VR	over bridge Pol (Spaarne on R)
5.3	CS	walk over footbridge, Oostkalk, T-Spaarndam
5.4	CS	Taanplaats (10 m), VL Sluissteeg
5.4	R	(50 m) IJdijk/Spaarndammerdijk
5.5	SS R	Hans Brinker statue
5.7	VL	dir. "Zaanstad," Zijkkanaal-C weg
9.5	-	ferry across Noordzeekanaal

Map 11.5. Utrecht & South Holland Tour, Day 7.

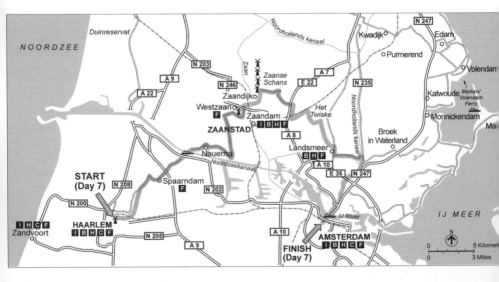

9.5	-	other side, bike path on R
9.7	R	sign "Nauerna," N246
9.8	R	sign "Nauerna"
11.8	CS	over locks, T-Nauerna
11.9	CS	Overtoom
14.2	L	dir. "Westzaan," Zuidende/Kerkbuurt
17.9	CS	T-Westzaan (Centrum), Stadhuis
18.1	R	sign "Zaanse Schans," N515
19.3	SS R	Schoolmeester Molen (windmill)
20.0	L	sign "Zaanse Schans" (under A8)
20.5	R	sign "Zaanse Schans," Dr. Jan Mulderstraat
21.0	L	sign "Zaanse Schans," cross railway tracks
21.1	R	cross N203 (50 m), VL sign "Zaanse Schans," Parklaan
21.3	VL	sign "Zaanse Schans"
21.4	R	sign "Zaanse Schans"
21.5	L	sign "Zaanse Schans"
21.6	L	sign "Zaanse Schans," over Julianabrug
21.6	SS L	view from Julianabrug
21.9	L	into Zaanse Schans (10 m), L (20 m) R
22.0	SS	Zaanse Schans
22.1	CS	(after first windmill) bike path along Kalverringdijk
23.6	R	sign "Neck and Purmerend"
25.4	R	over bridge (10 m), R sign "Zaanstad"
26.7	CS	cross N515 sign "Het Twiske," along canal
26.8	VL	along canal
27.6	R	sign "Het Twiske" (20 m), R along A7
29.4	U L	sign "Het Twiske," along railway tracks
31.3	R	Stationsstraat
31.7	CS	sign "Het Twiske and Amsterdam," alley for 20 m
32.0	R	#25209 Het Twiske

32.2	L	LF7a #25208
32.5	L	LF7a bike path (not road)
32.7	CS	LF7a
33.5	L	LF7a
33.7	R	along lake (90m), R (no LF7a sign here)
33.9	L	LF7a #25220 (10 m) R
34.1	L	LF7a #25219
34.7	L	LF7a #25218
35.0	R	LF7a
35.4	VR	LF7a #25213 sign "Landsmeer"
36.0	L	LF7a
36.3	R	LF7a
36.5	L	LF7a #25215, walk over long footbridge sign "Amsterdam"
36.8	R	LF7a sign "Amsterdam" Noordeinde/Dorpsstraat, T-Landsmeer
38.1	L	LF7a (at police station) Van Beekstraat
39.9	CS	do not follow LF7a
40.8	R	sign "Amsterdam," Kanaaldijk (along Noordhollandskanaal)
44.7	R	(50 m) L LF7a sign "Centrum" (along Noordhollandskanaal)
46.9	L	LF7a to the station, Buiksloterweg
47.3	-	IJ River ferry
47.3	L	De Ruijterkade
47.4	End	rear of Amsterdam Centraal Station

12.

Zeeland & Brugge

ZEELAND (literally Sealand) is made up of several islands in an extensive river delta, where three rivers, the Rhine, the Maas, and the Schelde, come together to drain into the North Sea. For centuries much of the Netherlands has battled the sea, but no area has struggled as much as Zeeland. On November 19, 1421, the St. Elisabeth's Day flood killed about 10,000 people and flooded the entire delta. More recently, on January 31, 1953, a flood killed about 2,000 people, caused ir-

Delta Project

Following the tragic flood in 1953, a massive engineering undertaking, the Delta Project, was begun in 1958. The initial idea was to heighten and strengthen the existing dikes and to dam the major estuaries of the delta, turning them into freshwater lakes. But in the 1960s, environmentalists voiced their concerns about the impact on fish, wildlife, and inland areas such as the sensitive Biesbosch National Park (see "North Brabant," page 244), not to mention the demise of the local fish industry.

As a result of revolutionary engineering innovations, there now exists an impressive system of dikes, locks, and storm surge barriers that can be opened and closed as the need arises. Only the Veerse Meer was closed off completely. The most incredible portion of the project is the Oosterschelde Stormvloedkering, three kilometers of movable barriers between Noord-Beveland and Schouwen-Duiveland. It took 10 years to complete and is the focus of the Delta Expo (see "Islands of Zeeland," Day 1).

reparable damage to dikes and landscape, and left 500,000 people homeless. As a result, the Delta Project (see Boxed text) was set into motion.

Zeeland today has huge sea dikes, farmland, and a coastline with seaside villages and recreation areas. Marvel at Middelburg, the capital, and visit other traditional towns, like Veere and Zierikzee. And be sure to try the famous Zeeland mussels and seafood.

Zeeland is also a jumping off point for northern Belgium. On the way, you will pass through the "other" Zeeland, Zeeuws-Vlaanderen (Zeeland-Flanders), which parallels the Belgian border and is separated from the rest of the Netherlands by water. Until recently, the only way across was by ferry, but since 2003, cars go by tunnel under the Westerschelde.

Middelburg

Middelburg, Zeeland's capital, is surrounded by canals. Laid out by the *Zee Guizen* ("Sea Beggars," as the Spanish rulers called the 16th-century Dutch rebels). They captured the town in 1574 and built the canals in 1595 as a line of fortification. The Nazis destroyed much of Middelburg's center in 1940, but many of the buildings have been restored, including the Gothic Stadhuis (tours daily), which dominates the Markt.

Allow time to visit the Abbey, built in 1120 and today the seat of the provincial governement. The complex has three churches, two museums, the Roosevelt Study Center, and an herb garden. On the Abbey grounds are also the Historama (open daily, April through October), which presents the abbey's history, and the Zeeuws Museum (www.zeeuwsmuseum.nl), which details Zeeland's history with archaeological finds and 18th-century tapestries and paintings depicting scenes in Zeeland.

The town has two main squares. The Markt is surrounded by shops and restaurants, and is the site of the Thursday market, where you can sometimes see Zeelanders in traditional dress. The Damplein, east of the Abbey, is ringed by 18th-century houses, many now shops and restaurants.

Information:	Instead of a VVV, Middelburg has Tourist Shop Middelburg at Markt 65C (Tel. 0118 674 333, www.touristshop.nl). The regional VVV for Walcheren and Noord-Beveland is in Domburg (www.vvvwnb.nl, see page 223). The ANWB is at Nieuwe Burg 40 (Tel. 0118 659 900). Check e-mail at the bookstore Drukkerij, Markt 51 (Tel. 0118 886 874), or at the library, Kousteensedijk 7 (Tel. 0118 644 000).
Bicycle Shops:	At the station, Fietspoint Middelburg, Kanaalstraat 22 (Tel. 0118 612 178), rents bicycles. In the center are Delta Cycle on the Zusterplein (Tel. 0118 639 245) and Halfords at Lange Delft 84 (Tel. 0118 651 351).
Where to Stay:	Near the station and overlooking the canal are three hotels and a B&B. On the corner, Grand Hotel du Commerce at

Loskade 1 (Tel. 0118 636 051, www.fletcher.nl) has singles
from €62 and doubles from €80. Next door, Hotel De
Nieuwe Doelen, Loskade 3-7 (Tel. 0118 612 121,
wwwhoteldenieuewedoelen.nl), has singles from €75 and
doubles from €91. Le Beau Rivage, Loskade 19, has the
same owners and prices as Hotel De Nieuwe Doelen.
Familiehotel Roelant, Koepoortstraat (Tel. 0118 627 659,
www.familiehotelroelant.nl), has singles from €50 and
doubles from €70. The bicycle-friendly owner has a shed
with tools for bike repair.

Wedged in amongst the hotels is one of the half dozen B&Bs
in Middelburg, B&B Alto Vista, Loskade 17 (Tel. 0118 651
265,www.altovista.biz); singles are €28 and doubles are €42.

Stayokay Hostel Domburg, Duinvlietweg 8 (Tel. 0118 581
254, www.stayokay.com/domburg), is housed in a castle,
Kasteel Westhove, about 10 km west of Middelburg (see
"Domburg Day Ride," page 222). It's worth the ride to stay
in this castle.

Camping Middelburg, Koninginnelaan 55 (Tel. 0118 625
395, www.campingmiddelburg.nl), is 2 km west of the
center.

Where to Eat: You'll find several restaurants on the Markt and the
Damplein. For fabulous French cuisine, head to Bistro
Provençal, in the cellar of Familiehotel Roelant (see "Where
to Stay," closed Sundays). For Italian fare, go to La Picola
Italia, Damplein 46 (Tel. 0118 674 780). For Indonesian
food, try the buffet at Surabaya, Stationsstraat 20 (Tel. 0118
612 160). Desafinado at Koorkerkstraat 1 (Tel. 0118 640
767, www.desafinado.nl) is a jazz eetcafé.

Islands of Zeeland Tour

Total Distance:	117.9 km
Duration:	2 days
Highlights:	Middelburg, Veere, Delta Project, Westenschouwen forest, dike-top cycling to Zierikzee, the Zeelandbrug, north coast of Zuid-Beveland
Terrain:	Level
When to Go:	Mid-April through early October. The most crowded months are the summer holiday months of July and August. Most

campgrounds don't open until Easter and close by early October.

Maps: Michelin 532 Zuid-Nederland/Pays-Bas Sud, ANWB/VVV
                       Toeristenkaart Zeeland

Start/Finish: Middelburg/Middelburg

Access: By train, Middelburg is about two hours from Amsterdam.

Connecting routes: Brugge: "Northern Belgium Excursion"; train to Breda or
                       Den Bosch: "South of the Big Rivers Ride"; train to
                       Amsterdam, Leiden or Den Haag: "Witches, Windmills, and
                       West Coast Ride"

This two-day ride takes you across the islands of Zeeland. Start in Middelburg on Walcheren and head north through Veere. The route touches the west corner of Noord-Beveland, crosses the Delta Project to the island of Schouwen-Duiveland, and goes through a forest and atop dikes to charming Zierikzee.

On the second day, the Zeelandbrug takes you to the eastern corner of Noord-Beveland. Enjoy relaxing cycling along the sheltered north coast of Zuid-Beveland and along the Veerse Meer, and then back to Veere and Middelburg.

Day 1: Middelburg to Zierikzee (66.9 km)

For the first part of the day, the route follows the signed LF1b Noordzee (coastal) route. Wind through the streets of Middelburg and exit via the Koepoort, the only remaining city gate, built in 1735. At 3.8 km, stop at the Kaasboerderij Schellach, a farm selling dairy products and bread (closed Sundays), and continue through farmland to Veere.

Entering Veere, you can't miss the massive 15th-century Gothic Grote Kerk (beside the VVV). The tower, never completed, was to be three times as tall (open April through October). Veere's prosperity resulted from the Scottish wool trade. Two Gothic houses, Schotse Huizen, Kade 25 and 27, now a museum, were the former offices and warehouses of Scottish wool merchants. On the water, the 15th-century tower, Campveerse Toren, was one of Veere's early fortifications. The 15th-century Stadhuis has a 48-bell carillon.

Leaving Veere, watch for the turns (10.0 km). There is an LF1b sign for the first turn, but no sign onto the small cobbled street. The road follows the Veerse Meer to Vrouwenpolder and over the Veerse Gatdam, which closes off the Veerse Meer from the North Sea. Look to your right for views of Veere.

The bike path from the island of Noord-Beveland to Schouwen-Duiveland, along the barrier dam (see boxed text "Delta Project"), is several meters above the sea. The wind on the exposed dam can make cycling difficult.

You may have to wait a few minutes at the Roompotsluis (23.5 km) as boats make their way through the locks from the North Sea to the Oosterschelde. At

26.3 km, take a side trip to the artificial island of Neeltje Jans (follow the signs to Waterland Neeltje Jans) and the Delta Expo (www.neeltjejans.nl, year-round, closed Mondays and Tuesdays November through March), where you can learn about the history of the Delta Project. The sheer scale of the project is sure to impress.

On Schouwen-Duiveland, the side trip (30.6 km) leads to a viewpoint, beach, and dune access. The turn at 30.6 km and the next few turns have no LF1b signs. Pass through the hamlet of Westenschouwen. Prior to entering the forest, Boswachterij Westenschouwen, there is beach access and a café (31.5 km), after which you will have 4 km of riding on a bike path through the pine forest.

The two towns Burgh and Haamstede were combined, forming Burgh-Haamstede. The prettier of the two is Haamstede, centered around an architecturally appealing central area with church and 14th-century castle, Slot Haamstede (info@vvvhaamstede.nl, tours Wednesdays at 11:30 a.m., June through September).

To go through Renesse, a rather plain resort town crowded with tourists in the summer, continue straight, following the LF1b and signs to Brouwershaven. At 47.6 km, continue straight; leave the LF1b route, which turns north. Follow the coastline east to Brouwershaven, keeping the water on your left. For part of this, you will be up on the dike. Pass the windmill and enter Brouwershaven, made famous as a trading port for beer (*brouwer* means brewer). The village has an elongated harbor, which allows boats to sail right up to the center. The Stadhuis dates to the 16th century.

From Brouwershaven, the route cuts inland through farmland. At 58.2 km, climb onto the Schouwsedijk for 5 km of dike-top cycling, with views in all directions. Zierikzee lies ahead, the huge St. Lievens Monstertoren acting as a beacon. Enter Zierikzee through the majestic Nobelpoort gate and ride south to the VVV by the harbor.

Cue Sheet

0.0	Start	Middelburg Railway Station go north on Stationsstraat
0.2	R	LF1b Londensekaai
0.4	L	LF1b Nieuwstraat
0.5	R	Korte Delft/Damplein
0.7	L	LF1b Damplein
0.8	R	LF1b Dam
0.9	L	LF1b Molstraat/Koepoortstraat
1.2	SS	Koepoort
1.3	VL	LF1b Veersesingel/Oordsingel

1.5	R	LF1b Sportlaan (20 m), LF1b Laan van Nieuwenhove
1.7	R	Nadorstweg
2.2	R	Prooijensweg
3.8	SS R	cheese farm
3.9	R	LF1b Golsteinweg
5.0	L	LF1b N663
5.3	R	LF1b Vioskeweg
5.7	L	LF1b Zanddijkseweg
8.2	R	LF1b
9.2	CS	church and VVV, Oudestraat

Map 12.1. Islands of Zeeland Tour, Days 1 & 2.

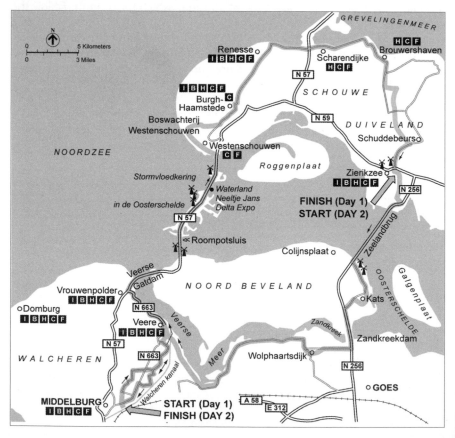

9.5	L	LF1b Markt, T-Veere
9.7	L	Kaai/Haven
10.0	R!	LF1b Bastion (10 m), L cobbled street
10.2	R	LF1b sign "Zierikzee," Langedam
10.4	R	LF1b N663
14.2	CS	LF1b N663
15.0	L	LF1b under N57
15.1	R	LF1b (20 m), L LF1b Dorpsdijk, T-Vrouwenpolder
15.4	R	LF1b (at church) Fort den Haakweg
16.5	R	LF1b sign "Delta Expo," Vroonweg
17.0	SS	views: beach to L, Veere to R
21.2	VL	bike path (to north) sign "Roompot"
23.5	SS	Roompotsluis (locks)
23.5	L	LF1b bike path
26.3	ST R	RT=1.4 km Delta Project
27.0	CS	alongside N57
29.9	L	LF1b bike path along dunes
30.6	R	(no sign) Kamperweg
30.6	ST CS	ST=600 m to point and beaches
31.3	L	Steenweg, T-Westenschouwen
31.5	R	Kraijensteinweg
31.8	R	Boswacherterij Westenschouwen (forest)
33.8	R	LF1b bike path
35.4	R	bike path
36.1	R	LF1b
36.4	CS	parking area
36.6	L	LF1b Hogeweg
37.6	CS	LF1b (to church), T-Burgh
37.8	L	LF1b Burghsering (at church)
38.0	L	LF1b Kerkstraat

38.9	L	LF1b T-Haamstede
39.0	SS L	Slot Haamstede (castle)
39.4	CS	LF1b R106
43.2	CS	LF1b sign "Centrum Brouwershaven"
43.7	CS !	T-Renesse
45.0	R	(no LF sign) Rampweg/N652
47.6	CS !	sign "Brouwershaven," (do not follow LF1b sign)
48.8	VL	keep dike on L, T-Scharendijke
49.6	R	"Platte van Schouwenroute" sign (gravel bike path) on Scharendijk
50.2	L	Langendijk
53.6	VR	onto bike path, Heeernisweg
55.0	CS	sign "Brouwershaven," Noorddijk
55.2	R	Nieuwe Jachthaven (windmill on R), Platte van Schouwenroute sign
56.0	L	Markt and Stadhuis, T-Brouwershaven
56.1	CS	small Platte van Schouwenroute sign, Zuiddijkstraat
56.3	CS	dir. "Zierikzee"
56.7	RA CS	cross N653 onto Zuidernieuwlandweg
57.8	L	unmarked road, Platte van Schouwenroute sign
58.2	VR	Schouwsedijk
63.2	R	N654 T-Schaddebeurs (on L)
65.8	L	sign "Zierikzee"
65.9	R	to Nobelpoort/Korte Nobelstraat
66.1	L	(at windmill) St. Anthoniesdam
66.2	R	Lange Nobelstraat
66.4	L	Mol/Havenplein
66.6	R	Visstraat
66.9	R	Nieuwe Haven (50 m)
66.9	End	VVV Zierikzee

Zierikzee

Zierikzee, founded around 800, was strategically positioned on shipping cross-roads, and obtained a lot of its early wealth from trade with the Hanseatic league (see boxed text "Hanseatic League," page 144). Other sources of prosperity were salt and madder (a root producing a red dye). The town fell into decline when the Spanish took it in 1576, but much of the architecture has been restored.

The town has three impressive city gates: the 16th-century Noordhavenpoort, the 14th-century Zuidhavenpoort, and the 14th-century Nobelpoort, which is flanked by two tall pepperpot towers (later additions).

The Stadhuis has an unusual 16th-century tower and onion dome adorned with a statue of Neptune. Inside, the Stadhuismuseum traces local history. Another notable museum, housed in 's-Gravensteen, the old 14th-century jail, is the Maritiem Museum (open daily), with maritime exhibits. The enormous tower, the St. Lievens Monstertoren, begun in 1454, was never completed due to lack of finances. It reached 56 m (184 ft) instead of the intended 130 m.

Information:	VVV Zierikzee is at Nieuwe Haven 7 (Tel. 0900 202 0233, www.vvvschouwenduiveland.nl). The library, Haringvlietplein 2 (Tel. 0111 414 548), has internet access.
Bicycle Shops:	Bike shop John Boon is at Meelstraat 31 (Tel. 0111 450 018), and Jan de Jonge Tweewielers is at Weststraat 5 (Tel. 0111 412 115).
Where to Stay:	Zierikzee has one hotel, one pension, and a handful of B&Bs; book early in the summer. Hotel Van Oppen, Verrenieuwstraat 11 (Tel. 0111 412 288, fax 0111 417 202) has singles from €35 and doubles from €60. Pension Klaas Vaak, Nieuwe Bogerdstraat 24 (Tel. 0111 414 204, klaasvaak@zeelandnet.nl), charges €24 for singles and €37 for doubles.
	B&B Meelstraat 56 (Tel. 0111 413 787, m.vanden.houten@freeler.nl) has rooms for €18 per person. The VVV has a list of more B&Bs.
	Camping De Val is at Straalweg 5 (Tel. 0111 413 429, camping.de.val@hetnet.nl). Mini-camping De Toren, Eerste Weegje 2 (Tel. 0111 412 308, campingdetoren@ zeelandnet.nl), 400 m from the harbor, is open mid-March to end October.
Where to Eat:	On the Havenplein is a good selection of restaurants, including Eetcafé Marktzicht at Havenplein 12 (Tel. 0111 415 195). For Greek food, try Delphi on the Schuithaven (Tel. 0111 422 393). China Garden is in Hotel Van Oppen (see "Where to Stay").

Day 2: Zierikzee to Middelburg (51.0 km)

A leisurely day takes you over the Netherlands' longest bridge and along the Veerse Meer. Start the day 17 m (56 ft) above the water on the 50-arch Zeelandbrug, Europe's second longest bridge. Built in 1955, the bridge links Zierikzee with Noord-Beveland. Eastern Noord-Beveland is mainly agricultural, punctuated with a few small villages such as Kats.

Cross Zandkreek on the Zandkreekdam to Zuid-Beveland. Turn right at ANWB post #20 and continue to Wolphaartsdijk. Just after the impressive two-story windmill (24.0 km), turn right onto Veerweg toward the coast, then onto the bike path along the Veerse Meer. For the next 4 km, the Veerse Meer, a playground for water enthusiasts, will be on your right. Watch birds at Middelplatten (28.4 km), with either your naked eye or the binoculars provided; there is a chart for bird identification.

The bike path veers away from the road (29.9 km) into the shady De Piet forest for 3 km, then goes back alongside the road until the route turns briefly into a camping area (36.0 km). At mushroom #24143 (36.1 km), the route turns away from the road and into an area of forests and pastures for the 4 km to Veere, where you emerge alongside the Kanaal door Walcheren.

After crossing the locks (42.1 km), turn south at 42.7 km (the route does not go into Veere), winding your way back to Middelburg along tiny canals and through open farmlands.

Cue Sheet

0.0	Start	VVV Zierikzee Go E on Nieuwe Haven
0.5	R	through Zuidhavenpoort (old city gate)
0.6	VR	sign "Zeelandbrug," 's Heer Lauendorp
0.8	R	sign "Zeelandbrug," Groenewegje
2.5	R	sign "Zeelandbrug"
2.9	CS	Zeelandbrug
8.4	U R	back toward Zeelandbrug
8.8	R	under bridge, Oost-Zeedijk
11.5	R	Bruggenroute sign
12.2	L	Noordlangeweg dir. "Kats"
12.4	CS	T-Kats
12.7	R	Kerkstraat
13.1	R	Dijkstraat/Boomdijk

15.5	L	Bruggenroute sign (under N256)
16.1	L	sign "Goes"
16.2	R	sign "Goes"
18.2	L	over Zandkreekdam
19.8	R	sign "Wolphaartsdijk," #20
19.9	R	sign "Wolphaartsdijk"
20.8	VL	sign "Wolphaartsdijk," Kaaidijk
23.0	CS	T-Wolphaartsdijk
23.3	R	Lepeistraat
23.4	L	Molendjk
24.0	R	Burg. Hackstraat dir. "Veerse Meer"
25.1	L	Aardbolweg/Muidenweg
27.2	R	onto bike path (alongside Veerse Meer)
28.4	SS R	Middelplatten
29.9	R	gravel bike path through forest De Piet
32.8	R	rejoin bike path on road
36.0	R	sign "Veere" (through campground)
36.1	L !	sign "Veere," #24143 Rammekensroute sign
36.5	L !	bike path, Rammekensroute sign
39.8	R	#24145 Wulpenborgseweg
42.0	L	bike path along Walcheren Kanaal
42.1	R	over locks (dismount)
42.2	R	sign "Veere," #17202
42.3	VL	Rammekensroute sign, "doorgaand verkeer Kanaalweg Westzijde"
42.6	L	sign "Centrum," Kanaalweg Westzijde
42.7	L	LF1a Veerseweg T-Veere (outskirts)
43.6	L	LF1a Kerkhofring
46.1	L	Oude Veerseweg, Rammekensroute sign (not LF1a)
47.2	R	Oude Kleverskerkweg

48.0	L	N663/Veerseweg/Nederstraat
50.1	R	Rotterdamsekaai
50.2	L	Rouaansekaai/ Londensekaai
50.8	L	Stationsstraat
51.0	End	Middelburg Railway Station

Domburg Day Trip

Total Distance:	46.5 km
Duration:	1 day
Highlights:	Coastal cycling, Domburg, cycling on the sea dike, Westkapelle's lighthouse, Aagtekerke
Terrain:	Level
When to Go:	From April through October the weather is best, but this ride would be suitable on a crisp winter's day.
Maps:	Michelin 532 Zuid-Nederland/Pays-Bas Sud, ANWB/VVV Toeristenkaart Zeeland
Start/Finish:	Middelburg/Middelburg
Access:	Middelburg Railway Station

Connecting routes: "Islands of Zeeland" and "Northern Belgium Day Trip"

The first 4 km replicates Day 1, "Islands of Zeeland Ride." Exit Middelburg via the Koepoort. At 3.8 km stop at the Kaasboerderij Schellach, a farm selling dairy products and bread (closed Sundays) and continue through farmland to Gapinge.

Leave Gapinge, passing the windmill. At 7.4 km, to your left, is the Vliedberg mound. Ancient mounds such as this, about 1 m high, were used as a refuge against floodwaters.

Head north through farmland to Vrouwenpolder, then along the edge of the dune area, accessed from several points. For a short time, you follow the Mantelingenroute. At 16.1 km, follow signs to Domburg, not Oostkapelle.

Farmlands give way to forests for the next 3 km after ANWB mushroom #23097. Should you wish to go to Oostkapelle, turn left on Duinweg (18.6 km), continuing for 1.2 km to Noordweg (N287). The VVV is on the corner. Turn right and continue 800 m to rach the center.

Otherwise, continue to Domburg. The short side trip at 21.1 km is to Kasteel Westhoeve, a 13th-century moated castle once the residence of Middelburg abbots, but now a Stayokay hostel (see "Where to Stay" in Middelburg). Next door, the orangerie houses the Zeeuws Biologisch Museum (www.zbm-westhoeve.nl, closed Mondays, plus Tuesdays November through March), a natural history museum and aquarium.

Domburg was one of the first beach resorts in the Netherlands, and a gathering place for artists such as Piet Mondriaan (which is the original spelling of the name, though often spelled Mondrian) in the early 20th century.

Leaving Domburg, pass the golf course. Stop to climb the steps (25.0 km) onto the 7 m high protective sea dike, which extends all the way to Westkapelle. About 1 km further, the bike path goes up onto the sea dike for an exhilarating 3 km ride to Westkapelle. At 29.3 km, the tank on the right is a remembrance of the 1944 bombing of the dike by the Allies, flooding the island and forcing out the Germans.

Westkapelle's most impressive sight is the lighthouse (30.2 km), perched on the remains of a Gothic church tower. The church was destroyed by fire in the 19th century.

From here, the route turns inland through pastures to Aagtekerke. Around the church is the compact village, a cluster of striking, traditionally-painted cottages with tarred black walls and contrasting white doors and window frames. At Dorpsplein 14, looking very sleek next to the old houses, is an enormous bike shop, Leo Joosse.

Further down the road (turn left onto Gasthuisstraat and go 200 m), Grijpskerke also centers on a church square. From here it's a quick ride back to Middelburg.

Cue Sheet

0.0	Start	Middelburg Railway Station go N on Stationsstraat
0.2	R	LF1b Londensekaai
0.4	L	LF1b Nieuwstraat
0.5	R	Korte Delft/Damplein
0.7	L	LF1b Damplein
0.8	R	LF1b Dam
0.9	L	LF1b Molstraat/Koepoortstraat
1.2	SS	Koepoort
1.3	VL	LF1b Veersesingel/Oordsingel
1.5	R	LF1b Sportlaan (20 m), LF1b Laan van Nieuwenhove
1.7	R	Nadorstweg
2.2	R	Prooijensweg
3.8	SS R	cheese farm

3.9	R	LF1b sign "Gapinge," Golsteinweg
4.1	L	Schellachseweg sign "Gapinge"
6.6	R	sign "Vrouwenpolder," T-Gapinge
7.1	L	sign "Vrouwenpolder," Snouk Hurgronjeweg
7.4	SS L	Vliedberg (mound)
9.4	R	sign "Vrouwenpolder" (50 m), L sign "Vrouwenpolder"
9.5	L	N663
10.3	VR	LF1b Mantelingenroute sign
11.0	L	LF1b under N57

Map 12.2. Domburg Day Trip.

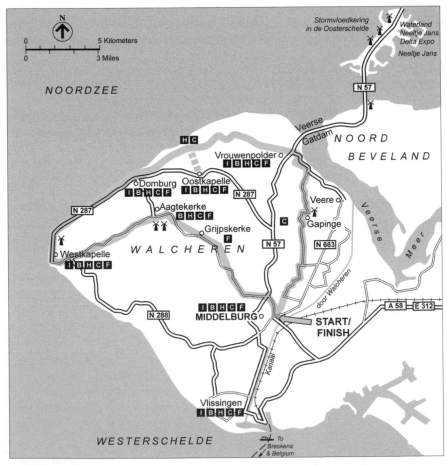

11.1	R	LF1b (20 m), L LF1b Dorpsdijk, T-Vrouwenpolder
11.4	R	LF1b (at church) Fort den Haakweg
12.6	L	Vroonweg sign "Oostkapelle and Domburg"
13.4	VL	Mantelingenroute
14.1	VR	Mantelingenroute, Noorddijk
15.4	VL	Mantelingenroute
15.5	R	Mantelingenroute
16.1	R !	unmarked road, Mantelingenroute sign "Domburg"
17.8	VR	#23097 gravel bike path
18.6	ST L	RT=4 km to Oostkapelle
18.6	CS	green bike signs sign "Domburg"
18.7	VR	#22258 sign "Domburg"
20.8	L	#22191
21.1	ST L	RT =400 m Kasteel Westhoeve and Zeeuws Biologisch Museum
21.2	R	sign "Domburg," N287
23.2	CS	N287/'tGroentje/Weststraat, T-Domburg
25.0	SS R	high point of dike and view
26.0	VR	onto sea dike
28.9	VL	N287
29.3	SS R	Tank memorial
29.4	L	sign "Centrum Aagtekerke," Achterweg
29.5	L	Kloosterstraat (80 m), R Zuidstraat, T-Westkapelle
30.2	R	Kerkeweg
30.2	SS	lighthouse church
30.3	L	Prelaatweg, sign "Aagtekerke"
35.3	L	Schoolstraat (just before windmill)
35.5	CS	T-Aagtekerke
35.6	R	Rijsoordselaan
35.7	L	sign "Grijpskerke," Pekelingseweg

39.8	CS	T-Grijpskerke (L 200 m)
44.4	L RA	Laan der Verenigde
44.6	R	N57/Seissingel sign "Centrum"
45.3	VL	cross canal into Seisstraat sign "Centrum and Station"
45.6	VL	Vlasmarkt sign "Centrum and Station"
45.8	CS	Markt
45.9	R	Gravenstraat
46.1	L	Hoogstraat
46.5	R	Stationsstraat
46.8	End	Middelburg Railway Station

Northern Belgium Excursion

Total Distance:	103.2 km
Duration:	2 Days
Highlights:	Sluis (Stadhuis and old ramparts), Schipdonk Kanaal, Damme, Brugge, Kanaal Brugge-Sluis
Terrain:	Level
When to Go:	This ride can be done year-round; cycling is mainly along sheltered canals. Try to avoid weekends. A popular vacation destination, Brugge is most crowded from April through October, and always on weekends.
Maps:	Michelin 532 Zuid-Nederland/Pays-Bas Sud, ANWB/VVV Toeristenkaart Zeeland
Start/Finish:	Middelburg/Middelburg
Access:	Middelburg Railway Station

Connecting routes: "Islands of Zeeland" and "Domburg Day Trip"

This ride takes you from Zeeland across the waters of the Westerschelde to Zeeuws-Vlaanderen, crossing the border to Belgium into the province of Flanders, and along tree-lined canals to the beautifully preserved ancient city of Brugge (the Flemish/Dutch name for the town called Bruges in English).

Day 1: Middelburg to Brugge (53.5 km)

The first part of the day follows the LF1a route from Middelburg along the Kanaal door Walcheren. This takes you to Vlissingen and the ferry to Breskens. Since the 2003 opening of the Westerschelde tunnel, the longest tunnel in the Netherlands, the ferry from Vlissingen to Breskens no longer takes cars. New high speed ferries are due to be operational by 2005.

Ferries depart once an hour, and twice an hour during weekday peak hours (5:50 a.m. to 8:50 a.m. and 3:50 p.m. to 5:50 p.m.); extra ferries are scheduled in the summer. One-way costs €2.20 per person plus 70 cents per bike (Tel. 013 549 9919, www.bba.nl).

After you exit the ferry, the route takes you 2 km along the N58 before turning right onto the N675 to Groede. At the time this was being written, the Breskens ferry holding area for cars, no longer needed, was being revamped, so directional signs from the ferry to the N58 may have changed.

Rural Zeeuws-Vlaanderen offers pleasant cycling. The route goes through Groede, to the left of the N675, and goes along the edge of Nieuwvliet. From tiny Zuidzande, cycle past the windmill and through pastures back to the N675. At the turn (23.6 km), there is a concrete marker with a maple-leaf and sign "Canadese Bevrijdingsroute" (Canadian Liberation Route), a reminder of Zeeland's liberation from the Nazis.

You will see Sluis, close to the Belgian border, packed with Belgians who come to the town for "border-bargain" shopping. From the 12th century until it silted up in the 15th century, Sluis was a port on the busy River Zwin. In the center is the turreted Stadhuis with its 14th-century belfry, and as you leave town, you will pass the windmill, Molen De Brak. At 28.6 km, do not follow the sign right to Brugge; instead, continue 700 m to the roundabout.

Just after Heille, you enter Belgium. There is no indication you have crossed the border until you reach Middelburg (B), somewhat smaller than Middelburg (NL). The route heads southwest across the N49 and to the Schipdonk Kanaal (39.0 km). The first 700 m is cobbled. Cycle 5 km of this picturesque tree-lined canal until you turn onto the Damse Vaart, an equally beautiful canal; this goes all the way to Brugge.

At 46.6 km is the town of Damme, the port for Brugge until the River Zwin (see "Sluis") silted up. The thriving port town then had a population of 60,000, but today has only 10,000. Damme is centered on the market square with its 15th-century Stadhuis, pretty gabled buildings, and statue of Damme native Jacob van Maerlant, a 13th-century poet. On Kerkstraat are the Museum Sint Jans Hospitaal and the 13th century Gothic Onze Lieve Vrouwekerk. Damme has lodging and restaurants, and is an alternative to staying in Brugge.

At the end of the canal (51.3 km) is Brugge's busy ring road. Cross the road and head to the center, keeping the canal alongside Wulpenstraat and Langerai on your left. Veer away from the canal at Genthof, following the route to the Markt and to the Burg, where the tourist office is on the eastern corner.

Cue Sheet

0.0	Start	Middelburg Railway Station go N on Stationsstraat
0.2	L	LF1a Turfkaai
0.7	L	LF1a sign "Vlissingen" (green bike signs)
0.8	L	LF1a sign "Vlissingen"
1.1	L	LF1a sign "Vlissingen," along canal (west side)
4.5	L	LF1a sign "Breskens ferry," over bridge

Map 12.3. Northern Belgium Excursion, Days 1 & 2.

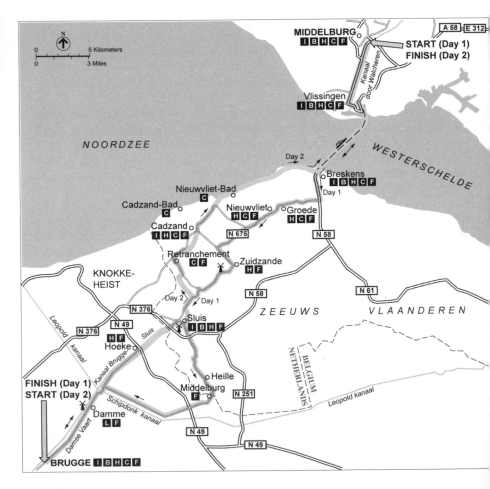

4.6	R	along canal (east side)
6.5	L	LF1a (at Westelijke Bermweg)
6.6	R	cross road
6.7	L	unmarked road to ferry
7.7	-	ferry to Breskens
7.7	L !	sign "Nieuwvliet"
7.9	R	to N58
9.9	R	sign "Groede, Sluis," N675
13.0	CS	T-Groede N675
15.7	CS	T-Nieuwvliet N675
19.2	L	sign "Oostburg," N674
21.0	R	sign "Sluis," T-Zuidzande, Zwinroute sign
22.0	SS R	windmill
22.5	R	sign "Sluis," Terhofstededijk, Zwinroute sign
23.6	L	sign "Sluis," Provincialeweg (N675)
23.6	SS	memorial marker
27.6	CS	Hoogstraat
28.0	L	Kappellestraat/Nieuwstraat, T-Sluis
28.4	SS R	De Brak mill
28.4	CS	Nieuwstraat (to Belgium)
29.3	RA CS	sign "Heille," Maerlant Route sign
31.2	R	#10928 sign "Heille, Middelburg (B)," Heilleweg
33.3	CS	T-Heille
34.5	R	T-Middelburg (Belgium)
34.6	CS	church on R
35.1	L	sign "Maldegem"
36.8	CS	cross N49
39.0	R	Schipdonk Kanaal (cobblestones 700 m)
39.7	CS	Schipdonk Kanaal
44.5	L	sign "Brugge," Damse Vaart (canal)

46.6	CS	T-Damme (on L) along Damse Vaart
51.3	R	ring road (Buiten Kruisvest)
51.4	L	cross road
51.5	CS	Sasplein/Wulpenstraat/Langerei
52.6	R	Genthof
52.9	VR	Academiestraat
53.0	L	Vlamingstraat
53.3	CS	Markt
53.4	L	Breidelstraat
53.5	End	Burg (Square) and Brugge Tourist Office

Brugge

Brugge, or Bruges, with its cobblestone streets, historic buildings, and pretty canals, is Belgium at its best.

Brugge centers on the impressive Markt, encircled by picture-postcard architecture, including the 13th-century Belfort Tower (open daily). Climb the 366 steps for a spectacular view, and, on the way up, look at the carillon.

The Burg has several remarkable buildings, including the 14th-century Gothic Stadhuis and its Gothic room (open daily). The Heilig-Bloed Basiliek (Basilica of the Holy Blood, www.holyblood.org, open daily) was built to enshrine a vial of Christ's blood; inside are various chapels and a museum.

Brugge boasts several excellent museums. The Memling Museum (open daily) at Mariastraat 38 houses works of Brugge native Hans Memling. The Groeninge Museum (open daily) at Dijver 12 has a collection of 15th to 20th-century Flemish art, including works by Van Eyck, Memling, Hieronymous Bosch, Delvaux, and Magritte. The Onze Lieve Vrouwekerk (Church of Our Lady, open daily), although not a museum, has Michelangelo's sculpture Madonna and Child. The church, built between the 13th and 15th centuries, has the tallest tower in Belgium, 122 m (400 ft). At the Lace Centre, Balstraat 14 (Tel. 050 330 072, kantcentrum@yucom.be, closed Sundays), watch the intricate process of lace making, Brugge's living tradition. The "bicyclists" statue at 't Zand Square is also worth a visit (see photo on page 25).

The Festival van Vlaanderen (Flanders Festival), around July 25 to August 8, is a fortnight of international music. Ascension Day sees Brugge come alive for the Festival of the Holy Blood.

Information: Toerisme Brugge is at Burg 11 (Tel. 050 448 686, www.brugge.be), and a small tourist office booth is at the railway station. There are several internet cafés in Brugge, including The Coffee Link, Mariastraat 38 (Tel. 050 349

973, www.thecoffeelink.com), and DNA Cybercafé, Langestraat 145 (Tel. 050 341 093, www.dna-cybercafe.com).

Pick up the brochure *5 x op de fiets rond Brugge* (5 Bike Rides Around Bruges), a guide for cycling in the immediate surroundings (available at Toerisme Brugge). The area around Brugge has many scenic backroads and picturesque bike paths. Quasimodo Tours (Tel. 050 370 470, www.quasimodo.be) offers guided bicycle tours in and around Brugge. Tours depart at 10 a.m. and 1 p.m., mid-March through September

Bike Shop: Closest to the center is Eric Popelier, Mariastraat 26 (Tel. 050 343 262).

Where to Stay: Advance reservations for are highly recommended in the summer months and on weekends. Between the railway station and the center, Hotel 't Breughelhof, Oostmeers 128 (Tel. 050 343 428, www.hotel-breugelhof.be), has rooms from €55, some with private facilities. Next door, Hotel 't Keizershof, Oostmeers 126 (Tel. 050 338 728, http://users.belgacom.net/hotel.keizershof), has singles for €25 and doubles for €38; showers are down the hall. Hotel Fevery Collaert, Mansionstraat 3 (Tel. 050 331 269, www.hotelfevery.be), near St. Gillis Church, is a few minutes walk from the Markt and has 10 rooms with private facilities from €60.

There are several dozen B&Bs in Brugge listed on the tourist office website.

The International Youth Hostel Europa, Baron Ruzettelaan 143 (Tel. 050 352 679, www.vjh.be), is south of the center, not far from the railway station. A few hundred meters north of the Markt is Snuffel Sleep-In Hostel at Ezelstraat 47 (Tel. 050 333 133, www.snuffel.be).

Camping Memling, Veltemweg 109, (Tel. 050 355 845, www.camping-memling.be) is about 2 km east of Brugge in Sint-Kruis.

Where to Eat: Several restaurants line the Markt, the Burg, and the streets around the two squares. Bistro Breughelhof (see "Where to Stay") has a restaurant. Brugge's specialty is *waterzooi*, a thick, creamy soup of chicken or fish. Mussels and waffles are also famous Belgian offerings.

'T Zand square has a Saturday morning market, and the Burg's market is every Wednesday.

Day 2: Brugge to Middelburg (49.7 km)

Day 2 of this route follows the classic long distance route, the LF1b from Brugge to Middelburg. The LF1b, the Noordzeeroute (North Sea Route), follows the North Sea coast for 610 km, commencing in Boulogne-sur-Mer, France, continuing through Belgium, and concluding in Den Helder, North Holland.

From the VVV, make your way back to the ring road where the Kanaal Brugge-Sluis begins (2.0 km). This is the same canal that you cycled along on Day 1; however, today you will be on the LF1b on the opposite, west side of the canal.

At 8.7 km, the Schipdonk Kanaal intersects the Kanaal Brugge-Sluis. The LF1b takes a rather circuitous path over the Schipdonk. Follow the signs carefully, and, after crossing the Schipdonk Kanaal, you will end up on the same side (west) of the Kanaal Brugge-Sluis (8.8 km).

Cycle along the canal for the next 8 km. The route leaves the canal prior to Sluis. Turn right onto a bike path of crushed shell (16.5 km) alongside a tiny canal. This bike path goes south of Sluis, following the old ramparts on the left. Cross Nieuwstraat (17.4 km) and continue on the other side. If you want to go into Sluis (on the left), this is the closest point to the town.

Pedal through the polders as the LF1b heads north to the coast. Pass through some rural farming communities and past several campgrounds. Once at the coast, you will notice an abundance of campgrounds (31.2 km) at Zwartepolder (marked #16). Climb the steps onto the high sea dike for water views or for cycling atop the dike.

Continue along the coast to Breskens. At Verklikker #20, there are steps leading to a wide beach with views across the Westerschelde. Your last chance for beach access before the ferry is 't Fort (40.2 km).

At 41.1 km, follow the LF1b signs south on the N58 to Breskens and the Vlissingen ferry. Go under the N58, swing back around, and follow the bike path to the ferry.

Once on the Vlissingen side, the LF1b follows the west side of the Kanaal door Walcheren all the way back to Middelburg. Follow the LF1b signs back to the station.

Cue Sheet

0.0	Start	Brugge Tourist Office go W on Burg/Breidelstraat
0.1	R	Markt
0.2	CS	Vlamingstraat
0.4	R	Academiestraat
0.5	VL	Genthof
0.8	L	Langerei/Wulperstraat
1.9	CS	cross ring road

2.0	CS	LF1b Noorweegse Kaai (canal)
6.8	CS	T-Damme
8.4	R	LF1b over bridge (20 m), L LF1b
8.5	L	LF1b over bridge
8.7	L	unmarked road (10 m), R unmarked road
8.8	L	over bridge (20 m), R LF1b
12.6	CS	under N49 T-Hoeke
16.3	VR	LF1b sign "Sluis," Maerlant Route sign (gravel 100 m)
16.4	L	LF1b over bridge
16.5	R	LF1b (crushed shell bike path 2 km)
17.4	CS	LF1b cross Nieuwstraat
18.7	R	LF1b #24536 sign "Breskens"
18.8	L	LF1b bike path
19.7	R	LF1b #15292 sign "Breskens," N675
20.6	L	LF1b sign "Breskens," bike path
21.6	VL	LF1b unmarked farm road
22.6	R	LF1b sign "Breskens"
23.5	L	LF1b T-Retranchement
24.0	R	LF1b
24.0	SS L	windmill
24.6	R	LF1b Bosweg
26.3	L	LF1b
27.4	L	LF1b
28.1	CS	LF1b N674 T-Cadzand
28.6	R	LF1b sign "Breskens"
28.8	VL	LF1b Mini-camping Wulpen
30.7	R	LF1b #21713
30.9	L	LF1b
31.4	SS	Zwartepolder #16 Nieuwvliet-Bad
32.1	VL	

34.1	SS	Verklikker #20
34.9	L	LF1b sign "Breskens"
35.2	VR	LF1b sign "Breskens"
35.5	L	LF1b (30 m) R
36.9	L	cross road (no sign) L LF1b 't Killetje
37.3	CS	LF1b (do not go to Breskens here)
37.6	SS	views
38.8	CS	LF1b
39.0	L	LF1b
39.6	CS	Strandplevier #29
40.2	SS L	't Fort
41.1	L	LF1b sign "Breskens & Vlissingen ferry"
41.2	R	bike path to ferry
42.0	-	ferry to Vlissingen
42.0	CS	LF1b sign "Middelburg"
43.2	CS	LF1b over bridge (Westelijke Bermweg) (40 m), R canal (west side)
48.6	VL	LF1b
48.7	R	LF1b through tunnel
48.9	R	LF1b sign "Station," Nieuwe Haven/Turfkaai
49.5	R	sign "Station," Stationsstraat
49.7	End	Middelburg railway station

13.

North Brabant

NORTH BRABANT, the largest province, is comprised largely of forests, heath, and farmland, and is crisscrossed by canals and rivers. Most of the province is above sea level. Art enthusiasts will delight in following the footsteps of Van Gogh, who was born in Zundert and lived and painted in Nuenen. History buffs will revel in the history and architecture of cities such as Den Bosch, Heusden, and Breda. Geographers will enjoy the "puzzling" twin-cities of Baarle-Nassau and Baarle-Hertog. And nature lovers will enjoy riverside panoramas, forested bike paths, and a visit to the Biesbosch National Park.

Cyclists relax on the banks of the Maas River en route to Heusden.

South of the Big Rivers Tour

Total Distance:	172.0 km
Duration:	4 days
Highlights:	St. Janskathedraal, dike along the Maas, Heusden, Dongedijk, Markkanaal-Zuid, Breda, Boven Mark, Baarle-Nassau/Baarle-Hertzog, Wilhelminakanaal, Oirschot, and Nuenen
Terrain:	Level
When to Go:	North Brabant is inland, so not subject to the strong coastal winds. This ride is good any time of year, but best between April and early October.
Maps:	Michelin 532 Zuid-Nederland/Pays-Bas Sud, ANWB/VVV Toeristenkaart Westelijk Brabant, Toeristenkaart Oostelijk Brabant, Fietsroute Netwerk De Baronie map, Fietsroute Netwerk De Kempen map
Start/Finish:	Den Bosch/Den Bosch
Access:	Den Bosch Railway Station, or Breda Railway Station. (This is a circular ride that can be started at either city.)
Connections:	Den Bosch is one mainline rail stop from Utrecht ("Witches, Windmills, and West Coast Ride," Day 2).

Begin in the capital, Den Bosch, head west along the Maas River, and stop at Heusden, one of the Netherlands' best preserved towns. Rivers, canals, and forests lead into and out of Breda, a city surrounded by parks and gardens. Quiet rural roads and canals, and a dip into Belgium via intertwined "twin" towns characterize the day from Breda to Oirschot. The return to Den Bosch takes you on a Van Gogh route and along tree-lined rural roads.

Den Bosch

Den Bosch is officially known as 's-Hertogenbosch (Count's Forest). Life centers around the triangular shaped Markt, where the 13th-century De Moriaan, the town's oldest building, houses the VVV. Alongside it stands the 15th-century Stadhuis, with a 35-bell carillon that chimes on the half hour. Markets are held (on the Markt) on Wednesday and Saturday mornings.

The St. Janskathedraal is one of the best examples of a Brabant Gothic church. Building began in the 14th century, and took nearly 200 years to complete. The church has an impressive interior that includes works by Den Bosch native Hieronymous Bosch. Next to the church is the Parade, a square that is the site of the Friday food market.

Behind the cathedral, at Choorstraat 16, is the Museum Slager (www. museum-slager.nl, closed Mondays), which contains the works of three generations of the Slager family of Den Bosch. The Noordbrabants Museum (www. noordbrabantsmuseum.nl, closed Mondays) is housed in the 18th-century former governor's mansion at Verwerstraat 41. It showcases the region's history, archaeological finds, paintings (including some by Van Gogh), sculptures, and works by Hieronymous Bosch.

Boat tours of the Binnen Dieze give an interesting perspective of the city, particularly because the river flows under many buildings and streets (mid-April through October, daily, 10 a.m. to 5 p.m.; a one-hour tour is €5). Tours depart from corner of Korenbrugstraat and Molenstraat.

Information: The VVV is at Markt 77 (Tel. 073 613 9629, www.vvvs-hertogenbosch.nl). The ANWB is located at Burg. Loeffplein 11-13 (Tel. 073 614 5354). Log on at Easy Internet Café, the first floor of the Free Record Shop, 28 Pensmarkt (Tel. 073 690 0021).

Bicycle Shops: Rijwielshop Van Deursen, next to the station at Stationsplein 77 (Tel. 073 613 4737), has rentals. Kemps Tweewielers is on Korenbrugstraat 10 (Tel. 073 613 7686, www.kempsbiketotaal.nl).

Where to Stay: Hotel Terminus, near the station at Boschveldweg 15 (Tel. 073 613 0666, www.hotel-terminus.nl), has singles for €28.50 and doubles for €54; shower and toilets are down the hall. Between the Markt and the St. Janskathedraal, Eurohotel Best Western at Hinthamerstraat 63 (Tel. 073 613 7777, www.eurohotel-denbosch.com) has singles from €65 and doubles from €85. On the high end, Golden Tulip Hotel Central, Burg. Loeffplein 98 (Tel. 073 692 6926, www.hotel-central.nl), has singles for €118 and doubles for €143.

There are several B&Bs in and around the city; the VVV has a list.

The closest camping is in Cromvoirt, 8 km southwest of Den Bosch. There are three campgrounds: Camping Brabant at Pepereind 13 (Tel. 0411 643 375, devonst@horizon.nl), Camping Zes Linden at Louvensestraat 7 (Tel. 0411 642 156, dezeslinden@horizon.nl), and De Leuvert at Louvensestraat 11 (Tel. 0411 641 406, www.deleuvert.nl). There is also a mini-camping, 't Ven, at Vendreef 3 (Tel. 073 511 6078, hetven@agronet.nl) in Vlijmen, east of Den Bosch.

Where to Eat: You'll have lots to choose from in two areas in particular. The first, Korte Putstraat, has 12 restaurants. The second, the intersection of Korenbrugstraat, Molenstraat, and Lepelstraat, has about eight restaurants. Look around for signs advertising *Bossche Bollen*. These scrumptious, chocolate-coated choux-pastry balls filled with whipped cream, a Den Bosch specialty, are available in many bakeries and cafés.

Day 1: Den Bosch to Heusden (18.1 km)

Leave Den Bosch on a long main road that has several name changes before you turn (2.2 km). At the traffic lights at 1.3 km, make a tiny turn to cross Aartshertogenlaan and then continue straight.

The turn into Orthen (2.3 km) takes you through a residential area. It's easy to miss the turn onto Engelsedijk, a small street right after the railway tracks. Once on Engelsedijk, you pass some lakes and polder.

Go 1.1 km along a service road along busy Treurenburg, then turn, go over the locks, Spuisluis Crevecoeur, and onto a dike alongside a canal. Cross the large locks, Sluis Engelen, and turn onto the dike road along the Maas River to Bokhoven, a tiny town where you'll see pretty houses with detailed brickwork, some with thatched roofs.

Watch carefully for the right turn (10.8 km) onto a tiny bike path on the dike; ride along the Maas River for 6 km of absolutely gorgeous cycling. Just before entering Heusden, pass through the small industrial area that is the town's shipyard. Just beyond that is the first of Heusden's three windmills. Turn into town by crossing the ramparts and wind your way to the center.

Cue Sheet

0.0	Start	Den Bosch Railway Station go E on Stationsplein
80 m	RA L	Koninginnelaan/Brugstraat/Orthenseweg
1.3	L !	(10 m), R (at Aartshertogenlaan) Orthenseweg
1.6	CS	under Orthen Viaduct
2.2	L	cross Hambakenweg at lights
2.3	R	Orthen
2.7	CS	cross railway lines
3.0	L !	Engelsedijk
4.4	CS	under A59

4.6	L	Engelsedijk/Gemaalweg
6.0	L	service road along Treurenburg
7.1	L	Crevecoeur
7.2	L	LF12b over Spuisluis Crevecoeur (locks)
7.3	R	Henriettewaard
8.0	L	Henriettewaard
8.3	CS	cross Sluis Engelen (locks)
8.4	R	LF12b dir. "Bokhoven and Heusden"
10.5	R	LF12b Graaf Engelbertstraat (at church), T-Bokhoven
10.8	R !	LF12b tiny bike path (after playground) to dike
16.0	R	bike path (at ferry access)
17.0	CS	LF7a
17.4	R	LF7a unmarked
17.5	L	LF7a (just after windmill)
17.6	L	LF7a Wielstraat

13.1. North Brabant Ride 1, South of the Big Rivers, Days 1 & 2.

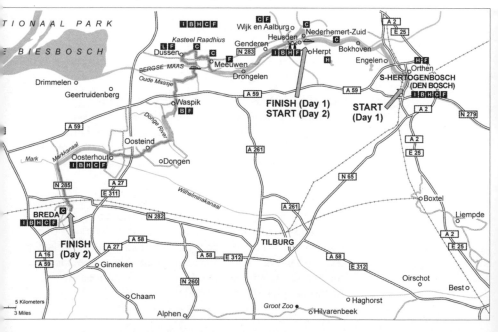

17.7	R	LF7a Herptsestraat
17.8	L	LF7a Putterstraat (10 m), R Zustersteeg
18.0	R	LF7a Hoogstraat
18.1	End	VVV Heusden

Heusden

Heusden is an old, restored, fortified town with 16th-century star-shaped ramparts. The architecture is mostly from the 16th and 17th century. The center is the Vismarkt (the old fish market) framed by lovingly restored buildings, several of which are now restaurants, some specializing in fish. Completing the picture are the Stadhuis, the Gothic church, a pretty harbor, and windmills.

Information: Heusden's Buro voor Toerisme is at Hoogstraat 4 (Tel. 0416 662 100, www.hbtheusden.nl).

Bicycle Shop: There is a small bike shop, Van Sterkenburg, at Burchtstraat 7 (Tel. 0416 661 395).

Where to Stay: Heusden has one hotel and two B&Bs, and there is another B&B in the next village, Herpt. Built in 1620, the gable-fronted Hotel In den Verdwaalde Koogel, Vismarkt 1 (Tel. 0416 661 933), has singles for €77.50 and doubles for €86.

B&B Hilwig, Burchtstraat 3 (Tel. 0416 665 220, open April through October) charges €40 for singles and €60 for doubles. Open all year is B&B Achter Sint Joris, Burchtstraat 8 (Tel. 0416 662 629, www.achtersintjoris.nl), with singles for €35 and doubles for €50.

Camping is across the Maas, at the secluded Natuurkamping Staatsbosbeheer-Nederhemert on Kastellaan (Tel. 0418 552 233, see Day 2 at 3.9 km), or Camping De Maashoeve, Maasdijk 181 (Tel. 0416 691 541), in nearby Wijk en Aalburg. The tourist office has a list of more campgrounds.

Where to Eat: Heusden's restaurants are clustered around the Vismarkt. The hotel (see "Where to Stay") has a fine dining restaurant. Brasserie-Restaurant Centraal, Vismarkt 9 (Tel. 0416 665 030, www.centraalheusden.nl), serves innovative meals. On the Vismarkt are also an eetcafé, a pizzeria, and a pancake restaurant. At Wijkestraat 6 is a Chinese-Indonesian restaurant (Tel. 0416 662 891).

Day 2: Heusden to Breda (55.5 km)

This route crosses the Bergse Maas twice by ferry. The first crossing takes you north of the river through the "Land van Altena," seven rural villages. (In a portion of this area, you will use the knooppunt system that is part of the small Altena-Biesbosch Fietsroute Netwerk.) After crossing the Maas the second time, the route heads southwest to Breda along two waterways, the tiny Donge River and the Markkanaal, both with bike paths away from traffic.

Leave Heusden the way you came in, heading 2 km back to the ferry. The ferry runs daily from 6 a.m. to 10 p.m. (until 6 p.m. November through March); cyclists ride free.

On the other side, the route takes you on a dike to a forest. At 3.9 km is Nederhemert campground (see Heusden, "Where to Stay"), and 200 m further is Kasteel Nederhemert (restoration began in 2003). Soon after the castle, you pass through Nederhemert-Zuid.

The road has no bike path after you cross the Heusden Kanaal, but it's only 500 m until you turn off. On your right you can see Wijk en Aalburg, the largest of the seven villages in the area known as the "Land van Altena." For the next 10 km, you will cycle on and along the Maas dike, partly on the signed ANWB Maasroute, passing three of the "Altena" villages—Genderen, Drongelen (most of which was destroyed in World War II), and Meeuwen. To go into Meeuwen's center, go right instead of left at Dorpsstraat (18.3 km). Leaving Meeuwen (18.8 km), look to the right at the small castle, now a private residence.

Enter Dussen along a tree-lined canal. Kasteel Raadhuis (21.8 km) can be seen from the road, and it's only 150 m to the drawbridge. You can wander through the courtyard area when it's open. There are picnic benches near the entrance.

The ferry (25.0 km) runs on the same schedule as the first ferry. At 25.8 km, turn just before the bridge and cycle on the north side of the Oude Maasje, a tributary of the Maas. After crossing over (28.3 km), cycle through 2 km of apple and pear orchards.

Leaving Waspik, an ordinary town, watch for the tiny Stadhoudersdijk, with a cluster of thatched houses on the left after you turn. From here, cycle through farms to Dongedijk along the tranquil Donge River for 3 km.

Cycle through Oosteind, a 3 km long linear village. From Hoogstraat (39.0 km), easy to overshoot, the route goes through suburban Oosterhout. At 45.4 km, the maneuver at the roundabout to the Markkanaal is tricky. Be sure to turn onto Hondstraat, which feeds onto the canal. Cycle along the shady Markkanaal for 5 km before making your way to the busy N285 for the last 3 km into Breda.

Cue Sheet

| 0.0 | Start | VVV Heusden |
| | | go NE on Hoogstraat |

60 m	R	Zustersteeg
0.1	L	Putterstraat (10 m), R Herptsestraat
0.2	L	Wielstraat
0.3	R	onto bike path
0.5	R	at windmill (50 m), L Mastdijk
2.0	L	to ferry
2.1	-	ferry
2.1	CS	other side
2.5	CS	LF7b Bernsedijk
2.7	VL	Moffendijk #04486 sign "Nederhemert-Noord," gravel 800 m
3.9	CS	Kasteellaan
4.1	SS L	Kasteel Nederhemert
4.6	CS	Kerklaan (unpaved 400 m)
5.3	R	N831/bridge over Heusden Kanaal
7.0	CS !	N831 (no bike path 500 m)
7.5	L	sign "K58," dir. "Genderen"
7.6	R	sign "K58," sign "Genderen"
8.9	CS	sign "K59," Tol
9.3	VL	sign "K59," bike path onto dike
11.4	R	sign "K59," Maasroute, sign Tol
12.6	VL	(at K59) Maasroute sign, Molensteeg
13.2	R	Burg. v/d Schansstraat (at church), T-Drongelen
13.3	L	Maasroute sign, Gansoyen
16.6	CS	Maasroute sign Meeuwensedijk
17.4	R	dir. "Meeuwen," Dijksteeg
18.3	L	Dorpsstraat, T-Meeuwen
18.7	L	N283/Baan, sign "Dussen"
18.8	SS R	small private castle
19.9	VR	sign "K52," Baan
21.8	SS R	Kasteel Raadhuis (ST: RT = 300 m)

21.9	VL	sign "K50," Molenkade, T-Dussen
22.6	L	cross N283, Oude Kerkstraat dir. "Sprang-Capelle and ferry"
24.6	R	Veerweg sign "ferry "
25.0	-	ferry
25.0	CS	Veerweg, other side
25.8	R !	(before bridge) Overdiepsekade
28.3	L	bridge over Oude Maasje, Polanenweg
29.8	L	over A59, then CS
30.5	R	Schepenhof
30.6	L	Schoolstraat dir. "'s-Gravenmoer," T-Waspik
31.6	R !	Stadhoudersdijk
31.9	L	Lage Weg
32.9	L	Wielstraat
33.2	R	LF9a Dongedijk (gravel 2.3 km)
35.5	CS	Dongedijk (hard-packed dirt 1 km)
36.4	R	Provinciale Weg, T-Oosteind
39.0	L !	Hoogstraat
41.6	CS	(over A27) Hoogstraat
42.6	CS RA	Ridderstraat
44.0	R	Bredaseweg, T-Oosterhout
44.2	L	Wilhelminalaan
45.1	SS	Sluis 1
45.4	RA R !	bike path on N629 (20 m), L Hondstraat
45.6	CS	Markkanaal-Zuid
47.4	CS	#20050 Markkanaal-Zuid
49.9	L	#22522 sign "Terheijden," Salesdreef
50.0	R	Hartelweg
51.2	R	bike path to N285
51.4	L	N285/Terheijdenstraat
54.9	R	Delpratsingel

55.2	R	Meerten Verhoffstraat
55.4	L	Stationsplein, Breda Railway Station
55.5	L/end	Willemstraat, (30 m) VVV Breda

Breda

Breda has an old city center ringed by canals. The entire city is dotted with attractive parks such as the Burg. Sonsbeeck Park to the south and Valkenburg Park, once part of the castle grounds, to the north. Alongside Valkenburg is the serene Begijnhof, dating to 1535, with houses grouped around a courtyard and a medicinal herb garden. Within Valkenburg Park is the moated castle surrounded by fortified walls, part of which is Het Spanjaardsgat (Spanish Gate), two large towers with onion domes. The castle now belongs to the Netherlands Military Academy and isn't open to the public.

Breda is the party city of North Brabant on weekends and Mardi Gras. Breda's heart is the Grote Markt. Markets are on Tuesdays and Fridays. On the Grote Markt is the Stadhuis and Het Wit Lam (The White Lamb), the old meat market. On the Havermarkt is the 16th-century Grote Kerk, an immense Brabant-style Gothic church with a 97 m (318 ft) onion dome belfry and a 49-bell carillon. The mausoleum of Count Engelbrecht II is inside, as are several other tombs of the Oranje-Nassau dynasty.

Breda is a good base for trips to the enormous Biesbosch National Park (www.biesbosch.org), a unique wetland formed as a result of floodwaters flowing inland during the flood of 1421 (see "Zeeland," page 211). Although cycling is possible, the best way to experience the park is by boat from Drimmelen or Geertruidenberg (about 12 km north of Breda). You can take a regular boat trip, but in July and August, there are combination boat/bike trips. VVVs in Breda, Heusden, and Oosterhout have information. There is a visitor center in Drimmelen.

Information:	VVV Breda is at Willemstraat 17-19 (Tel. 0900 522 2444, www.vvvbreda.nl). The ANWB is at Nieuwe Ginnekenstraat 27 (Tel. 076 522 3232). Internetcafé Knowledgebase at Veermarktstraat 37(Tel. 076 515 6729) has internet access.
Bicycle shops:	Bike shop Schietecat is on Korte Boschstraat (Tel. 076 521 2830). Rijwielshop Breda, Stationsplein 16 (Tel. 076 521 0501), has rentals. Halfords is at Grote Markt 17 (Tel. 076 520 2052).
Where to Stay:	In the center, Hotel Van Ham at Van Coothplein 23 (Tel. 076 521 5229, hotel.van.ham@hetnet.nl) has simple singles and doubles for €40 and €60 respectively; toilets and showers are down the hall. Next to the station is the modern chain hotel, Mercure Breda Centre, Stationsplein 14 (Tel.

076 522 0200, www.mercure.nl). Singles start at €115 and doubles at €126; add €14 per person for breakfast.

The most comfortable and convenient place to stay in Breda is B&B Aan de Singelgracht, Delpratsingel 14 (Tel. 076 521 6271, www.desingelgracht.nl). This B&B in three adjoining canal houses is near the station and a five-minute walk from the center. Singles start at €25 and doubles at €57; some rooms have private facilities.

The closest hostel, Stayokay Chaam, Putvenweg 1 (Tel. 0161 491 323, www.stayokay.com/chaam), is about 15 km away in Chaam (see Day 3 at 20.4 km).

There is no campground in the vicinity of Breda. The closest is Camping Liesbos, Liesdreef 40 (Tel. 076 514 3514, www.camping-liesbos.nl, open April through October), about 7 km southwest. There is also a campground in Ulvenhout (southeast), three campgrounds in Oosterhout (see Day 2), and two in Chaam (see Day 3).

Where to Eat: Several restaurants, many with outdoor seating, line the Grote Markt and the Havenmarkt. The VVV has a free booklet, *Restaurants Breda*. For the most reasonably priced meals in Breda (if not the entire country), go to Den Boerenstamppot, Schoolstraat 3 (Tel. 076 514 0162, closed Sundays). Three-course traditional Dutch meals with main courses of everything from *stamppot* to *nasi goreng* are an astonishing €7. Humphrey's, Catharinastraat 1 (076 520 4406, www.humphreys.nl), has three-course meals for €18.

Day 3: Breda to Oirschot (59.9 km)

Cycle out of Breda past a castle, along a river, and through forests to the two "Baarles" for a tiny taste of Belgium. Head east on quiet bike paths to historic Hilvarenbeek, and along the Wilhelminakanaal to Oirschot. (The knooppunt system you will use today is part of the Fietsroute Netwerk De Baronie.)

Head south through the suburbs of Breda on Ginnekenweg, lined with rows of neat brick and sandstone buildings. The Ginnekenmarkt (3.9 km) is a cute little triangular plaza that feels like a separate village but is the southern outskirts of Breda.

Stop at the Kasteel Bouvigne (4.8 km). Built in 1612, this petite, picturesque castle (not open to the public) is flanked by octagonal turrets and surrounded by a moat. Continue on the road alongside the Mastbos, one of the forests surrounding Breda. At 6.8 km, begin 7 km of serene cycling along the small Bovenmark River.

After the river, cycle for 3 km on a path of hard-packed dirt through rural areas and a quiet forest, and then on Oude Bredasebaan almost all the way to Baarle-Nassau. At 20.4 km, the route continues straight, but if you want to visit Chaam (or stay at the hostel), turn left on Ulicotenseweg and ride for 2.3 km, following signs to K48. (Note: This isn't the quickest way to Chaam from Breda, but it is the most scenic.)

From just beyond here to Baarle-Nassau, the road goes through a forest. The road itself becomes dirt, but the bike path alongside it is paved the entire 5 km.

Arriving in Baarle-Nassau/Baarle-Hertog, you begin to see Belgian flags, but Dutch flags are also still visible. In fact, the VVV has both flags displayed. You will see both Dutch and Belgian banks, churches, post offices, and shops, but each country also has its own town hall, police department, schools, and tax system (see Boxed Text "The Two Baarles").

VVV Baarle-Nassau/Baarle-Hertog is at Nieuwstraat 16 in Baarle-Nassau (Tel. 013 507 9921, www.groendriehoek.nl). If it's lunchtime, go across the road to Nieuwstraat 23, to the mouth-watering Van Eijl bakery/deli/chocolate shop. Bike shop Jansen-Oomen, Gen. Maczeklaan 13, is in Baarle-Nassau (Tel. 013 507 9228). Should you decide to stay, there are three hotels (one in Baarle-Nassau, two in Baarle-Hertog), and one B&B (in Baarle-Hertog). There are many camp-grounds in the area, mainly north of town in the Dutch area.

To venture into Belgium proper, ride 14 km mostly through forest to Turnhout on a bike path called *Belse Lijntje* (the old railway line between Tilburg and

The Two Baarles

Baarle-Nassau is Dutch, while Baarle-Hertog is Belgian, but they are not simply one town with a border in the middle: In the 12th century, the town was divided between the two countries, but parts were re-absorbed over time. Today, there are 21 Belgian enclaves scattered throughout what is otherwise a Dutch territory, as well as several Dutch enclaves located within the Belgian enclaves. The VVV has a sheet explaining the full history of the two Baarles, a "geographical curios-ity." Not surprisingly, the symbol of the towns is two interlocking jig-saw puzzle pieces.

Look at the house numbers; houses on the same street do not always have consecutive numbers. The numbers with a white center banded by red and blue are Dutch houses, while Belgian house numbers have a small Belgian flag in the corner. As you go down some streets, you are actually crossing borders several times. The house on Loveren with the numbers 2 (Belgian) and 19 (Dutch) has the border go through the house. The family cooks in one country and sleeps in another.

Today you pay for items in the common currency, the Euro, but pre-Euro, you could pay in either Dutch or Belgian currency. If you call Belgium to book a hotel or even call the shop next door in Baarle-Hertog from Baarle-Nassau, you will need to dial the Belgian country code.

Turnhout). Just out of the "Baarles," you leave the Netherlands and enter Belgium. Then you leave Belgium and re-enter Dutch territory. After 5.0 km, you cross once again into Belgium. Continue straight, crossing the N119 after 2.5 km, and go straight ahead through the forest. Using the knooppunt system, begin at K82, and go to K87, K5, K3, K2, and finish in Turnhout at K1.

Turnhout is a lively town centered on its Grote Markt. Turnhout's castle was originally built as a hunting lodge for the Dukes of Brabant in the 12th century. Don't miss the Begijnhof, one of the finest and most intact in Belgium.

Once on the route again, pass several small farm communities. At 33.5 km, join the LF13a, which the route follows to Oirschot. At mushroom #24701, once again the road becomes dirt, but the bike path is paved for 3 km until, at 38.3 km, it also becomes hard-packed dirt.

At 39.7 km, at mushroom #21308, watch for the turn to Hilvarenbeek off busy Turnhoutsebaan, on which you cycle for 30 m. Then turn onto a well-maintained dirt road through a forest. At mushroom #21311 (42.0 km), the road becomes paved again. Just past this point, notice the small turreted hunting lodge, De Licenhof, and 600 m further (if it's May) a 300 m row of blooming rhododendrons.

Approaching the town of Hilvarenbeek, you will see the tall, ornate, double onion domed steeple of the 15th-century St. Petruskerk. Continue past the church and turn left to Diessen. Ride through Diessen. Watch for the turn at 50.0 km. In 800 m, turn onto Trimbaan, a tiny bike path through a forest of birch, oak, and pine, and then through farmland. At 53.0 km, campers may want to consider staying at the farm/mini-camping D'n Bobbel (Oirschotsedijk 4, Tel. 013 504 2702, www.denbobbel.nl). Pitch your tent or stay in one of the six gypsy caravans.

Ride through an evergreen forest (54.0 km) until the turn onto the Wilhelmina Kanaal (55.5 km), and end the day with a 4 km ride on the dike into Oirschot.

"You are approaching *Knooppunt* No. 44."   Route options at a typical *Knooppunt*.

Cue Sheet

0.0	Start	VVV Breda go S on Willemstraat
0.2	L	Willemstraat/Sophiastraat/Nassaustraat
0.8	R	Wilhelminasingel
2.4	R	Wilhelminastraat/Ginnekenweg
2.9	VR	Ginnekenweg
3.2	VR	LF9a Ginnekenweg
3.9	R	LF9a Ginnekenmarkt
4.0	R	Duivelsbruglaan
4.3	L	#24538, sign "Bouvigne," Bouvignelaan
4.8	SS L	Kasteel Bouvigne
6.2	L	sign "K36," #21861, sign "Ulvenhout," Reepteind
6.8	R	after bridge, sign "K41" (at K36), #24540 and #62744 Bovenmark River
8.8	VR	LF13b/LF9a sign "K41," #24543 sign "Galder and Meersel Dreef"

Map 13.1. North Brabant Ride 1, South of the Big Rivers, Days 3 & 4.

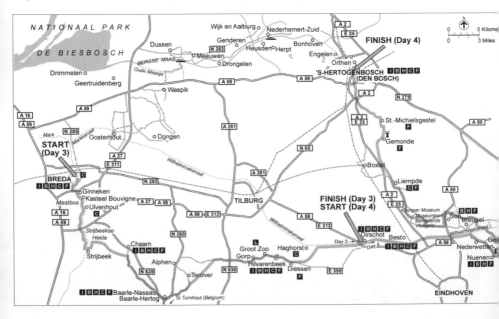

9.9	R	LF9a sign "K43" (at K41), #24544 bike path, Mark
10.1	L	LF9a sign "K43," #24545 sign "Galder, Meersel, Dreef, and Strijbeek," along the Mark
13.4	L	sign "K44" (at K43) #24547 sign "Strijbeek," (at Markbrug) Markweg
14.3	L	sign "K44," #21342 sign "Ulvenhout," Strijbeekseweg
14.7	R	sign "K44," Erikaweg (hard-packed dirt)
16.0	CS	sign "K45" (at K44)
17.0	L	sign "K45," Oude Bredasebaan
18.2	CS	sign "K46" (at K45)
18.3	CS	#21316 sign "Baarle-Nassau"
20.4	CS	sign "K24" (at K46) #21301 sign "Baarle-Nassau" (L sign "Chaam")
20.6	VR	#23583 sign "Baarle-Nassau," Oude Bredasebaan
22.6	CS	sign "K79" (at K24) Oude Bredasebaan
25.1	CS	sign "K63" (at K79) Oude Bredasebaan
26.2	CS	N639/Hoogsbraak (do not follow sign "K63")
27.3	CS	VVV on L, Chaamseweg/Nieuwstraat, T-Baarle-Nassau and Baarle-Hertog
27.4	VL	Singel/St. Annaplein (50 m), L sign "Alpen and Tilburg" Alphenseweg
27.6	VR	Oosteinde
28.0	CS	Oordeelsestraat
29.4	L	sign "K78," dir. "Alpen," Oordeelsestraat
31.4	CS	sign "K76" (at K78) Terover
33.0	R	LF 13a sign "K75" (at K76) sign "Hilvarenbeek," Hondseind
33.5	VL	sign "K75," Hondseind
35.5	L	LF13a sign "K75," #24701 Baarlsebaan
37.0	CS	LF13a sign "K77"
38.3	R	LF13a sign "K53," #24700 sign "Hilvarenbeek," Nieuwkerk Baantje

39.7	L !	LF13a #21308 sign "Hilvarenbeek," Turnhoutsebaan (30 m), R "Gorp a/d Lay"
41.6	CS	LF13a #21310 sign "Hilvarenbeek"
42.0	R	LF13a #21311 sign "Hilvarenbeek"
42.1	SS L	De Licenhof (a small hunting lodge)
42.7	SS R	row of rhododendrons
44.3	VL	LF13a Groot Loo/Loostraat
45.9	R	LF13a Schoolstraat
46.0	L	(no LF sign) Wouwerstraat, T-Hilvarenbeek
46.2	L	LF13a Vrijthof sign "Diessen"
46.4	L	LF13a Diessenseweg/N395
49.6	VR	Julianastraat (service road), T-Diessen
50.0	L	LF13a Emmerseweg sign "Oirschot"
50.8	R !	#22517 sign "Oirschot," Trimbaan (bike path)
53.0	SS R	Mini-camping D'n Bobbel
53.2	VR	LF13a #22516 sign "Oirschot," Oirschotsedijk/Achterste Heistraat
54.7	L	LF13a #22512 sign "Boxtel," Jhr. de la Courtweg
55.5	R	LF13a sign "Oirschot," Kanaaldijk-Zuid (Wilhelmina Kanaal)
58.7	L	LF13a sign "Oirschot," (over the Wilhelmina Kanaal)
58.8	R	LF13a sign "Oirschot," Provincialeweg
58.9	L	(20 m) R LF13a Den Heuvel
59.3	CS	Koestraat
59.7	L	sign "VVV," Markt (at church)
59.8	R	sign "VVV," Deken Frankenstraat (north side of church)
59.9	End	VVV on L (beside museum)

Oirschot

Oirschot is a quiet town with an attractive square framed by shade trees and congenial cafés and restaurants. Across from the striped, 15th-century St. Pieterskerk is the Stadhuis, dating to 1463. Off the square is the Vrijthof, with a small, 12th-century church. Originally built as a Catholic church, it was used as a

Boterwaag (Butter Market) from the mid-17th-century until 1800, when it became a Dutch Reformed church. Restored in 1961, it is known today as the Boterkerkje (Little Butter Church). Near the square, on the corner of Rijkesluisstraat and Gasthuisstraat, you will see the biggest chair in Europe, which represents the furniture industry of Oirschot. The Museum De Vier Quartieren, St. Odulphusstraat 11, focuses on life in North Brabant.

Information:	VVV Oirschot, St. Odulphusstraat 11 (Tel. 0499 550 599, www.vvvoirschot.nl), is adjacent to the Museum de Vier Quartieren.
Bicycle Shops:	Oirschot has two bike shops with rentals: Smetsers at Spoordonkseweg 28 (Tel. 0499 571 231, www.smetsersfietsen.nl) and R.V. Overdijk at Spoordonkseweg 91 (Tel. 0499 572 959).
Where to Stay:	In the center, Hotel de Kroon, Rijkesluisstraat 6 (Tel. 0499 571 095, www.hoteldekroon.nl), has singles from €72.50 and doubles from €92.50.
	The VVV has a list of the six B&Bs in town. Pension Het Merelnest, Spoordonkseweg 11 (Tel. 0499 571 771), is in a residential setting. Doubles are €45. The friendly B&B de Notelhoeck, Snellaertstraat 1 (Tel. 0499 572 025, www.denotelhoeck.nl), is 1 km from the center; singles are €25 and doubles are €45.
	Oirschot has many campgrounds; the VVV has a comprehensive list. Camping De Bocht at Oude Grintweg 69 (Tel. 0499 550 858, www.campingdebocht.nl), and Camping Latour at Bloemendaal 7 (Tel. 0499 575 625, www.campinglatour.nl) are larger facilities. There are also four mini-campings, plus Camping d'n Bobbel (Day 3, 53.0 km).
Where to Eat:	For a small town, Oirschot has lots of restaurants, especially around the Markt and on Rijkesluisstraat. Restaurant La Couronne is at the Hotel De Kroon (see "Where to Stay"). Next door, at Rijkesluisstraat 4, La Fleurie has fine dining, and across the road, at Rijkesluisstraat 3, is De Oude Smidse. For more casual dining, good Italian food can be found at Il Tavolino, Rijkesluisstraat 11, and across the road is Eetcafé 't Stoeltje, Rijkesluisstraat 18. The trendy pub De Wildeman is at Markt 7. Dine in an old windmill, De Meulen, at De Korenaar 49 (closed Mondays and Tuesdays, open for dinner only).

Day 4: Oirschot to Den Bosch (65.4 km)

Cycle along the Wilhelmina Kanaal and visit Nuenen, where Vincent van Gogh lived and worked. Ride on straight stretches of tree-lined roads through pastoral landscape and villages to Den Bosch. (The knooppunt system you will use today is part of the Fietsroute Netwerk De Kempen.)

After leaving Oirschot, there is a tricky turn at the roundabout (1.0 km). Go straight through the roundabout; after 10 m, turn right toward the Wilhelmina Kanaal. Just after the roundabout, you will see signs for both the LF13a and LF13b. Follow LF13a.

You will cycle for 15 km on the bike path beside the tree-shaded Wilhelmina Kanaal, skirting the town of Best. If you do not want to go to Nuenen, thereby shortening the route to Den Bosch, turn off the route (6.7 km) at Batabrug (turn left at Julianaweg-Zuid). Make your way north through Best to the Klompen-museum (Wooden Shoe/Clog Museum) at Broekdijk 14 (39.5 km) and rejoin the route there.

To continue on the route to Nuenen, stay alongside the canal. At 9.0 km, cross on the bicycle bridge, Fietsbrug Ekkersweijer. On the other side, at mush-room #24670, the LF13a shows two options, one to Eindhoven and the other along the canal to Son en Breugel. Unless you have a burning desire to go into Eindhoven, a large industrial city built up around the huge Philips electronics com-pany, then stay on the route. You will cross the canal twice more before turning left (15.1 km) onto a tree-lined road flanked with fields to Nuenen.

Vincent van Gogh lived and worked in Nuenen from 1883-1885, where he did his first paintings of peasant life, including the famous *Potato Eaters*. Many Van Gogh landmarks, tributes, and scenes from his paintings can be seen in and

Left: Vincent van Gogh statue in Neunen, where he lived and worked.
Above: The church at Neunen, which was depicted in a Van Gogh painting.

around the town. Pick up a self-guided route description in English of places associated with Van Gogh at the VVV, 600 m from the turn at 19.3 km, at Berg 17 (Tel.
040 284 4868, closed 12:30 p.m. to 1:30 p.m. and Sundays), or the Van Gogh
Documentation Center, Papenvoort 15 (Tel. 040 283 9615, open daily, 10 a.m. to
noon and 2 p.m. to 4 p.m.), where photos, works, and reproductions from the artist's Nuenen period can be viewed.

To go to Nuenen, a side trip (19.3 km), turn right onto Berg at the windmill,
which is in many of Van Gogh's paintings. The first Van Gogh landmark you come
to, 500 m from the turn (19.3 km), is a small square with a huge linden tree, a
stone monument to Vincent, and the old town water pump. In another 300 m you
reach a larger square with a pond, gazebo, and statue of Van Gogh. Next to the
park is a large church, and next to it is the house where Van Gogh had his studio.
Other points of interest are Van Gogh's parent's house, the tiny church where his
father was the vicar (recognizable as a well-known Van Gogh painting), and the location of the *Potato Eaters* house.

After your "Van Gogh" tour, return to the windmill and cycle to Gerwen. The
left turn (20.2 km) just after the town sign for Gerwen is easy to miss. The route
weaves through farmlands as you head back to the Wilhelmina Kanaal (24.1 km),
which you cross over. Then cycle through rural landscape to Planetenlaan, which
skirts Son en Breugel and becomes busier as it nears the A50. (Note: The roads in
this area are incorrect on some maps because of ongoing construction on major
arteries around the freeway.)

To cross the freeway, turn north (29.3 km) on Afrikalaan, west over the freeway, and south to Sonseweg. At Sonseweg 39 (35.2 km), nestled in the forest, is
the Museumpark Bevrijdende Vleugels (Wings of Liberation Museumpark, Tel.
0499 329 722, www.wingsofliberation.nl, open daily), a museum detailing southern Netherlands' liberation in World War II.

Follow the signs to K19, which lead to the Klompenmuseum (Wooden
Shoe/Clog Museum) at Broekdijk 14 (Tel. 0499 371 247, open daily, April through
October). Soon after the Klompenmuseum, turn right onto Koppelstraat. You will
see signs for the LF7b Overlandroute, which the route follows to Den Bosch. You
will cycle on straight, rural roads through the villages of Liempde and Gemonde
and past the white grain mill (54.5 km).

The route skirts St.-Michielsgestel and takes you on a bike path and quiet
roads to the outskirts of Den Bosch. After the freeways (61.6 km), follow the bike
path through the green area, Bossche Broek. In the center of Den Bosch, the
route passes the St. Janskathedraal and the VVV (on the Markt) and ends at the
station.

Cue Sheet

0.0	Start	VVV Oirschot
		go SE on Markt
80 m	L	Rijkelsluisstraat

1.0	RA CS !	LF13a Bestseweg (10 m), R unmarked street (to canal)
1.2	L	LF13a Dijkpad Wilhelmina Kanaal
2.4	CS	sign "K12" (at K13)
5.9	CS	LF13a #25028 sign "Son en Breugel"
6.2	SS L	Beatrix Kanaal merges
6.7	CS !	LF13a Batabrug (L Julianaweg-Zuid to Best)
6.7	CS	sign "Son en Breugel," Kanaaldijk
8.1	VR	LF13a along the canal sign "Son en Breugel"
8.5	CS	LF13a sign "K10" (at K11) sign "Son en Breugel" (cross road)
9.0	L	LF13a LF7a sign "K10, Fietsbrug Ekkersweijer" (bike bridge across canal)
9.1	L !	LF13a (x 2) #24670 sign "Son en Breugel"
12.3	L	LF13a sign "K9" (over canal) (30 m), R bike path on other side of canal
12.5	CS	LF13a sign "K9," #21524 and #62730
13.8	R	LF13a sign "K9," over canal (60 m), L LF13a, T-Son en Breugel
14.1	L	LF13a bike path
15.1	R !	LF13a Hooidonk/Eikelkampen
19.3	ST R	RT = 1.6 km Nuenen, Berg
19.3	L	dir. "Gerwen," sign "K74," Gerwenseweg (at windmill)
20.2	L !	sign "K74," Gerwenseweg
20.7	L	sign "K73" (at K74) Heuvel
20.9	R	LF13b sign "K73," Heuvel (10 m), L De Huikert/Rullen/ Nieuwe Dijk
23.1	R	LF13b sign "K72" (at K73) Nieuwe Dijk
23.8	VR	Nieuwe Dijk (60 m), L sign "K72"
24.1	R	sign "K17" (at K72), cross canal (not LF13b)
24.1	L	#22673 Kwadestraat sign "Son en Breugel" (50 m), R unmarked road
25.8	L !	(main road) Planetenlaan (not sign "K17")

26.3	R	Planetenlaan (bike path to the R in the trees)
27.2	L	sign "K17"
27.4	R !	Planetenlaan (cross road) sign "K17"
28.1	CS	Planetenlaan/Gentiaanlaan (not sign "K17")
29.3	RA R	Afrikalaan
29.8	L	Hazeputtenroute sign, Aziëlaan
30.1	R	Hazeputtenroute sign, Brabantlaan
30.6	L	Hazeputtenroute sign, unmarked
31.0	L	sign "K17," Alpenlaan
32.1	R	sign "K17," Vogezenlaan
32.4	CS	over A50
32.5	L	(no sign) bike path along freeway
33.6	R	sign "K17," Sonseweg
35.2	SS R	Museumpark Bevrijdende Vleugels
36.3	R	sign "K19" (at K17) sign "Boxtel," Molenheideweg
36.7	L	sign "K19," #21593 sign "Boxtel," Oude Baan
37.7	L	sign "K19," Klavershoekseweg
37.9	R	sign "K19," Herkseweg
38.8	R	sign "K19," dir. "St. Odel"
39.0	L	sign "K19," Molenkampseweg
39.3	L	sign "K19," # 25024 Broekdijk
39.5	SS R	Klompenmuseum (wooden shoe/clog musuem)
39.8	R	Peppelroute sign, Koppelstraat
41.4	L	LF7b Vleutstraat
42.1	L	LF7b Hamsestraat
44.1	VR	LF7b Hamsestraat/Oude Postbaan
44.6	R	LF7b Oude Postbaan
44.8	VR	LF7b Raadhuisplein, T-Liempde
45.4	R	LF7b Tooseplein
45.6	L	(no LF sign) Smaldersestraat (500 m unpaved)

46.6	VR	LF7b Molendijk/Kasterensestraat
47.4	L	LF7b (cross railway tracks) Gemondsestraat
48.4	VL	LF7b Onrooi/Koppenhoefstraat/St. Lambertusweg
50.8	L	LF7b Boomstraat
51.3	VR	LF7b Boomstraat
52.3	L	LF7b St. Lambertusweg, T-Gemonde
52.7	L	LF7b #22618 Kruisstraat/Loopstraat
53.8	L	LF7b De Wiesle Hoeve
54.5	SS R	white windmill
55.3	L	(no LF sign) "overige richtingen Spijt"
55.6	R	LF 7b Nieuwestraat, T-St.-Michielsgestel
56.4	VL	LF7b sign "Den Bosch," Ruwenbergstraat
56.9	L	LF7b Kapelbergstraat/Lookerstraat
57.5	VL	LF7b Muddakkersedijk (bike path)
57.8	CS	Muddakkersedijk (gravel bike path for 600 m)
58.5	L	LF7b Venstraat/Haanwijk
59.7	L	LF7b Dooibroek
61.6	CS	under A2 and N65
64.0	L	LF7b Pettelaarsweg (20 m), CS (cross Hekellaan) Trineitstraat
64.3	L	Parade/Lange Putstraat
64.5	R	LF7b Verwerstraat
64.7	L	Achter het Stadhuis (10 m), R Ridderstraat
64.8	CS	Markt (50 m), VVV (20 m), L Hoge Steenweg
65.0	L	Visstraat/Stationsweg
65.4	End	Den Bosch Railway Station

14.

Limburg

LIMBURG, the southernmost Dutch province, bisected by the Maas river, is a hilly finger of land wedged between Belgium and Germany. The Netherlands' highest elevation is at Drielandenpunt (Three-Country Point), in the southeast of Limburg, where the Netherlands, Belgium, and Germany converge. The maps of Limburg have the symbols < and > to indicate the direction of the inclines. Limburg is a land of castles, forests, rolling hills, and apple orchards, which change color with the seasons. It is predominantly Catholic, and you will come across many statues of Christ and the Virgin Mary. The cosmopolitan Maastricht is the main city, while Valkenburg is the major tourist town. Late April to early May is the season for the luscious white asparagus, a Limburg specialty. Also try a piece of

Verdant rolling hills characterize cycling in Limburg.

Limburgse Vlaai, a type of flan. Limburg has the country's only vineyards, and local wines are often on menus.

The two rides in this chapter vary considerably. The first ride, "Two Limburgs," takes you through Belgian Limburg, west of the Dutch border, along canals, through forests, to Maaseik, and the "white village" of Thorn. You will return to Maastricht by weaving past lakes, islands, and canals of the Maas River in Dutch Limburg.

The second ride, in South Limburg, leaves the flatlands behind, with side trips into Belgium and Germany. Day 2 of the ride takes you into all "Three Countries in a Day."

Maastricht

Maastricht, the capital of Limburg, is a lively city divided by the Maas river. The train station is on the east of the river; crossing the Maas on the St. Servaasbrug leads to the city's core on the western bank. The city has two main squares. The Vrijthof is dominated by two impressive churches: the St. Servaasbasiliek, dating to around 1000, and the smaller Gothic St. Janskerk. The Markt is the site of a busy outdoor market (Wednesdays and Fridays) and the Stadhuis, built in the mid-17th century. A little further south is the Onze Lieve Vrouweplein, a smaller, cobbled square named for the Onze Lieve Vrouwebasiliek. All three churches can be visited.

On the east bank, the Bonnefanten Museum, Ave. Céramique 250 (www. bonnefantummuseum.nl, closed Mondays), houses an excellent collection of Old Masters and contemporary work by Limburg artists.

A trip to Maastricht would not be complete without visiting the winding tunnels of the caves of Mount St. Pieter, created by centuries of marlstone mining. More tunnels created by marlstone excavation between 1575 and 1825 can be found at the casemates. Both sites offer daily, one-hour tours lead by VVV guides.

Information:	Maastricht's VVV is located in Het Dinghuis, Kleine Straat 1 (Tel. 043 325 2121, www.vvvmaastricht.nl), from where both rides begin. From the station, go west on Stationsstraat, cross the St. Servaasbrug, and, after 150 m, turn right onto Kleine Straat. Go 100 m; the VVV is on your right. The ANWB is at Wycker Brugstraat 24 (Tel. 043 362 06 66). Internet access is available at the library at Ave. Céramique 50 (Tel. 043 350 5600).
Bicycle Shops:	Next to the railway station, Cycle-shop "Aon de Stasie," Parallelweg 40A (Tel. 043 321 1100, www.aondestasie.nl), has rentals. In the center is Courtens Bike Sports, Calvariestraat 16 (Tel. 043 321 3820).
Where to Stay:	Several hotels can be found around the Markt. La Colombe, Markt 30 (Tel. 043 321 5774, www.hotellacolombe.nl), has simple singles from €59 and doubles from €80. Off the Markt, Maison du Chêne, Boschstraat 104-106 (Tel. 043

321 3523, www.maastrichthotel.com), has singles from €50 and doubles from €60; breakfast is €8.50. Hotel Botticelli, Papenstraat 11 (Tel. 043 352 6300, www.hotelbotticelli.com), in a building from 1620, has rooms from from €92 to €175; breakfast is €13.

You can also stay on a boat: The Botel on the Maas, near Onze Lieve Vrouweplein at Maasboulevard 95 (Tel. 043 321 9023), has single cabins for €34 and doubles are €53.

The VVV has a list of B&Bs. Two options are Batta 4, Alex. Battalaan 4 (Tel. 043 321 7761), and a few doors away, Crets, Alex. Battalaan 14 (Tel. 043 325 3248). Singles are around €40 and doubles around €50 at both.

Stayokay Hostel Maastricht, Dousbergweg 4 (Tel. 043 346 6777, www.stayokay.com/maastricht), is located about 5 km west of Maastricht in Dousberg Parc, a sporting complex. Guests can use the facilities, including the swimming pool.

Camping De Oosterdriessen, Oosterweg 1 (Tel. 043 409 3215, www.oosterdriessen.nl), in Oost Maarland, is at 6.5 km of Day 1 of the "South Limburg Ride."

Where to Eat: Head for the Markt and the Vrijthof for a good selection of restaurants. On the Markt, Tijl Uilenspiegel in the Hotel La Colombe (see "Where to Stay") and the restaurant in Maison du Chêne (see "Where to Stay") are good bets, as are Mincklers at Markt 35 and La Chine at Markt 33 (www.lachine. nl). Opposite the St. Servaasbasiliek, the street along the Vrijthof is lined with restaurants and cafés.

Maastricht's skyline viewed from across the Maas River.

Tour of Two Limburgs

Total Distance:	132.9 km
Duration:	2 days
Highlights:	Maastricht, Zuid-Willemsvaart Kanaal, Maaseik (Belgium), Thorn, Sluis Osen and Sluis Linne, Maasbracht, Elsloo, Juliaanakanaal
Terrain:	Hilly south of Maastricht, flat along the Zuid-Willemsvaart Canal and the Maas River
Maps:	Michelin 532 Zuid-Nederland/Pays-Bas Sud, ANWB/VVV Toeristenkaart Limburg; Fietsroute Netwerk Zuid-Limburg map; Fietsroute Netwerk Kempen in Maasland map
Start/Finish:	Maastricht/Maastricht
Access:	Train to Maastricht
Connections:	"South Limburg Ride," train from Nijmegen (end of "Hanzeroute"), train to/from Den Bosch ("South of the Big Rivers Ride")

Day 1: Maastricht to Thorn (58.5 km)

On this day, you will first ride past hills covered in vineyards, then along peaceful canals for most of the day. The ride through a forest leads to the pretty Belgian town of Maaseik. Cycling through farmlands will bring you to Thorn.

Soon after leaving Maastricht, the hills of southern Limburg come into view. At 3.0 km, grapevines cover the hills to the right. This is the Dutch wine country. The Jeker Valley is ideally suited to white varietals such as Müller-Thürgau, Riesling, and Pinot Gris. If you would like to try Limburg wines, go to Apostelhoeve (the largest producer) or Hoeve Nekum.

You will enter Belgium just before Kanne (4.7 km). Here you will see a *fietsnetwerk* board for Kempen in Maasland and use the first knooppunt of the day (see boxed text on page 45 and photos on page 247). At 5.9 km is the 17th-century Chateau Neercanne (www.neercanne.com), but only the gardens can be visited (closed Mondays). At 5.9 km, begin the only climb of the day, a rather steep 1 km; however, you will be rewarded with a descent of equal distance.

From the bridge at 8.7 km, view the massive Albertkanaal. Continue on a small, forested road above the Albertkanaal, to which you cycle down at 12.3 km and ride beside for 3 km. At 15.0 km, the canal veers left and you soon join the Zuid-Willemsvaart Kanaal. The first 800 m of the 20 km ride along the Zuid-Willemsvaart Kanaal has some industry; but after that, the ride is serene along the tree-lined canal. At 17.0 km and 19.8 km, detour around two sets of locks.

For a canal-side break, enjoy the café at 36.7 km. After you leave the Zuid-Willemsvaart Kanaal (38.6 km), head east toward Maaseik through a cool forest on a lovely bike path for about 8 km.

Life in Maaseik centers on its shady Markt surrounded by impressive 17th and 18th-century buildings. The Tourist Office is on the Markt. Should you want to spend the night here instead of in Thorn, Maaseik has hotels and restaurants.

A circuitous route takes you from Maaseik to Aldeneik. Its 8th-century church, originally an abbey church, was enlarged in the 14th century and renovated in the 19th century.

At 50.1 km, the route turns onto the Maasdijk along the Maas River before turning at Ophoven past a huge marina, through farmlands to Kessenich, and on to Thorn.

Cue Sheet

0.0	Start	VVV Maastricht
		Go S on Kleine Straat
60 m	L	Maastr. Brugstraat
0.1	R	Vissersmaas/Het Bat sign "Kanne"
0.4	R	Graanmarkt sign "Kanne"
0.5	L	Onze Lieve Vrouweplein/Cortenstraat
0.7	L	Achter de Molens sign "Kanne"
0.9	L	Kleine Looiersstraat sign "Kanne"
1.0	R	St. Pieterstraat/St. Hubertuslaan/Luikerweg sign "Kanne"
1.8	VR	Mergelweg
4.7	R	Berkenlaan sign "K88"
5.1	R	Brugstraat sign "K88," T-Kanne
5.3	R	Statiestraat
5.9	SS	Chateau Neercanne
5.9	L	Kapelstraat
6.1	R	Muizenberg
6.3	VR	onto bike path
8.7	L	N79 sign "K88"
8.9	R	Kapitein-Vlieger Glorie Straat sign "K88"
10.2	CS	at K88 sign "K59"
12.2	CS	cross N2 sign "K59," T-Veldwezelt

12.3	VR	down to the Albertkanaal
15.0	R	bridge (N78) over the Albertkanaal
15.1	CS	bike path sign "K54"

Map 14.1. Limburg Ride 1, Tour of Two Limburgs, Days 1 & 2.

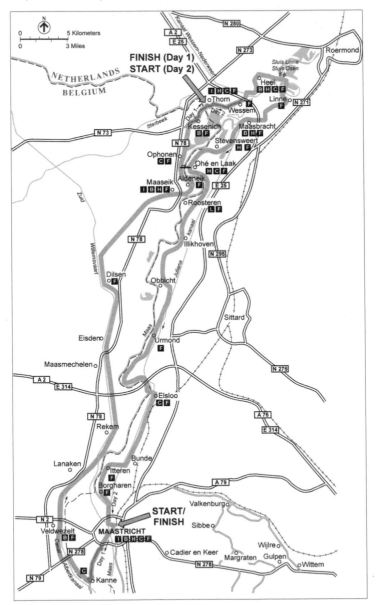

15.2	R	bike path sign "K54"
15.3	R	unmarked road, sign "K54," (to Zuid-Willemsvaart)
17.0	VL	locks (no entry)
17.3	VR	to K54
18.9	CS	along canal sign "K54"
19.8	VL	locks (no entry)
20.0	CS	at K54 sign "K58"
22.8	UL	at K58 sign "K57," T-Rekem
22.9	L	over Zuid-Willemsvaart
23.1	UR	sign "K57"
27.8	CS	at K57 sign "K56"
28.6	CS	at K56 sign "K55"
31.1	CS	at K55 sign "K48," T-Eisden
34.1	L	sign "K48," still along Zuid-Willemsvaart
35.7	VR	sign "K48"
36.7	CS	at K48 sign "K44," T-Dilsen
38.6	R	at K44 sign "K43"
39.4	CS	cross road sign "K45"
43.5	CS	at K45 sign "K27"
45.1	L	Werfelermolenweg sign "Centrum Maaseik"
45.2	L	N78 sign "Centrum"
45.4	R	sign "Centrum" unnamed farm road/Eerste Straat
47.2	L	sign "Centrum," sign "K24," Hepperstraat
47.3	CS	Markt, T-Maaseik
47.4	-	Tourist Information
47.5	CS	Eikerstraat/Venlosesteenweg sign "K25," LF7b
47.9	R !	Maasweg sign "K25"
48.0	L	(10 m) Kluisstraat sign "K25," LF7b
48.2	L	sign "K25"
48.3	R	sign "K25," under N296/N78 sign "Aldeneik"

48.4	R	sign "K25," LF7b
48.5	L	sign "K25"
48.8	VR	Hamontweg sign "K25," T-Aldeneik
49.1	R	Aldeneik sign "K25," (at church)
49.3	R	Leugenbrugweg sign "K25"
49.4	L	Leugenbrugweg/Broekstraat sign "K25"
50.0	L	sign "K2"
50.1	R	Leeuwerikstraat/Maasdijk at K25 sign "K22"
52.1	L	at K22 sign "K21," LF7b
52.4	R	Dalerstraat sign "K21"
53.3	L	Vroenhof sign "K21"
53.7	R	Geistingen sign "K21," T-Ophoven
54.2	L	Steenpad sign "K21"
54.4	R	Kessenicherweg/Kempweg sign "K21," LF7b
55.5	R	Meierstraat/Dorpsstraat sign "K21"
56.3	R	(to church) sign "K2"
56.4	L	Kerkstraat (at church) sign "K21"; T-Kessenich
56.6	R	at K21 sign "K33," sign "Thorn"
56.8	L	Thornerweg sign "K33"
58.1	CS	Beekstraat/Holstraat (don't follow sign "K33")
58.4	R	Hoogstraat
58.4	R	(30 m) Vinkenstraat
58.5	End	VVV Thorn

Thorn

Known as the "white village" on account of the color of its houses and buildings. By day, this picturesque village is often crowded with tourists but regains its serenity in the evening. The focal point is the 1,000-year-old Abdijkerk (abbey church) in the center (open daily, March through October). Adjacent to the VVV is a small museum, Museum Het Land van Thorn (open daily, April through October), which details Thorn's history. The forested walking trail along the tiny Itterbeek River east of town makes a pleasant evening stroll.

Information:	VVV Thorn, Wijngaard 14 (Tel. 0475 562 761, www.lekker-genieten.nl), is in the center.
Bicycle Shops:	There are no bicycle shops in Thorn; the closest are at Meierstraat 27 in Kessenich (Tel. 089 564 791, see Day 1) and Wilhelminaplein 4 in Heel (Tel. 0475 578 096) (see Day 2).
Where to Stay:	Hostellerie La Ville Blanche, Hoogstraat 2 (Tel. 0475 562 341, www. villeblanche.nl), has singles for €80 and doubles for €104. Next door, Hotel Crasborn at Hoogstraat 6 (Tel. 0475 561 281, www.hollandhotels.nl/crasborn) has singles from €59.50 and doubles from €79.
	In the residential area, Pension Lindeveld, Manderscheidtsingel 26 (Tel. 0475 562 185, m.beunenstraetemans@tref.nl), has two spacious rooms; singles are €32 and doubles are €53.
	Camping Vijverbroek, Kessincherweg 20 (Tel. 0475 561 914), is about 500 m south of Thorn on the bank of the Itterbeek River.
Where to Eat:	Most of Thorn's restaurants are on Hoogstraat. The two hotels (see "Where to Stay") have good restaurants. For fine dining try Restaurant Drie Cronen, Hofstraat 1 at the corner of Hoogstraat (Tel. 0475 561 219). De Pannekoekenbakker, Bogenstraat 2 (Tel. 0475 563 327), serves pancakes. The MeerMarkt supermarket, Casino 33 (near Akkerwal), and the bakery on Akkerwal are about 500 m south of Hoogstraat.

Day 2: Thorn to Maastricht (74.5 km)

You can break this ride into two days by staying in the twin villages of Ohé en Laak (24.5 km-26.6 km), where there are hotels and camping. It may seem strange to cycle north from Thorn to head south to Maastricht, but today's route twists and winds around and over the lakes, canals, locks, and bridges of the Maas River, giving a sense of the vast area this massive river covers. Many LF routes and the *fietsroute netwerk* of *knooppunten* crisscross the area, so carefully follow the signs indicated on the cue sheet.

Heading north, you soon cycle along the Maas in Wessem, then cross the Polderplas (6.2 km), one of the lakes created by the Maas. After Heel, a short ride through a forest brings you to the huge Linne-Buggenum Kanaal, where you cycle over the double locks, Sluis Osen and Sluis Linne. Take the time to watch the operation of the locks as barges wait their turn for the water to fill the gated chambers.

After crossing the locks, cycle along a Maas lake toward the dam. Follow the LF3a signs across the dam on the bicycle bridge. Walk your bike over the dam (the sign *"fietsers afstappen"* means "cyclists dismount"); continue through a forested area. Note the small castle on the left (14.0 km), now a private residence. Continue through the forest on an unpaved path (which starts 200 m after the castle). Unfortunately, you will see the ugly towers of a power plant for a few kilometers. Once beyond these, you will approach Maasbracht (16.0 km) through apple and pear orchards. Watch for the left turn (17.0 km), which comes shortly after you go under the A2.

Maasbracht is an inland port teeming with pleasure boats and barges. Alongside the harbor, Tipstraat has several restaurants from where you can watch the scene. At 18.6 km, cross the impressive triple locks; the only way to see them is by climbing onto the viewing platform on the left.

At 20.7 km, cross to an island created between two arms of the Maas. Centered on a cobbled market square, Stevensweert (22.1 km), surrounded by lakes and the Maas itself, has a lovely insular atmosphere. The quiet villages of Ohé en Laak have a similar atmosphere. Ohé and Laak have hotels, B&Bs, camping, and restaurants. The pedestrian/bike ferry to Ophoven (Belgium, see Day 1) from Laak (24.5 km) operates May 1 through September, from 10 a.m. or 11 a.m. until 8 p.m. or 9 p.m., depending on the day.

At 30.0 km, ride alongside the dike of the Julianakanaal. Shortly after Roosteren, the route takes you up onto the Ruitersdijk (with views of the Maas), through farmlands, and again onto the dike after the hamlet of Visserweert (37.0 km). Follow the narrow bike path (42.5 km) next to the Maas to Obbicht, and the bike path along the Julianakanaal to Urmond.

The route crosses the bridge at Elsloo, a spectacular town with red rooftops and cobbled streets, high above the Julianakanaal. The steep descent (58.4 km) comes as quite a shock, as you bounce down the cobblestones from Elsloo to Kasteel Elsloo (now a restaurant). For the next 10 km, cycle atop the forested dike along the Julianakanaal, and, later, on the banks of the Maas to Bogharen and to Maastricht.

Cue Sheet

0.0	Start	VVV Thorn
		Go W on Daalstraat
0.1	L	Beekstraat
0.2	L !	Onder de Bomen (no sign after river)
0.5	R	Waterstraat
1.0	L	Grootheggerlaan
1.1	L	Grootheggerlaan sign "K33"
1.6	L	sign "K33," R 30 m Weiserweg

2.1	VR	sign "K33," LF5a
2.7	R	at K33 sign "K42," LF5a Haggenbroek (900 m unpaved road)
4.0	L	sign "K42," LF5a
4.1	VR	sign "K42," LF5a Thornerweg (bike path)
4.3	R	LF5a Oude Thornerweg (through sport fields)
4.7	R	Maasboulevard, T-Wessem"
5.2	L	LF5a Havermansstraat/Markt/Van Horneplain
6.0	R	LF5a sign "K35," dir. "Pol"
7.1	L	LF5a sign "K35"
7.6	CS	do not follow the LF5a here
8.0	VR	unmarked street
8.1	L	sign "K35" (past church)
8.3	R	Dorpsstraat, T-Heel
8.8	R	Dorpsstraat at Wilhelminaplein (10 m), L sign "K35"
9.1	R	sign "K35," unpaved road
9.2	L	sign "K35," unpaved road
9.5	R	sign "K35," paved road
10.3	L	sign "K35"
10.9	R	LF5a sign "Linne," at K35 sign "K84"
11.0	SS	Sluis Osen (locks)
11.2	L	LF5a sign "K84"
11.5	R	LF3a sign "K36," sign "Linne"
11.6	SS	Sluis Linne (locks)
12.2	VR	LF3a sign "K36" (along the Maas)
12.7	CS	bike path (alongside dam)
12.8	SS	cross Maas on bicycle bridge above dam (walk bikes)
13.2	R	LF3a sign "K36"
14.0	VR	LF3a (at small castle on L)
14.2	R !	LF3a unpaved bike path

14.6	L	LF3a sign "K37," unpaved
14.8	R	LF3a sign "K37," unpaved
15.9	CS	LF3a sign "K37," unpaved, T-Linne
16.3	L	LF3a Hofstraat, paved
16.6	R	LF3a Kloosterstraat
17.0	L !	LF3a Europlein
17.3	L	LF3a (10 m), R Kalverstraat
17.5	R	LF3a (10 m), L Sintelstraat, T-Maasbracht
17.9	L	Tipstraat (no LF3a sign)
18.5	R	LF3a Oude Maasweg dir. "Stevensweert"
18.6	SS	triple locks
19.9	CS	Oude Maasweg (do not follow LF3a signs)
20.7	R	LF3a Schuttersweg dir. "Stevensweert"
21.3	RA CS	Schuttersweg
21.5	L	LF3a Nieuwedijk
22.1	VL	Singelstraat West, T-Stevensweert
22.3	L	Maasdijk (along the Maas)
22.6	R	LF3a Roumerweg
23.0	R	St. Annadijk
24.5	CS SS	ferry, T-Laak (SS only: route does not cross the river here)
26.6	R	LF3a Bosstraat, T-Ohé
27.0	R	LF3a sign "K3," small castle on L, gravel 700 m
28.5	R	LF3a along small canal
29.8	L	LF3a Endepoelsdijk
30.0	R	LF3a sign "K13," alongside dike
33.2	R	LF3a sign "K13" (10 m), L Maasheuvel (20 m), R Drs. J. Lebbensstraat, T-Roosteren
33.5	R	LF3a Passtraat
33.6	L	LF3a sign "K13" (10 m), R
33.7	L	LF3a sign "K13," Kempstraat

34.9	CS !	LF3a sign "K19," cross N296 (busy road)
35.2	L	LF3a sign "K19," Ruitersdijk
36.2	R	LF3a sign "K19," bike path
37.0	VR	LF3a sign "K19," T-Visserweert
37.4	R	LF3a sign "K19"
37.8	R	LF3a sign "K19," T-Illikhoven
38.0	R	LF3a sign "K19," Ruitersdijk
40.3	R	LF3a sign "K19"
41.1	R	LF3a sign "K19," Door den Dreesj
41.2	L	LF3a sign "K19," Staai
41.7	R	LF3a (10 m), L dike
42.5	VL	LF3a to K27, narrow, unpaved bike path (on dike)
44.2	VL	LF3a Maasstraat, T-Obbicht
44.4	L	LF3a Kasteelweg
44.8	R	LF3a sign "K27," Koestraat/Brugstraat
46.0	VL	bike path along the Julianakanaal
49.3	R	Walstraat (after Urmond bridge)
49.5	R	Bergstraat
49.7	L	Beekstraat sign "K45"
49.9	VL	sign "K45" (not LF3a) alongside dike
52.3	R	sign "K45"
53.2	L	sign "K45," Veldschuurdijk T-Maasband
54.2	R	LF3a sign "K45"
54.7	VL	LF3a Grote Straat/Koevaart, T-Meers
55.2	U L	LF3a sign "K45," onto dike
55.9	R	LF3a sign "K45"
56.8	CS	under Scharberbrug/A2
57.8	CS	at K45
57.9	L !	Elsloo bridge
58.1	R	LF3a Scharberg (10 m), R Julianastraat/Op den Brug

58.4	U R !	LF3a Maasberg, 200 m steep descent, T-Elsloo
58.7	SS	Kasteel Elsloo on L
60.6	R	LF3a bike path onto dike (Julianakanaal)
63.8	L	LF3a up (at Brug Bunde)
64.0	U R	over Bunde bridge
64.1	R	LF3a down
64.1	R	50 m onto bike path on other side of dike (Julianakanaal)
65.2	R !	LF3a off dike, Weg naar Hartelstein/Bundervoetpad
66.7	CS	Keizerstraat/Geneinde, T-Itteren
67.3	R	LF3a farm road
69.8	SS	Kasteel Borgharen on L, T-Borgharen
70.5	L	LF3a sign "Maastricht," Schutkolkweg
71.2	CS !	LF3a onto road/Sluisdijk (no bike path for 800 m)
71.4	CS	over Sluis Limmel (locks)
72.0	CS	onto bike path, sign "Centrum," Borgharenweg
73.0	R	LF3a sign "Centrum," beside the Maas
73.4	VL	stay on red bike path beside the Maas
73.8	VL !	LF3a sign "Centrum and Station," cross road
74.4	End	St. Servaasbrug (L 500 m to the station or R 400 m to the VVV)

Grazing cattle are a common sight in Limburg.

Tour of South Limburg (including "Three Countries in a Day")

Total Distance:	108.8 km
Duration:	1–4 days (You can do the entire ride in four days. Days 1, 3, and 4 can be connected to make a great 60-km day ride from Maastricht. If you are returning to Maastricht on Day 3 and are not staying in Valkenburg, combine days 3 & 4 for a 33.6-km ride.)
Highlights:	Maastricht, hills, Limburg villages, expansive views, *vakwerk* houses, highest point in the Netherlands, side trips to Belgium and Germany, cave biking.
Terrain:	Hilly
When to Go:	South Limburg is a popular vacation destination not only for the Dutch, but also for Germans, Belgians, and the French. It is crowded on weekends from mid-April through September, and especially busy during July and August. Hotel rates are better in the off months. Spring, particularly the end of April through early May when the apple trees are blossoming, is especially beautiful.
Maps:	Michelin 532 Zuid-Nederland/Pays-Bas Sud, ANWB/VVV Toeristenkaart Limburg, Fietsroute Netwerk Zuid-Limburg map.
Start/Finish:	Maastricht/Maastricht
Access:	Maastricht
Connections:	"Tour of Two Limburgs"

Day 1: Maastricht to Slenaken (26.4 km)

The route starts off with flat cycling along the Maas River, then turns east away from the river valley, offering sweeping views for the rest of the day.

Leave Maastricht to the south with the Maas on your right. At 2.0 km, the hills of Limburg are visible across the river. The route is flat along the Maas to Eijsden.

Eijsden is an attractive old town with cobbled streets. The center is 100 m left of the Mariaplein (9.4 km). The quay, Bat, offers views across the river to Lanaye in Belgium. In 2004, a pedestrian/bicycle ferry began operating between the two towns (May through September, €1). Kasteel Eijsden (10.1 km), built in 1636, can't be visited, but the gardens surrounding the moated castle offer a pleasant place for strolling.

At 12.3 km, shortly after crossing the A2, the Maas Valley gives way to Limburg's hills, with its grazing cows, apple orchards, and cute villages. The roads, except for a few main arteries, are quiet farm roads.

Your first major climb begins at 13.3 km en route to Libeek, a tiny hamlet where you will see the first examples of *vakwerk* houses. (*Vakwerk* houses are half-timbered houses with dark, exposed beams and whitewashed walls that are found throughout southern Limburg.) More can be found in the next town, Mheer. At 17.3 km, a side trip to St.-Geertruid, its church on a small hill in the center, offers a roller-coaster ride.

From Mheer, there is a steep descent with stunning views of Noorbeek. At 20.4 km, the warning sign *"Fietsers Afstappen"* advises cyclists to dismount on this 10% grade, but you will see cyclists whipping down the hill.

From Noorbeek, the roads wind through pastures and apple orchards. From Ulvend (blink and you'll miss it), the small farm road you are on denotes the Dutch-Belgian border. Be ready to use your brakes for the last kilometer as you drop down steeply into Slenaken.

Cue Sheet

0.0	Start	VVV Maastrict
		Go S on Kleine Straat
60 m	L	Maastr. Brugstraat/St., Servaasbrug (bridge)

Map 14.2. Tour of South Limburg.

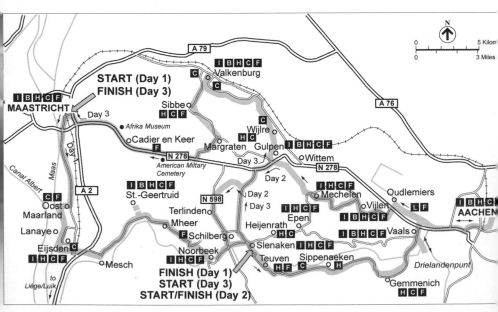

0.7	R	Wilhelminasingel/Ave. Ceramique
1.4	R	sign "K4," Serpentilunet/Limburglaan/N591
4.9	CS	at K4 sign "K75," N591
6.5	CS	Camping De Oosterdriessen
6.9	R	at K75 Kasteellaan
7.4	L	Trichterweg
9.4	R	Mariaplein sign "K76," T-Eijsden
9.4	L	(20 m) Bat (beside the Maas River)
9.6	L	at K76 sign "K77," Diepstraat
9.8	R	sign "K77," Graaf de Geloeslaan
10.1	SS R	Kasteel Eijsden (castle)
10.3	L	at K77 Caestertstraat
10.4	L	sign "K78," T-Mariadorp
12.2	R	Eikenlaan dir. "Mesch"
12.3	CS	overpass over A2
12.5	L	sign "K78"
12.6	CS	Kommelsweg
13.3	L	sign "K80," dir. "Mheer," Heiweg
16.4	VR	dir. "Libeek"
17.3	CS	at K80 sign "K81," sign "Mheer," T-Libeek
17.3	ST L	RT = 2.2 km to St.-Geertruid
18.9	R	dir. "Noorbeek," T-Mheer
19.2	CS	at K81 sign "K84," Dorpsstraat/Duivenstraat
20.4	CS !	fietsers afstappen (walk your bike)
21.3	VL	Dorpsstraat
21.4	CS	the VVV on R, T-Noorbeek
21.6	R	sign "K84," St. Martensweg
22.2	VL	sign "K84," Vroelen
22.4	U R	sign "K84"
22.7	R	sign "K84," sign "Ulvend"

23.5	VL	sign "K84"
23.8	L	sign "Schilberg," T-Ulvend
25.1	CS	sign "K84," cross N598, border marker to R
25.4	CS	at K84 sign "K92," sign "Slenaken"
25.9	R !	sign "K92," Kerkdel, steep descent
26.4	End	Slenaken Tourist Office

Slenaken

The village of Slenaken, nestled at the bottom of the Gulp River Valley, and surrounded by velvety green hills, is more reminiscent of the lowlands of Switzerland than of the Netherlands. Eye-catching views are at every turn. Other than residential dwellings, there are six hotels, a few restaurants, some basic retail stores, and camping nearby.

Alternatives for overnight accommodations can be found in the neighboring villages of Noorbeek, Heijenrath, Epen, and Mechelen, each offering hotel, pension, and camping options. There are also two hotels in Teuven, Belgium (see 2.3 km cue on Day 2).

Information: Slenaken's Tourist Office (not an official VVV) is at Dorpsstraat 21, on the corner of Schildbergerweg. The closest VVV is in Epen (5 km away) at Julianastraat 15 (Tel. 043 455 2443) or Noorbeek, Dorpsstraat 8 (Tel. 043 408 3571). (See Day 1 at 21.4 km.) For comprehensive tourist information about southern Limburg, go to www.vvvzuidlimburg.com (see "Valkenburg," page 280).

Bicycle Shops: There are no bicycle shops in Slenaken. The closest is Jef Abels Bikes, Cobbejennegats 1 (Tel. 043 450 4000), 6 km away in Gulpen.

"Drielandenpunt"

Drielandenpunt (Three-Country Point) is where the Netherlands, Belgium, and Germany meet. At 322.5 m high, this is the highest point in the Netherlands, denoted on a plaque next to the official Drielandenpunt monument (19.4 km). The plaque also indicates the lowest point in the country, Nieuwekerk a/d IJssel, 6.74 m below sea level.

Peaceful walking trails lace the forests at the top, whereas less peaceful restaurants and a labyrinth (19.3 km) draw the tourists. €3 takes you to the top of the observation tower for a view over the area (19.5 km).

Where to Stay: At Grensweg 1, cozy Hotel de la Frontière (Tel. 043 457 4302, www.delafrontiere.nl) has six rooms. Singles are €40 and doubles are €70. Up the hill, Hotel De Zevende Heerlijkheid, Grensweg 9 (Tel. 043 457 3259, www.zevendeheerlijkheid.nl), has phenomenal views from its terrace and restaurant (which has excellent meals created by the owner/chef). Rooms start at €40 for singles and €54 for doubles. Next to the tourist office, Hotel Berg en Dal, Dorpsstraat 19 (Tel. 043 457 3201, www.hotel-bergendal.nl), has single rooms without bath for €35 and with bath for €50. Doubles without bath are €60 and with bath, €70.

Campers will have to cycle either 2 km uphill to Kampeer-boerderij Welkom, Hoogcruts 27 (Tel. 043 457 1296. www.vekabo.nl/welkom, open mid-March through October), or head uphill 1.7 km toward Epen to Camping Heijenrade, Heijenratherweg 13 (Tel. 043 457 3260).

Where to Eat: Both of the hotels have a restaurant of excellent quality, with half-pension (dinner, bed, and breakfast) available. Other restaurants include 't Stegelke at Waterstraat 7, with pizzas, waffles, and pancakes, and De Boswachter, at Heijenrather-weg 2, with Dutch meals.

There is a small supermarket/bakery across from the tourist office.

Day 2: Three Countries in a Day (48.8 km)

On this ride, weave in and out of three countries, cycle to the highest point of the Netherlands, visit one of Germany's most historic cities, meander through some of Limburg's prettiest villages and countryside, and climb some tough hills.

Stretch before you begin the short climb up Grensweg to Teuven (Belgium) and the 1.2 km climb through a forest out of Teuven. The monument at the top (4.7 km) is to those in World War I who tried to escape, but perished at the electric fence on the border. The descent offers views across the Geul Valley and of Kasteel Beusdael, a private residence.

The route rolls through Belgium until Gemmenich, where it returns to the Netherlands. After a steep climb on tiny Chemin du Duc (12.6 km), views over Gemmenich appear to the right. At 13.6 km re-enter the Netherlands on the way to Drielandenpunt (see boxed text "Drielandenpunt" on page 274). Skirt Vaals and, at 17.5 km, begin the 2 km ascent to the highest point in the country. Once down again, the route goes through the busy border town of Vaals. To visit Aachen (Aken in Dutch, and worth the 40-minute round-trip ride), continue straight at 23.5 km on Vaalserstraße (you are now in Germany) for 3.4 km, veering left at the St. Jakob Church (3.6 km) on Jakobstraße, and following Jakobstraße another 700 m to the Markt in the center.

The crowning glory of the Markt is the Dom, a most impressive cathedral. Don't overlook the Rathaus (Town Hall) and the medieval and baroque buildings surrounding the Markt. Near the Markt is the Couven Museum (named for the architect of many of the city's Baroque buildings, closed Mondays). If you decide to stay overnight, there are plenty of lodging options. Return by the same route.

From Vaals, the route continues along the tiny Senserbach Creek. The road beside the creek, Senserbachweg (24.1 km to 26.8 km), is the Dutch-German border. The turn along the creek (26.8 km) brings you back to the Netherlands, to Oud Lemiers, and past several *vakwerk* houses and the St. Catharinakapel, a little stone chapel dating to 1350.

Vijlen's church, high on a hilltop, is a landmark as you approach, with valley views to the left as you enter and leave the village. In the small farming community of Rott, as well as in neighboring Mechelen, see several good examples of *vakwerk* houses. At 34.5 km, turn right and go about 200 m to reach the pretty center of Mechelen.

Overgeul is a quiet little road overlooking the Geul River Valley and the town of Wittem and its abbey.

Gulpen is a busy town on the N278, a main artery through the area. The route avoids the N278, also Gulpen's main street, by paralleling the N278 on Burg. Teheuxweg, 100 m south.

Gulpen is home to Gulpner beer, famed throughout Limburg and the rest of the country. If you're hungry, stop at De Pannekoeken Molen at Molenweg 2A (38.6 km) for pancakes (www.depannekoekenmolen.nl, closed Mondays). It's housed in a huge old water mill.

At the base of the parking area, it's easy to miss the tiny road (38.9 km) along the Gulp River to Pesaken. At 41.8 km, the last climb of the day is a hefty one. The bike path atop the ridge provides for expansive views: apple orchards to your right,

Idyllic cycling through the rolling hills of South Limburg.

hops for the Gulpner brewery on your left (42.7 km), and asparagus mounds further along on your left (44.2 km).

End the day with the same speedy descent into Slenaken as on Day 1.

Cue Sheet

0.0	Start	Slenaken Tourist Office go SE on Dorpsstraat
80 m	R	sign "K92," at Hotel de la Frontière dir. "Teuven"
0.1	VR	sign "K92," Grensweg (at church)
1.3	L	sign "K92," sign "Teuven"
2.3	CS	past church, T-Teuven
2.5	R	sign "K92," Dorpsstraat
3.1	L!	sign "K92," Kasteelstraat
4.1	L	unmarked
4.7	SS	monument
7.1	CS	at K92 sign "K91"
8.0	CS	T-Sippenaeken
8.2	L	sign "K91," Evenbaeg sign "Gemmenich"
12.5	L	at K91 sign "K93," Rue des Ecoles, T-Gemmenich
12.6	L	sign "K93," Chemin du Duc
13.6	L	sign "K93," Rue de Vaals
14.4	L	sign "K93," Schuttersbergweg
15.7	R	sign "K93," Eschberg to Drielandenpunt
15.8	CS	not sign "K93," Eschberg
16.5	R	sign "Drielandenpunt," Randweg
16.8	VR	sign "Drielandenpunt," Nieuwe Hertogenweg
17.5	CS!	Viergrenzenweg
19.2	SS	labyrinth
19.3	R	toward monument and tower
19.4	SS	monument
19.5	SS	tower (turn around)
19.6	VR	one-way road to descent

21.6	VL	Nieuwe Hertogenweg (under bridge)
22.1	R	Tentstraat
22.4	L	sign "Centrum," Bosstraat
23.1	R	Maastrichterlaan
23.2	CS	VVV on L, T-Vaals
23.5	L	Grensstraat
23.5	ST CS	RT = 9.0 km to Aachen (Aken)
23.9	CS	bike path
24.1	L	at K95 sign "K94," Senserbachweg
26.8	L	sign "K93," along creek
26.9	R	sign "K93," Oud Lemiers
27.1	L	sign "K93," Oud Lemiers
27.3	CS	cross N278 Klaassvelderweg, T-Lemiers
28.1	R	at K93 sign "K90," sign "Harles," LF6b
28.8	L	sign "K90," T-Harles
29.6	R	sign "K90," sign "Vijlen," Vijlenberg
30.6	CS	VVV, T-Vijlen
30.8	L	sign "K90," Vijlenerstraat
30.9	R !	LF6b bike path (steep descent)
31.1	L	farm road
31.2	CS	sign "Rott"
32.0	CS	T-Rott
32.7	R	LF6b sign "K90," Kleebergerweg
33.7	R	LF6b at K90 sign "K86"
34.1	L	sign "K86," Burgpappersweg
34.5	L	LF6b sign "K86," Hoofdstraat, T-Mechelen
34.8	R	LF6b sign "K86," Overgeul (900 m unpaved)
36.8	L	LF6b at K86 sign "K85"
36.9	R	Oude Akerweg/Burg. Teheuxweg
38.0	CS	sign "K85," T-Gulpen

38.6	L	Molenweg, "De Pannekoeken Molen"
38.7	R	at K85 sign "K83"
38.9	R !	sign "K83," sign "Pesaken," Pesakerweg
41.4	R	sign "K83," Slenakerweg
41.8	L !	sign "K83," Groendals-Bergweg (steep climb)
42.3	L	sign "K83," bike path
44.6	L	sign "K83," Provincialeweg/N598 (10 m), R Gulperstraat
44.9	CS	at K83 sign "K84," Gulperstraat, T-Terlinden
45.0	L	sign "Hoogcruts"
45.5	R	sign "K84," Provincialeweg/N598
46.7	L	sign "K84," dir. "Slenaken"
46.7	R !	(60 m) sign "K84," Maastrichterweg
47.8	R	at K84 sign "K92," sign "Slenaken"
48.4	R !	sign "K92," Kerkdel (steep descent)
48.8	End	Slenaken Tourist Office

Cave Biking

Ever thought of cycling in a cave? As far as I know, the only place on earth where you can do this is 2 km outside Valkenburg. For an hour, ASP Adventure (www. aspadventure.nl) takes you below the earth's surface and through the tunnels of the longest man-made cave in Europe, with depths varying from 20 m (60 ft) to 70 m (210 ft).

The caves themselves, still mined for marlstone by three families, are approximately 140 km long, and have been worked since the 17th century. The 8 km guided ride is on mountain bikes equipped with lights. You will be taught basic cave biking skills, as well two essential Dutch words: *afstappen* (get off), for some of the narrow passages, and *bukken* (duck), for lower ceilings (height varies from 1.40 m to 2 m). The cycling isn't difficult, and this is a truly unique experience. Public tours are offered April 1 to November 30, Saturdays and Sundays only, and daily in July and August, noon to 5 p.m.

For reservations, contact VVV Zuid Limburg in Valkenburg (Tel. 043 609 8518, info@vvvzuidlimburg.nl) or ASP Adventure (Tel. 043 604 0675). Guided tours are €14 per person, and include a good mountain bike and helmet.

Day 3: Slenaken to Valkenburg (16.5 km)

The short ride to Valkenburg starts with easy cycling through the Gulp Valley to Pesaken and Gulpen. Climb out of Gulpen and head to Wijlre, turning off at Gulpenerweg past the Kasteel Wijlre (not open to the public). At 9.9 km, join the bike path Kaizer Willempad, crossing the Geul River at 10.2 km.

Valkenburgerweg/N595 is a busy road, but has a separate bike path for the 4 km before you turn off to go to the Kasteel Schoelen. Go through the forest on a hard-packed dirt bike path to Valkenburg.

Cue Sheet

0.0	Start	Slenaken Tourist Office
0.0		Go NW on Dorpsstraat
0.7	R	Beutenaken/Slenakerweg
3.4	R	Pesakerweg
5.9	VR	sign "K85" (parking area) (30 m), L
6.1	CS	at K85 sign "K58," Landsraderweg
6.2	CS	Tramweg
6.4	L	sign "K58," Aan het Veld
6.6	R	cross N278, then CS
6.7	R	sign "K58," past stone church
6.8	VR	Rosstraat
7.0	L	sign "K58/K69," VVV Dorpsstraat/Gulpenerweg
8.7	L	sign "K58," Wijlreweg
8.8	SS	Kasteel Wijlre on L (no visits)
9.6	R	sign "K58," Stokhem
9.9	CS	Kaizer Willempad
10.4	L	sign "K58," Valkenburgerweg/N595
10.9	CS	at K58 sign "K59"
14.4	R	sign "K59," Kasteeltuin sign
14.5	SS	Kasteel Schoelen
!4.5	R	bike path
14.9	L	sign "K59," sign "Valkenburg"

16.2	CS	sign "K59," Oosterweg
16.3	CS	at K59
16.5	L	sign "VVV," Louis v.d. Maesenstraat
16.7	End	VVV Valkenburg

Valkenburg

Valkenburg, on the Geul River, is southern Limburg's tourist center. The Netherlands' first tourist office was opened here in 1885. There are several castles in the area. High atop a hill, the castle ruins of the Lords of Valkenburg, dating to the 12th century, dominate the town. Two of the town's gates, the Berkelpoort and the Grendelpoort, remain.

The town is well-known for its "underground" tours of the Gemeentegrot, a Roman quarry, the Steenkolenmijn, a coal mine, and Roman catacombs. Valkenburg also offers an unusual adventure: "*grotbiking*," or cave biking—cycling underground in marlstone caves (see boxed text "Cave Biking" on page 279).

Information:	The VVV is at Theodoor Dorrenplein 5 (Tel. 043 609 8500, www. vvvzuidlimburg.nl). Internet access is available at Internetcafé: The Attic, Tienschurstraat 2 (Tel. 043 601 1193).
Bicycle Shops:	Tintelen at Statenlaan 2 (Tel. 043 601 3025) is a full-service bike shop. Cycle Center Bicycle Rental at De Valkenburg 8B (Tel. 043 601 5338, www. cyclecenter.nl) rents bicycles.
Where to Stay:	Valkenburg has a huge range of hotels and pensions. Close to the cave biking location, Hotel Vogelzang, Daelhemerweg 140 (Tel. 043 601 2098, www.hotelvogelzang.nl), has simple rooms without private shower/toilet for €25 per person per

Kasteel Schoelen, on the outskirts of Valkenburg.

night. In town, Hotel De Guasco, De Guascostraat 3-9 (Tel. 043 601 3204, www. hoteldeguasco.nl), has singles for €35 and doubles for €70.

There are a few camping options. The most convenient to town and the cave biking location is Stadscamping Den Driesch, Heunsbergerweg 1 (Tel. 043 601 2025, www. campingdendriesch.nl). Be prepared to walk your bike up the steep hill to the campground, but once you're there, enjoy views of Valkenburg and the castle ruins.

Where to Eat: Valkenburg is Limburg's tourist mecca, and the streets, particularly Grotestraat, are lined with dozens of restaurants.

Day 4: Valkenburg to Maastricht (17.1 km)

Leave Valkenburg by walking your bike through the pedestrian passage, named Passage, for 100 m.

If you're up for a challenge, instead of veering left at 0.4 km, go right onto Cauberg and climb its 12% gradient for 800 m. This is part of the annual Amstel Gold bicycle race, and just about the toughest climb anywhere in the country.

Leaving town, a gradual 2 km climb will warm you up. This is the hardest climb of the day; you will notice the hills leveling out as you head back to Maastricht.

Near Margraten, the American Military Cemetery and Memorial (7.4 km) are sobering reminders of American soldiers who lost their lives during World War II in the Allied effort to liberate the Dutch. Row upon row of simple white crosses and stars of David mark the 8,301 graves. (Open daily, 9 a.m. to 5 p.m.)

From 12.1 km, just outside Cadier en Keer, you begin a 2 km glide down to Maastricht. The interesting Afrikamuseum (12.4 km), Rijksweg 15 (Tel. 043 407 7383, www.afrikacentrum.nl, 1:30 p.m. to 5 p.m., closed Mondays), houses a collection of African art, masks, and artifacts.

LF6b signs will guide you through Maastricht to the railway station.

Cue Sheet

0.0	Start	VV Valkenburg walk NW on Passage
0.1	L	Wilhelminalaan/Grendelplein
0.3	CS	at K60 sign "K68"
0.4	VL !	sign "K68," Daelhamerweg, 2 km climb
0.4	ST CS	RT = 1.6 km Cauberg climb
2.3	SS R	ASP *Adventure: Grotbiking* (cave biking)

2.4	RA CS	dir. "Margraten"
2.5	L	dir. "Margraten," Kerkersweg
2.9	VL	Sibberkerkstraat Plateauroute sign, T-Sibbe
5.2	R	at K69 sign "K70," Scheuldersteeg, T-Scheulder
6.9	L	sign "K70," Eijkerstraat
7.2	VR	at K70, sign "K71," Pastoor Brouwerstaat, T-Margraten
7.4	R	N278, sign "American Military Cemetery"
8.5	SS L	American Military Cemetery
10.6	R	Kerkstraat
10.8	VL	Kerkstraat
11.1	R	sign "K66," Kerkstraat, T-Cadier & Keer
11.7	R	at K66 sign "K65," N278
12.1	CS !	N278 (do not follow sign "K65")
12.4	SS R	Afrikamuseum
14.0	R	sign "Centrum," bike path/Keerderstraat
14.9	L	Bemelerweg/Wethouder van Caldenborghlaan
15.6	L	LF6b Scharneweg
16.5	L	sign "Centrum, Station," along railway tracks
16.7	R	cross over tracks (20 m), Spoorweglaan (beside railway)
17.1	End	Maastricht Railway Station

Appendix

I. Glossary of Terms

Abdij	Abbey
Begijnhof	Beguinage, i.e., Enclosed residential community for beguines, an order of lay nuns; usually a group of buildings surrounding a small, peaceful courtyard.
Brink	Central square (often grass, similar to a village green)
Brug	Bridge
Carillon	Church tower chimes
Casemates	Tunnels resulting from mining or built into natural hills for military defense
Centrum	Center
Dorp	Village
Gables (stepped)	Building facades shaped like steps on upper level
Gemaal	Pumping station for controlling water level
Gracht	Canal (also *Kanaal*)
Grote	Great or large (such as *Grote Markt*, or *Grote Kerk*)
Gildehuis	Guild Hall, Offices of the medieval guilds
Haven	Harbor
Huis	House
Jaagpad	Towpath along a canal
Kasteel	Castle
Kerk	Church (*Grote* and *Kleine*: Big and Small)
Linear, or Ribbon Village	Long, narrow village built alongside a canal
Markt	Market square
Molen	Windmill
Onze Lieve Vrouw (*O.L. Vrouw*)	Our Lady (as in "Church of")
Plein	Square

Polder	Area of reclaimed land
Pont	Ferry
Poort	Gate
Raadhuis	Town hall
Rooster	grate or grill (e.g. *veerooster* - cattle grate)
Sluis	Locks; gate mechanism in a waterway or canal to raise or lower water level for boats
Speeltoren	Bell tower
Stadhuis	Town hall
Veer	Ferry
Vrijthof	Regional term for a church square (used in southern Netherlands)
Waag	Weigh house

II. General Vocabulary

This is a very basic selection of words and terms. A small phrasebook or pocket dictionary is recommended.

English	**Dutch**
Hello	*Dag*
Good-bye	*Tot ziens*
Please	*Alstublieft*
Thank you (very much)	*Dank u wel*
Excuse me	*Pardon*
Yes	*Ja*
No	*Nee*
Do you speak English?	*Spreekt u Engels?*
I don't speak Dutch	*Ik spreek geen Nederlands*
Where is...?	*Waar is...?*
The station	*Het station*
The post office	*Het postkantoor*

Supermarket	*Supermarkt*
Library	*Bibliotheek*
How much does ... cost?	*Hoeveel kost...?*
Open	*Geopend*
Closed	*Gesloten*
New	*Nieuw(e)*
Old	*Oud(e)*
Entrance	*Ingang*
Exit	*Uitgang*
Battery	*Accu*
One	*Een*
Two	*Twee*
Three	*Drie*
Four	*Vier*
Five	*Vijf*
Six	*Zes*
Seven	*Zeven*
Eight	*Acht*
Nine	*Negen*
Ten	*Tien*
Eleven	*Elf*
Twelve	*Twaalf*
Twenty	*Twintig*
Hundred	*Honderd*
Monday	*Maandag*
Tuesday	*Dinsdag*
Wednesday	*Woensdag*
Thursday	*Donderdag*
Friday	*Vrijdag*
Saturday	*Zaterdag*

Sunday	*Zondag*
Tomorrow	*Morgen*
Bread	*Brood*
Cheese	*Kaas*
Butter	*Boter*
Tea	*Thee*
Coffee	*Koffie*
Milk	*Melk*
Water	*Water*
The bill	*De rekening*
Daily dish/Special	*Dagschotel*

Additional Terms

Eetcafé: Cross between a restaurant and café, with a casual atmosphere and reasonably priced menus.

Bruin Café ("Brown Café"): Neighborhood café that takes its name from all the brown woodwork; they generally have a warm, old-fashioned atmosphere.

Starters	*Voorgerechten*
Soup	*Soep*
Main courses	*Hoofdgerechten*
Desserts	*Nagerechten*

III. Cycling Vocabulary

Bicycle	*Fiets*
Cyclist(s)	*Fietser(s)*
Bike path(s)	*Fietspad(en)*
Bicycle parking	*Fietsenstalling*
Handlebars	*Stuur*
Light	*Licht*
Brakes	*Rem*

Front fork	*Voorvork*
Pump	*Pomp*
Tire	*Buitenband*
Spoke	*Spaak*
Inner tube	*Binnenband*
Rim	*Velg*
Air	*Lucht*
Crank	*Crank*
Pedal	*Pedaal*
Chain	*Ketting*
Hub	*Wielnaaf*
Rack	*Bagagedrager*
Wrench/Spanner	*Moersleutel*
Screwdriver	*Schroevedraaier*
Wheel	*Wiel*
Lock	*Slot*
Front	*Voor*
Rear	*Achter*

Other useful words and phrases

Map	*Kaart*
North	*Noord*
South	*Zuid*
East	*Oost*
West	*West*
Left	*Links*
Right	*Rechts*
Straight on	*Recht door*
Direction	*Richting*
Through traffic	*Doorgaand verkeer*
Cyclists cross over	*Fietsers oversteken*

Cyclists dismount	*Fietsers afstappen*
Caution	*Let op/Pas op*
Road/Path	*Weg/Pad*
Street	*Straat*
Bike tunnel	*Fietstunnel*
Bike bridge	*Fietsbrug*
Excepted	*Uitgezonderd*
Private road	*Eigen weg*
You are approaching/nearing....	*U nadert...*

V. Weights and Measures

All of Europe uses the metric system of weights and measures. Here is a basic conversion table:

39 inches = 1 meter

1 inch = 2.54 centimeters

1 mile = 1.6 kilometers

1 kilometer = 0.6 mile

2 pints = 1.1 liters

1.1 pounds = 500 grams

2.2 pounds = 1 kilogram

Distance:	To convert miles to kilometers, multiply by 1.6.
	To convert kilometers to miles, multiply by 0.62.
Examples:	10 miles = 10 x 1.6 = 16 km
	10 km = 10/1.6 = 6.2 miles.
Electricity:	Voltage is 220 volts; sockets are for 2-round-pin type plugs, with or without ground.

Temperatures: Fahrenheit to Celsius (For an approximate conversion from Celsius to Fahrenheit, double the Celsius figure and add 30.)

Celsius	0	10	15	20	25	30	35
Fahrenheit	32	50	59	68	77	86	95

Decimal Note: In the Netherlands, as everywhere else on the Continent, the decimal point is denoted by a commas, and the period is used to separate 1000s. Example: 8.765,43 on the continent corresponds to 8,753.43 in English-language countries.

V. Further Reading

Background reading before you leave and supplemental guidebooks and literature will greatly enhance your trip.

Guidebooks

The following books are all general guidebooks. No publication dates have been given, as these books are updated frequently, some annually. Look for the most recent edition for the most up-to-date information.

Insight Guide: Holland (APA Publications)

Insight Guide: Amsterdam (APA Publications)

Insight Guide: Belgium (APA Publications)

Rick Steves' Amsterdam, Bruges, and Brussels (Avalon Travel Publishing)

Eyewitness: Holland (Dorling Kindersley)

Eyewitness: Amsterdam (Dorling Kindersley)

Cadogan: Holland (Globe Pequot Press)

Cadogan: Amsterdam and the Randstad (Globe Pequot Press)

The Netherlands (Lonely Planet Publications)

Amsterdam (Lonely Planet Publications)

Belgium and Luxembourg (Lonely Planet Publications)

Green Guide: Netherlands (Michelin Travel Publications)

Green Guide: Amsterdam (Michelin Travel Publications)

Green Guide: Belgium and Luxembourg (Michelin Travel Publications)

Red Guide: Benelux (Michelin Travel Publications)

Blue Guide: Netherlands (W.W. Norton)

Blue Guide: Amsterdam (W.W. Norton)

Rough Guide: The Netherlands (Penguin)

Rough Guide: Amsterdam (Penguin)

Rough Guide: Belgium and Luxembourg (Penguin)

Time Out: Amsterdam (Penguin)

Fodor: Holland (Random House)

Fodor: Amsterdam (Random House)

Frommer: Belgium, Holland, and Luxembourg (Wiley Publishing)

Frommer: Amsterdam (Wiley Publishing)

Culture

Hunt, Janin and Ria van Eil. *Culture Shock! Netherlands* (Graphic Arts Publishing, 2003).

White, Colin and Laurie Boucke. *The UnDutchables: An Observation of the Netherlands, Its Culture and Its Inhabitants* (White-Boucke Publishing, 2001).

Literature

Tracy Chevalier. *Girl with the Pearl Earring* (Plume, 2001). Set in Dutch painter Johannes Vermeer's Delft household during the 1660s, this book centers on a 16-year old servant.

Mary Mapes Dodge. *Hans Brinker, or The Silver Skates* (Aladdin Paperbacks, 2002). This children's novel is set in the area of the *Randstad* over 100 years ago.

Alexandre Dumas. *The Black Tulip* (Oxford). This historical novel is about the tulip craze in the 17th century.

Anne Frank. *Anne Frank: Diary of a Young Girl* (Bantam, 1993). The diary chronicles the experiences of Anne and her Jewish family, who lived in hiding in Amsterdam during the Holocaust.

Manfred Wolf, ed. *Amsterdam: A Traveler's Literary Companion* (Whereabouts Press, 2001). Short stories and literary excerpts about Amsterdam.

Mysteries

The Dutch have some excellent mystery writers, among whom are Janwillem van de Wetering and A.C. Baantjer. Both expertly set the scene in the Netherlands and are available in English translations.

Index

Van der Plas Publications / Cycle Publishing

We publish many books of interest to cyclists, including books about bicycle touring and bicycle maintenance and repair.

To obtain a copy of our current catalogue, please call toll-free 1-877-353-1207 or visit our website at http://www.cyclepublishing.com.

Van der Plas Publications / Cycle Publishing
1282 7th Avenue
San Francisco, CA 94122, USA